# TELEVISION PRODUCTION TODAY

# TELEVISION PRODUCTION TODAY

## 3RD EDITION

**MARK BIELAK**

**Radio and Television Director**
**Maine Township High School South**
**Park Ridge, Illinois**

National Textbook Company
a division of *NTC Publishing Group* • Lincolnwood, Illinois USA

Cover photo: David Joel, photographer/Tony Stone Images

**1996 Printing**

Published by National Textbook Company, a division of NTC Publishing Group.
© 1995 by NTC Publishing Group, 4255 West Touhy Avenue,
Lincolnwood (Chicago), Illinois 60646-1975 U.S.A.
Manufactured in the United States of America.
Library of Congress Catalog Card Number: 94–66602

6 7 8 9 QB 9 8 7 6 5 4 3 2

# Contents

# Preface

*Television Production Today* is a practical book, containing information and advice that will help you actively produce television programming. Television production requires the combination of equipment, people, and ideas. Every time you are part of a different TV production, you can add to your knowledge. Only after working on a variety of programs in different roles can you acquire a true understanding of what can be done and a greater appreciation of programs created by others. *Television Production Today* will provide helpful information for those new to TV, as well as for those who already have some experience in creating programming.

## NEW EDITION

Now in its third edition, this textbook provides a contemporary look at television production from the various perspectives of audio, video, recording, writing, teamwork, completed programs, and media career planning. Reflecting what is happening today in the constantly changing field of television, this text includes coverage of technological developments that are creating an environment wherein television, computers, film, and video are merging into one integrated medium.

## TEXT FEATURES

*Television Production Today* supports conceptual learning and practical skills development. Activities are offered for both individual and collaborative work at the end of each chapter. "It's a Wrap" provides a quick chapter summary. "Take Two" section activities are opportunities to evaluate, discuss, and extend chapter content. "Video Labs" are creative activities providing experience in television production techniques. Sample scripts, storyboards, and floorplans are provided as models and examples of production processes. Each chapter offers an additional readings and resource list. The text concludes with a glossary of terms related to television, broadcasting in general, and video production.

## TEXT ORGANIZATION

The book is divided into eight chapters. Chapter One discusses the growth of technology and television in the U.S., reports on television viewing habits, and examines the organization and economics of broadcasting and cable TV.

Chapter Two focuses on the importance of audience analysis and the communication process, in order to help you select the program or genre to transmit your message.

Chapter Three discusses the variety and uses of studio cameras and video equipment, lighting, switching, and special-effects equipment.

Chapter Four discusses the characteristics of audio—including coverage of radio techniques—and focuses on the variety and uses of microphones and other sound equipment.

Chapter Five covers the creation of scripts, introducing the various genre related to writing for television and movies. This chapter includes examples and methods of script creation and timing and introduces the storyboard and teleplay formats. Script evaluation guidelines and issues of copyright/clearance for broadcasting are also addressed.

Chapter Six discusses production processes and the importance of teamwork. The role of each team member, including that of the director and performer (talent), is explained. The importance of collaborative effort and teamwork is stressed.

Chapter Seven surveys the variety of videotaping and editing equipment available today, explaining the uses of video recorders, camcorders, and digital recording.

Chapter Eight considers the variety of careers in the media industry today and the preparation needed to enter the field. This chapter features an address by Brianne Murphy, A.S.C., to students considering a future in television and moviemaking. Murphy is a renowned professional in television and film production—the first woman to become a member of the American Society of Cinematographers.

## ACKNOWLEDGMENTS

The author and publisher gratefully acknowledge the assistance of Patricia Metzinger, Maine Township High School South, Park Ridge, Illinois, and John Holmes, John Marshall High School, Milwaukee, Wisconsin. Acknowledgment is also extended to Frank Stokes, who assisted in the preparation of this third edition, and to James Kirkham, the author of the second edition, and his students at Thornton Township High School, Harvey, Illinois. Finally, special thanks go to the wonderful broadcasting students at Maine Township High School South who are pictured in this textbook.

# Viewing the Message

By the time the average person graduates from high school, he or she has watched more than 17,000 hours of television and spent only about 10,800 hours in the classroom. Surprised? You shouldn't be. Think about how much time you spend watching television and compare it with the time you spend in a classroom. According to the A. C. Nielsen Company, a media research group that monitors your viewing habits for advertisers, the average household now watches television for an all-time high of seven hours and thirteen minutes a day. In recent years, diversified programming, cable TV, and video-cassette recorder usage have made TV viewing an even more addicting pastime.

No one has proven TV viewing is good or bad for you. One thing is clear: When you choose to watch TV you opt to give up something else you might do. Currently, television is the most widely used form of recreation as well as the *only* information source for many Americans.

## WHY DO YOU WATCH TELEVISION?

It's late in the afternoon. You come home from class, grab a snack from the refrigerator, and sit down in front of the TV set, perhaps to catch the latest video on MTV or to watch a rerun. Later your favorite movie may be shown on cable, or you may watch a video-cassette you rented from a local video store. To many people, TV is a constant companion, a friend, a way to avoid boredom, a way to

> The average household watches 7 hours, 13 minutes of TV each day

add structure to any amount of unorganized time. In cold weather, you can watch a movie on TV rather than trudge through the snow to a movie theater. If you are a sports fan, you can watch football, basketball, or even a tennis match almost any time of day thanks to cable TV. Today's TV audience has an ever-growing selection of sports, movies, and upscale network productions.

According to the A. C. Nielsen Company, young adult males spend an average of 23.3 hours per week in front of the TV set, while young adult females watch 28.5 hours of TV weekly. Sound like a lot? If you kept a diary every time you sat down to watch TV, you might be surprised to find out how important the TV is to your recreational time.

Television is an entertainer, a journalist, a teacher, and a salesperson. Your reasons for watching TV determine your attitude toward different types of programs and influence your interpretation of the messages they convey. Just as the purpose of a program determines its point of view, your reason for viewing it affects your perception of the program. If you expect to be entertained, for example, you will be unhappy to receive a lecture on economics. Some people look to TV only for one thing, such as entertainment. However, the uses of television are limitless. You can learn to become a critical viewer of programming by learning more about how media is created.

## WHAT DETERMINES WHICH PROGRAMS YOU WATCH?

Until recently, what you watched was determined by the television stations in your area. Many cities could pick up only one or two stations. New technology has expanded your options. Let's examine all the factors that determine what you watch.

### Broadcast Stations

You probably still receive the majority of your TV programs from commercial or educational TV stations. Commercial television is an expensive enterprise. Networks and advertisers spend millions of dollars on programs to attract viewers and, in turn, earn profits for the network or TV station. Advertisers spend millions of dollars for ads they hope will influence what you buy, think, and feel. Networks and production companies spend millions of dollars creating programs to get your attention so you watch the ads.

## FIGURE 1.1

## Hours of Household TV Usage

**Average hours:minutes of TV usage per day**

|          | Annual | February | July |
|----------|--------|----------|------|
| 1981–82  | 6:48   | 7:22     | 6:09 |
| 1982–83  | 6:55   | 7:33     | 6:23 |
| 1983–84  | 7:08   | 7:38     | 6:26 |
| 1984–85  | 7:07   | 7:49     | 6:34 |
| 1985–86  | 7:10   | 7:48     | 6:37 |
| 1986–87  | 7:05   | 7:35     | 6:32 |
| 1987–88  | 6:59   | 7:38     | 6:31 |
| 1988–89  | 7:02   | 7:32     | 6:27 |
| 1989–90  | 6:55   | 7:16     | 6:24 |
| 1990–91  | 6:56   | 7:36     | 6:26 |
| 1991–92  | 7:04   | 7:32     | 6:39 |
| 1992–93* | 7:13   | 7:41     | 6:47 |

Source: Nielsen annual estimates are based on total U.S. households, September-August (48 week average excluding unusual days). February and July data are based on the National Audience Demographic reports for each year.

1981–87 data based on NTI Audimeter/Diary

1987–present data based on Nielsen People Meter

*TV usage for 1992–93 is based on September 1992–July 1993.

Reprinted by permission of Nielsen Media Research from the *1992–1993 Report on Television,* ©1993 Nielsen Media Research.

You should understand that American television is different from television in many parts of the world. In some European countries there are no commercial breaks. Sounds great, doesn't it? No commercials during your favorite show! But there is a catch. Some European countries impose a yearly tax on each TV set in a home. Many countries broadcast on only one or two channels, and a majority of the shows are educational TV or government programming. American-made television shows and movies are shown around the world, while American audiences see very little programming not made in America. Of course, American commercial TV is not entirely free. You pay for the programs with your time. The time you spend watching commercials is the price for seeing a program. TV stations are paid for the length of time commercials are run and the number of people believed to be watching. The program is a filler between commercials. More money is spent to make each minute of commercial than each minute of program. From the station's point of view, the commercials are more important because they generate the profit.

A majority of the programming shown on local TV stations is provided by one of the larger networks. Local stations cannot afford to create a full day's worth of programs. Most educational TV stations receive their programs from PBS (Public Broadcasting Service).

Independent TV stations (those not affiliated with a network) purchase syndicated TV programs from private distributors or purchase older network reruns. Some of the larger independent TV stations, such as WOR in New Jersey, WTBS in Atlanta, and WGN in Chicago, are called "superstations" because, with the help of cable TV, they reach as many viewers as the major network stations. These superstations use low-power satellites to beam their programs across the nation; local cable companies then pick up the signals. On any given day only about 11 percent of the programs you view on any local TV stations are actually produced by that station. The remainder come from networks or syndication.

## Ratings

Perhaps the most important influence on TV programming is *you*. Advertisers try to reach as many people as possible. They have created a system that estimates the number of people viewing specific programs at one time. Ratings are a scientific method of estimating how many people viewed a program. Advertisers use them to determine if they are getting the largest possible audience for their advertising dollar. If advertisers run their commercials during programs that do not "pull a good rating," the advertisers are not reaching the largest potential audience. Advertisers also try to match the age and sex of audience members with those who typically buy their products.

Ratings are important to broadcasters because ratings estimate how many people are viewing the television program. The more popular a program is, and the larger its audience, the more advertisers must pay for airing their commercial during the program.

For example, if the program is very successful in the ratings, the network might charge as much as $400,000 for a 30-second "spot" (commercial), and there will probably be at least three opportunities to air this spot during the program. That adds up to $1,200,000 for commercial time during this particular show. If the program runs poorly in the ratings, the network may charge only $100,000 to run the same commercial; this means the network earns a gross profit of only $300,000. Losing $900,000 is a strong reason for the network to drop a program that you might like. Programs are often dropped if they do not create the maximum possible profit. Some programs are seen only a few times before a network drops them in favor of a more popular one. Some "pilot programs" are created but never aired because it is believed that they will not gain high ratings.

Ratings services, such as A. C. Nielsen, ARB, Trendex, and Pulse, poll a number of randomly selected viewers at a specific time. They check overnight in large cities such as New York, Chicago, and Los Angeles to get instant ratings on important programs. One rating service uses computer terminals connected to the television sets of a carefully selected sample of about 1,200 viewers. When their televisions are on, the channel is automatically monitored by a computer. The rating service can instantly determine which shows these viewers are watching. Using a scientific method known as sampling, the ratings service estimates how these 1,200 viewers represent other viewers across the country. Other sampled viewers are given diaries to keep for one month. Although these methods are often criticized by people in the radio and TV industry, the ratings strongly influence network schedules. During a ratings week, as the result of the competition for viewers, the four networks may air four attention-getting programs at the same time.

Pay TV, cable, and home VCRs have made selling products to TV viewers increasingly difficult. These technologies make it hard to direct viewers to the network programs where the ratings are taken. People with VCRs who have recorded a network program are likely to "zap" commercials by using the fast forward button on the recorder. Advertisers are also finding that during *prime time,* the period in which most viewers have traditionally tuned in network programs (from 7:00 P.M. to 11:00 P.M. Eastern time), many people are turning on VCRs, cable channels, or computers instead. This trend is creating problems for networks and ratings companies.

> **Higher ratings= higher advertising revenue.**

## FCC Regulations

Another influence on the programs available to you is the FCC, the Federal Communications Commission. Made up of seven commissioners appointed for seven-year terms by the President with the approval of the Senate, the FCC directs the development of the nation's broadcasting services. The commissioners decide who gets to use limited spectrum or wavelength space for police, shortwave, and cellular phone broadcasts. They assign frequencies to radio stations and channels to television stations. They decide that Station A will transmit on Channel 5, that Station B will broadcast at 710 on your AM radio, and that Station C will broadcast at 95.2 on your FM radio. Without regulation and assignments, you might not be able to hear or see anything because the broadcasts would jam each other. There is talk of deregulating radio and TV stations. Soon stations may be granted licenses for life instead of having to renew their commitment every three years. Until recently the FCC stated

**FIGURE 1.2**

Cable companies use earth-station antennas to receive programs transmitted from satellites in space. *Artist's rendering of satellite courtesy of NASA.*

that no one person or company could own more than seven radio or TV stations; the new limit is twelve. The FCC is studying possible new rules to cover changing technologies such as HDTV (High Definition TV) and DBS (Direct Broadcasting Satellites). The FCC staff also investigates how new technologies may impact older, established systems.

The FCC grants broadcasting licenses to applicants who can meet technical broadcasting standards and agree to operate in the "public interest, convenience, and necessity." Furthermore, the FCC reviews each station's performance to determine whether it has met the requirements of its license. Therefore, the commission directly affects what the stations show, or do not show, on television. However, FCC regulations are less strict now than in the past. During the 1980s the television industry was deregulated. The Fairness Doctrine, an FCC ruling dating from 1959 requiring TV stations to present both sides of any issue, was dismantled. Although the FCC still regulates licensing and controls some aspects of advertising, the television industry now sets its own standards on most issues.

## Cable TV

Cable TV was developed in the 1950s to improve television reception in areas that were too far from TV stations or where reception was blocked by mountains or other terrain problems. In the beginning, TV repair shops installed huge TV antennas and charged customers to hook up to them. This hookup enabled the customer to receive clear reception from distant TV stations. Now the cable situation has changed. Instead of providing improved reception, a cable hookup gives viewers access to up to 500 channels instead of the five or six offered by off-the-air reception. Some predict that by the year 2000, over 90 percent of the homes in the United States will have cable or will receive programs by the use of satellite dishes on the roof. This transmission, called DBS (Direct Broadcasting Satellite), operates with the use of a small two- to three-foot dish that receives transmissions from satellites located in space.

Most superstations such as WGN and WTBS can now be seen in all states. Cable television offers uncut movies through premium channels such as HBO, Showtime, and Cinemax. News broadcasts are offered twenty-four hours a day on the Cable News Network, and weather, once a minute review on a newscast, is now continuously offered by one cable channel. Diversity of programming is perhaps the greatest advantage of cable TV (where the programs are paid for by subscriptions rather than by advertisers solely interested in numbers of viewers).

Some say we are becoming a nation divided between information-rich people, who know how to access and can afford many cable channels and databases, and information-poor people, who cannot afford cable TV, computers, modems, or other means of accessing the increasing amounts of information available.

Cable offers those interested in TV production another feature. Local cable companies and others interested in TV production can produce programs for their local cable channels. These channels fall into two categories—local origination channels and public access channels. Locally originated programs are produced by the cable company for the viewers. These may include local high school and college sports, panel discussions, local newscasts, or any program the cable company chooses to produce for the viewers. Some of the cable companies charge local advertisers for commercials. The second type of programming offered by cable companies is *public access programming.* This is the most exciting for those interested in TV production because it offers anyone with a program idea the opportunity to bring it to viewers' screens. In order to use the cable company's studio or TV equipment, in most areas served by cable, you must take a short "access course." After a test, you are certified to check out the equipment and produce programs for local viewers without charge. Some schools enroll their TV classes in the access course so that the class can use the cable company's equipment to produce programs. You can put your school's basketball or football game on the cable. Perhaps you or your class can produce a weekly newscast for the access channel on your cable system. Some communities have required the cable company to locate its access studio in a local school so students can create programs for the access channel. This allows smaller towns to begin to use TV to communicate ideas. Some consumer equipment such as Hi-8 video camcorders can provide a signal good enough to use on cable or broadcast TV.

## Home Video Recorders

Until recently, only television stations, schools, or large businesses could afford large videotape recorders. Often costing many thousands of dollars, they were too expensive for most people. However, technology has changed all this, and now most homes have portable video recording equipment and camcorders. Viewers can now view two programs at once by recording one channel while viewing another. If your favorite movie comes on at 1 A.M., you can set the recorder to tape the movie and then view it at your convenience. It is now common to purchase or rent the latest movies. Virtually all movies can be rented for home VCRs soon after they are shown in theaters. Most libraries lend movies.

Some programming is created only to be shown on VCRs with no plan for it ever to be released at theaters or broadcast on TV. You can buy your favorite movie in the supermarket as you check out or at a fast-food restaurant. With this newer technology, you no longer have to depend on the major television networks for entertainment and information.

Video also has overtaken film as a medium for recording family activities. Many weddings are now recorded on videotape as well as in a traditional picture album. Smaller video companies tape weddings, dance recitals, anniversary parties, and almost any event that a still photographer was once employed to photograph. In addition, people are hiring aspiring video enthusiasts to videotape entire rooms and their contents for insurance purposes. Some realtors use video to "show" homes to prospective buyers, thus saving them from having to actually visit the homes. With video, entire new industries are being created because only imagination and public demand can limit the possible uses of video. "Virtual reality walk-throughs," creations of environments or total sensory experiences, are the latest technology.

## HISTORY OF BROADCASTING

Television is still a relatively young medium. Newspapers, for example, have been in the United States since about 1700. The telegraph was invented in 1844. The telephone was developed in 1876, and the first commercially licensed radio station went on the air in 1920. KDKA in Pittsburgh, Pennsylvania, transmitting from an attic in a Westinghouse radio factory, began broadcasting on November 2, 1920, with the Cox-Harding election results, and still broadcasts today.

Television really did not begin to come into homes until 1948. Before television, people listened to the radio. In fact, many of our favorite TV types of programs developed from earlier radio broadcasts. Daytime audiences listened to their favorite soap operas on radio. Instead of watching "As the World Turns," "General Hospital," and "All My Children," they listened to "Ma Perkins" and "Romance of Helen Trent."

In the evening, the family turned to adventure programs or to variety and situation comedies. "The Lone Ranger" was one of the longest running radio programs. Other programs included "Suspense," "Inner Sanctum," and "Gangbusters." Long before "Roseanne" came to television, families were laughing about the problems of "Blondie," "Henry Aldrich," and "The Nelson Family" on the radio.

Of course these shows were different in some respects from the situation comedies we watch today. For example, during the 1930s, one of the most popular radio programs, "Amos 'n' Andy," was very racist. The characters on the program portrayed negative stereotypes of African Americans at a time when few minorities were present in the media.

For more information on broadcasting's past, see the following chronological listing of significant events.

**FIGURE 1.3**

## CAPSULE HISTORY OF BROADCASTING

**1897:** Guglielmo Marconi patents the "wireless" in Great Britain.

**1901:** Marconi sends radio signals across the Atlantic.

**1909:** Professor Charles D. Herrold begins commercial radio broadcasts in San Jose, California. Lee De Forest calls it "the oldest broadcasting station in the entire world."

**1915:** University of Wisconsin begins experimental radio station. WHA becomes first educational radio station.

1920: KDKA, Pittsburgh, begins regularly scheduled programs.

1922: WEAF, New York, broadcasts first sponsored program. Advertising begins.

1923: WEAF, New York, and WNAC, Boston, complete first network hookup (a football game).

1923: Vladimir Zworykin invents iconoscope, an early CRT (cathode-ray tube).

1926: RCA buys AT&T's radio properties and forms NBC, with twenty-four stations. David Sarnoff is first president.

1927: NBC broadcasts first coast-to-coast radio program (Rose Bowl game).

1927: United Independent Broadcasters (UIB), later Columbia Broadcasting System (CBS), begins with sixteen stations. Cigar heir William S. Paley buys the network.

1927: Federal Radio Commission (FRC) begins. Issues station-only licenses, frequencies, and bands. Acts against "radio pirates."

1929: Crosley Radio Company begins first broadcast rating service.

1931: CBS begins, on an experimental basis, first regularly scheduled TV with New York City Mayor Jimmy Walker and singer Kate Smith.

1932: "Amos 'n' Andy" goes on air from Chicago on NBC.

1933: President F.D. Roosevelt uses all radio networks for four "Fireside Chats" to talk directly to the American people.

1934: Federal Communications Commission (FCC) established to issue all radio licenses and renewals, allocate frequencies and call letters.

1938: Radio's Golden Age begins. Networks expand. Variety, drama, and action shows flourish. Golden Age lasts until 1948 when TV begins to take over variety, drama, and adventure programming.

1941: World War II begins. Radio brings the war into the home. CBS, alone, beams 35,700 war programs. By war's end there are 56 million radios and 16,500 TV sets.

1943: Edward G. Nobel buys the NBC Blue Network and changes its name to the American Broadcasting Company (ABC).

1945: FM radio established. Development of both FM and TV held up by WW II.

1945: Dr. Peter Goldmark of CBS develops long-playing (LP) 33-rpm record. Also color TV first developed.

1948: "Ed Sullivan Show" and "Milton Berle Show" begin on TV.

1952: Golden Age of TV begins with shows like "Playhouse 90" and "Studio One."

1955: Edward R. Murrow does exposé on Senator Joseph McCarthy. Spells end of McCarthyism and blacklisting.

1956: Ampex demonstrates first workable videotape recorder.
1963: President J.F. Kennedy is shot in Dallas. Networks abandon all commercial broadcasting for four straight days and nights.
1969: The world watches over twenty-four hours continuous coverage of man's first steps on the moon's surface.
1970: Public Broadcasting Service (PBS) is formed.
1971: National Public Radio (NPR) begins operation.
1977: QUBE system (interactive CATV) begins in Columbus, Ohio.
1980: Corporate TV studio operations now outnumber broadcast TV stations in U.S.
1982: Toshiba of Japan introduces the LCD, flat-screen, pocket TV set.
1984: Stereo AM and TV go on the air.
1984: FCC begins to deregulate radio and TV stations, concentrating on technical rules. Limits on permitted numbers of commercials are lifted.
1985: FCC rules that one person or group can now own up to twelve radio and TV stations. HDTV demonstrated.
1986: FCC overturns many local laws that prohibit viewers from owning TV satellite dishes. FCC rules that communities may not regulate against program reception by satellite.
1986: HBO begins scrambling satellite transmissions so that those with satellite dishes must now pay to receive programming.
1993: Closed Captioning for the hearing impaired required on all new TVs.
1993: Both Warner Bros.-Tribune and Paramount-Chris Craft announce plans to launch new national broadcast networks. SKY CABLE satellite launched.

## HOW DO YOU WATCH TELEVISION?

People watch television for a variety of reasons. What do you watch? And, more importantly, how do you watch? Do you absorb like a sponge? Are you critically selective? Are you a spectator or a participant? Can you tell from the commercials what kind of viewer the advertiser thinks you are—perceptive, gullible, conservative, liberal, critical, adventurous, romantic, creative, unimaginative, young, old, sophisticated?

When you watch the news, do you consider all the newscasters fair and unbiased? In his book *The Newscasters,* critic Ron Powers charges that the late evening newscasts (11:00 P.M. in the East)

**FIGURE 1.4**
Edward R. Murrow was a highly-respected and popular American radio and television broadcaster. He is shown here during one of his Voice of America radio broadcasts during the early 1960s. *Photo courtesy of the United States Information Agency.*

often design stories to attract viewers and earn higher ratings. He claims that often uninteresting or nonvisual stories are dropped to make room for emotional or stimulating stories designed to catch attention. "Soft news" features such as reports on soap operas, nutrition, or film review are added because it is thought viewers will pay more attention to them than they would to more traditional news stories. Newscasts now are big money-makers for stations and often become entertainment.

Can you observe any clues, verbal or nonverbal, that indicate what the newscaster's personal opinion is about the news he or she is presenting?

> "Soft news" features are designed to draw more viewers to newscasts.

## Background

How you watch television and how critically you react depend on your personal background, interests, prejudices, and knowledge. If you lived in New York City for several years before moving to Keokuk, Iowa, you will watch a television play about a fire in a New York City subway more critically than your Keokuk friends. They do not know, as you do, what it means to travel on the subway, and therefore they cannot judge as well as you can how true to life the story is. It is easy to believe what you have seen on TV if you have no real-life examples for comparison. If your father and two older brothers have been varsity football players in high school and college, you watch the pro-football games on television with the understanding you have absorbed by listening to their conversation. The doctor sees a different medical show, the teacher a different education documentary, the police officer a different crime drama. Because of their personal experiences, viewers differ in their opinion of those programs and even in the television personalities with whom they are most familiar.

It is frequently hard to believe there are actually families like those as portrayed on TV. Yet many people view these programs because they can identify with the characters or problems in the television families. Archie Bunker on "All in the Family" was a character created to show the foolishness of racism, yet some people with racist values liked Archie and felt he stated their outlook.

How you watch and react also is determined to a considerable degree by how you tend to react to all elements of your environment. According to legend, John Burroughs, the naturalist, and a banker friend were strolling together along a noisy side street near Times Square, New York. Suddenly Burroughs halted and grabbed his companion by the arm. "Listen! Hear that cricket?" The banker ridiculed the idea that anyone could hear the chirp of a cricket in all that traffic din. What would it be doing there anyway? Burroughs, however, insisted he had heard a cricket and proved he was right when he spotted it among the fruits and vegetables on a peddler's pushcart at the curb. A few blocks farther up the street, the banker grabbed Burroughs' arm and halted him with the exclamation, "Someone dropped a coin. I heard a quarter hit the pavement." This time, it was Burroughs' turn to scoff at the audio acuity of his friend until the banker pointed to a coin on the metal sewer grill at the curb. The story may be fictional, but the idea is clear. We see and hear what we have been trained to pay attention to.

How do you watch? Do you select only the programs you know and like? If a show does not appeal to you, does the reason lie in you or in the program? When you watch a dramatic show, can you separate the shoddy from the artistic? Can you analyze what you see and hear well enough to evaluate what you watch? Note the standards for evaluation of productions created for the International Student Media Festival (Figure 1.5) and the criteria used by the International Television Association (Figure 1.6).

## FIGURE 1.5
## International Student Media Festival

### Categories

**Use these descriptions to choose a category for your production:**

(1) **Comedy:** Primary Purpose—To entertain and amuse. Tell a humorous story with a beginning, middle, and end, incorporating comedic elements such as: misunderstanding; choices, needs, goals; exaggeration; sight gags; reactions; characters; satire; obstacles; dialogue/arguments; scenes that help advance the plot. Humorous material often deals with universal or serious issues, obstacles, pain, and conflict.

(2) **Drama:** Primary Purpose—To tell a story using emotion and feeling in a dramatic way. Drama can incorporate elements such as: a character learning something; a slice of life; a specific story that examines a general idea; beginning, middle, and end to the story; choice, needs, goals; dialogue/arguments; scenes that help advance the plot; obstacles, pain, conflict.

(3) **News:** Primary purpose—To report real current events. A sincere attempt made to provide fair, factual, logical coverage of real world events within the time constraints of real-world newscasting. Extensively edited features, shot over more than one day, are documentaries, not news.

(4) **Documentary:** Primary Purpose—To provide a personal view of real events and people while remaining objective enough not to become propaganda. Created from interviews, analysis, and audio or visual presentation of facts selected by the producer. A viewpoint should be the focus of the effort but not to the total exclusion of alternate opinions.

(5) **Instructional:** Primary Purpose—To develop a program that helps people to learn something.

### Judging Criteria

**To be used to evaluate your production:**

(1) **Creativity/Originality:** Provide fresh, interesting insights into the subject of your video.

(2) **Organization/Purpose:** Show evidence of planning and choice through all parts of your production as you focus on achieving the program's purpose.

(3) **Continuity/Structure:** Show that the information or story is paced and developed in a way that keeps viewers interested and helps them understand your meaning.

(4) **Relevancy/Importance:** Will anyone care about the content of your video? Is the subject or idea big enough to sustain the entire program?

(5) **Documentation:** Have you provided the outlines, questions, scripts, storyboards, that you used to help plan and complete your video? (The thing professional directors regret most after completing a project is not having planned completely before beginning.)

(6) **Use of Available Resources:** Have you used the media opportunities available to you to their maximum effect? The judges will try to assess the level of effort and skill used under very different circumstances.

(7) **Clarity/Universality/Meaning:** Could everyone understand it? Did you tell a unified story or message that provides an insight into your subject or the human condition?

(8) **Energy/Emotion/Residue:** Does your program heighten viewer attention and interest? Does the program touch human emotions or feelings? When the program is over, does it leave a meaning with the viewer more general or beyond the specific presentation or story you have told?

### Categories

(6) **Promotional:** Primary Purpose—Program longer than sixty seconds designed to present an idea, concept, organization, or individual in a positive and credible way, so as to encourage audience approval, support, and/or participation.

(7) **Music Videos:** Primary Purpose—To entertain, express ideas and emotions, through a combination of music and visual material. Original musical composition and performance is encouraged. Nonoriginal music requires written permission.

(8) **PSA's:** Short thirty- or sixty-second messages designed to change public opinion, actions, or feelings.

(9) **Sports:** Primary Purpose—to capture the essence of a sport such as surfing, skating, motorcross, biking, etc. Creative editing of action may be accompanied by original music, interviewing, or narration.

### Judging Criteria

*This festival, held annually, is administered under the auspices of the Association for Educational Communications and Technology (AECT) headquartered at 1025 Vermont Ave. N.W., Suite 820, Washington, DC 20005-35470. The work of the committee and the judges is totally voluntary. No honorarium is given to the committee or judges.*

### FIGURE 1.6
### Modified ITVA Evaluation*

#### Message Design Elements
OBJECTIVES: To what degree does the program accomplish its stated objectives?
DESIGN STRATEGY: Are good principles of communication or instruction applied to the development of the material? Is the content organized? Is there a logical, understandable flow?
TREATMENT: To what degree is the treatment of the subject matter effective? Are appropriate production techniques used to focus on the critical components of the message design?

#### Creative Element
WRITING: Is the script clear and understandable? Is the language appropriate for the program treatment, subject matter, and audience level?
DIRECTION: To what degree did the director successfully manage the integration of all program elements to achieve the stated objectives?
EDITING: To what degree did the editing techniques contribute to the program's effectiveness (pacing, shot selection, flow, etc.)?
ARTISTIC USE OF MEDIUM: To what degree do the following elements contribute to the quality of the material presented?

| | |
|---|---|
| Music Selection | Set Design |
| Talent Selection | Graphics Design |
| Lighting Design | Animation |
| Special Effects | |

Would the program still achieve the stated objectives without these elements? Do these items improve or enhance the program and not cover up poor program design?

### Production Elements
CAMERA: To what degree was the videography effective? Was the camera steady? Were the moves smooth? Was the exposure correct?
LIGHTING: To what degree did the lighting contribute to the overall effectiveness of the program? Was there the proper ratio of key, back, fill, etc.? Was lighting consistent from scene to scene?
TALENT: To what degree did the talent's performance (whether pro/amateur/on-camera or VO) contribute to the program's effectiveness?

\* based on a form used by the International Television Association. Courtesy of John Holmes, John Marshall High School, Milwaukee, Wisconsin.

# EFFECTS OF TELEVISION VIEWING

How do you let TV affect you? Can you avoid its influence? Should you avoid its influence?

Television certainly has affected the amount of information easily available to you. Adult experiences are yours at the flick of a

**FIGURE 1.7**

*Courtesy: Magnavox/Philips Consumer Electronics Company.*

switch. Even the youngest member of your family acquires information formerly reserved for adults. Kindergarten teachers report that "detergent" is now in the vocabulary of the preschool child, who can also, thanks to television commercials, select cereals and packaged foods from the shelves of the supermarket before he or she has learned to read. Educational programs such as "Sesame Street" have taught children how to read and count long before they enter kindergarten.

Think of the misconceptions that have been avoided because television brings people with lifestyles totally different from your own into your life. A city person can see something of life on a farm; the suburban student can witness conditions in a city; the ranch hand in Montana can watch a nightclub act in Las Vegas. Through TV newscasts everyone can see the starving children of Somalia or a grieving family whose son or daughter has been shot. It is said TV has made the world smaller by bringing us events from all over the world and transmitting them instantly into our homes. This instant transmission has made us more aware of the world around us. Has it made us more sympathetic or more numbed and apathetic? Do we watch because we care or because we feel relieved that a similar tragedy hasn't happened to us? You, as a critical viewer, can heighten your sensitivity if you study what you see and use your information for making judgments.

As in any field, understanding media increases your ability to criticize poor work and your ability to enjoy quality programs. Similarly, the more you know about baseball, the more you can enjoy the skillful maneuvering of the pitcher and base stealer, and the more critical you are when you see stupid blunders and errors. The more you learn about music, the more you can appreciate musical skills and styles. The tone-deaf listener who knows nothing about music does not cringe at the "sour" note; the same note is agonizing for the musician.

It is the same with your knowledge of television. The more media-literate or visually literate you become, the more you will enjoy and appreciate some programs, and the more you will dislike others. You may decide to turn the set off and do something else, such as make your own programs, your own way. The decision to watch TV is always the decision to give up the opportunity to do something else.

## IT'S A WRAP

Many of you watch television programs mainly for enjoyment, sometimes for education. You can become a more critical viewer by learning how TV is created. Much of the programming you watch is provided by commercial television stations. Many of these stations are part of larger networks, but independent and cable stations are becoming more important. Television stations use ratings to estimate how many viewers watch a program. Advertisers depend on ratings to see if their products are reaching a large audience. The FCC (Federal Communications Commission) directs the development of the nation's broadcasting services and grants licenses.

Viewing habits are being affected by the growth of cable and pay-TV systems; also home video recorders (VCRs) now enable viewers to record one program while viewing another.

As you increase your understanding of the visual media, you will become a more discerning viewer, better able to enjoy and appreciate the programs you watch.

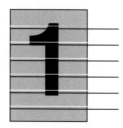

# Video Lab

1. Two popular programs on TV are "Siskel & Ebert," a syndicated TV program on which two critics review the latest movies, and "Sneak Previews," a PBS offering with basically the same format.

Set up a program on which you and/or a partner review the latest TV programs. This program, if done well, could be an excellent program for a public access cable TV channel or a closed-circuit TV channel within a school. Select two or three TV programs, preferably of different types, and review them. Reviews could address the following:

a. For whom is the program intended?
b. What is the point of view of the program?
c. Does the program portray life realistically?
d. Does it entertain, inform, instruct, influence feelings, or sell?
e. What is the message of the program?
f. What kind of person would enjoy this program?
g. Would you watch the program again?
h. Use the International Student Media Festival standards to evaluate a program.

2. Create a two-minute radio program called "Who's Who in Media." This program should contain a musical opening and closing and portray someone influential in the field of radio or television. If your school has a low-power radio station or a cable TV station, this would be an excellent program. It could feature early radio pioneers such as Edward R. Murrow or David Sarnoff, the founder of NBC, or today's broadcasters, such as David Letterman of CBS.

3. Keep a log for a thirty-minute television newscast. List each story used, and note if the story had accompanying film or videotape. Which reports were more interesting? Did the order follow from the most to least important? Did many stories contain exciting visuals such as floods, fires, or car crashes?

4. Keep another log for a local newscast for one week. Determine which stories were used to hold your attention. How many stories were "soft news" (special reports, consumer affairs, movie reviews, and other non-news items)?

5. Watch "The MacNeil/Lehrer NewsHour" on PBS and compare its format with the network news.

6. Television commercials are the mainstay of American TV. These thirty-second interrup-

tions are the price we pay for viewing our programs. Advertisers spend millions of dollars analyzing the audience, refining the message, and producing the commercial. Most ads are based on an emotional appeal and claims that the product fills a need. Some common emotional appeals used by advertisers include:

a. Love for family (insurance ads, film commercials)
b. Acquisition and savings (sales, giveaways)
c. Adventure (car ads)
d. Sex appeal (beer, perfume, cars)
e. Better taste (coffee, soft drinks)
f. Health (caffeine-free and sports drinks)
g. Testimonial (favorite actor or sports figure selling a product)
h. Use of humor
i. Guilt (product causes people to like or dislike you)

Keep a log of twenty-five TV commercials. For each one, note the product, identify the emo-tional appeal used in the ad, and explain how the ad was made visually appealing for TV.

7. Bring in at least one ad from a newspaper or magazine that is an example of the emotional appeals mentioned above. Be sure to identify which appeal is used in the ad.

8. Become familiar with trade journals by reading a copy of *Broadcasting and Cable.* Write a two-page report on what you found inside. Why are so many radio and television jobs listed?

9. Pretend you are a radio/TV critic for a local newspaper. Using the criteria found in this chapter, write a review for a program such as "Seinfeld" or "Star Trek: The Next Generation."

10. Keep a diary for two full weeks listing everything you watched on TV. Include the time, the program, the date, the channel, and the number of viewers in your home. Compare your diary with those of your classmates. Then set up a class ratings system to determine if your viewing habits differ from your classmates'.

## Take Two

1. Why do you think the government regulates radio and television stations but does not regulate newspapers?

2. Broadcasters must promise to broadcast in the public "interest, need, and convenience." Do you think most broadcasters are providing programs that meet these requirements? Why or why not?

3. Why are ratings so important to radio and television stations? How do the ratings affect programming?

4. If you were a TV producer or network president, how would you feel about video recorders and video discs? How do you think they will affect TV in the future?

5. In your opinion, how important is visual appeal (film or tape) in television news?

6. How does radio differ today from the programs heard before television? Why do you think radio changed after television?

7. Why is the local newscast so important to a TV station?

8. The average family spends seven hours and thirteen minutes viewing television every day. Keep a daily record of viewing in your family for several days. How does your family compare with the average? Using the following categories, describe the types of programs your family prefers.

**Program Categories**

Situation comedies

Family shows

Medical, detective, police shows

Sports

Game shows

News and public affairs programs

Talk, variety, interview shows

Soap operas

Specials

Children's shows

Dramas

Public Broadcasting Service programs

Music, concert programs including MTV

Religious programs

Nature shows

**9.** In order to keep its license, a TV station promises to air local programs for public service. This includes newscasts, local documentaries, public affairs programs, public service announcements (PSAs), children's programs, and other programs of importance to local viewers. Check the program schedule from the local paper for a week, keep a log for one of the stations, and write down the time a public affairs program is aired. After checking this for one week, come to some conclusion regarding the number of programs offered by the station for public affairs as compared with entertainment programs offered by the same station.

**10.** If you have cable TV in your area, has it changed the viewing habits of your family? Does your family watch the public access channel offered by your cable company? Keep a family TV viewing log for a week to determine how much TV viewing comes from cable programming rather than from off-the-air stations.

**11.** With cable TV "R"- and even "X"-rated programs can be received directly into the homes. Small children can now tune in to uncut movies usually reserved for adult viewers. What regulation, if any, do you think should be imposed on cable companies to prevent sensitive viewers from seeing such programs? Who, if anyone, needs to be protected? How would you categorize acceptable and unacceptable programs? Who should make the categories?

## ADDITIONAL RESOURCES

Bianculli, David. *Teleliteracy: Taking Television Seriously,* (New York, Continuum Publishing Company, 1992).

*Broadcasting and Cable.* (New York, Cahners Consumer/Entertainment Publishing Division, weekly publication).

*Broadcasting Bibliography.* (Washington, D.C., NAB Library, 1984).

Ellmore, R. Terry. *NTC's Mass Media Dictionary*, (Lincolnwood, Ill., National Textbook Company, 1991).

Fiske, John. *Television Culture: Popular Pleasures and Politics,* (New York: Routledge, 1988).

Foster, Eugene. *Understanding Broadcasting,* (New York, Wesley Publishing Co., 1982).

Head, Sydney, and Christopher Sterling. *Broadcasting in America, sixth edition,* (Boston, Houghton Mifflin Company, 1991).

Hilliard, Robert. *Radio Broadcasting: An Introduction to the Sound Medium, third edition,* (New York, Longman, 1985).

Rather, Dan. *The Camera Never Blinks,* (New York, Ballantine, 1987).

Schrank, Jeffrey. *Understanding Mass Media, fourth edition,* (Lincolnwood, Ill., National Textbook Company, 1991).

Sklar, Robert. *An International History of the Medium,* (New York, Henry A. Abrams Publishers, 1993).

Stephans, Mitchell. *Broadcast News, third edition.* (Ft. Worth, Tex., Harcourt Brace, 1993).

**Organizations Interested in Media Literacy and Education**

National Alliance for Media Education
c/o NAMAC
655 Thirteenth Street #201
Oakland, California 94612 (510/451-2717; 213/483-0216)

National Telemedia Council
120 E. Wilson Street
Madison, Wisconsin 53703 (608/257-7712)

# 2

# Assessing the Medium

"Go Wildcats!" cheer two dirty tennis shoes as they alternately hit the pavement with the verb and noun lettered on their sides.

"This lemon was purchased from McWhorter Motors, 16 West Broad Street" is the message in ten-inch high, iridescent letters on the side of a new station wagon in the shopping center parking lot.

A teenager and a disgruntled car owner selected what they considered the most appropriate medium to communicate an idea. But it is not always easy to decide the best way to get a message across. Advertisers have an increasing variety of media from which to choose in their quest to reach the public. Radio, television, magazines, newspapers, and billboards are a few ways they can publicize their products.

In most schools, students also have a variety of media from which to choose. If your message is "Come to the school play," you may tell your story on posters, on the public address system, in the school newspaper, on the school radio or television station, on the auditorium stage, in conversation in the cafeteria, or in visual exhibits in a display case. Before making a choice, you listen to student reactions and comments. "Nobody ever listens to the P.A. bulletin." "Everyone will see that kind of poster—why don't we make fifty?" "That idea's just plain stupid." You consider comments from fellow students and then select the most effective means, instrument, or medium for getting students to attend the play. You learn quickly which medium (newspaper, radio, television, posters) is the most powerful in your school.

If you are campaigning for an office on the student council, how do you select the medium through which you will sell yourself to student voters? How should students decide which of their activities will be reported in the school paper, which will be memorialized in the yearbook, and which recorded in a video yearbook? Which messages are most effective in print? Supermarkets prefer to publish their price lists and coupon sales in the newspaper for consumers to reread and use in making shopping lists. Which messages leave the most lasting impression? Does a live theatrical performance, with its three-dimensional, physical reality, communicate some ideas more effectively than a video laser disc? Does television have a characteristic impact of its own, or is it merely a combination of the pictures and sounds of other media? How does theater differ from television? Can television do anything theater cannot?

## TWO KINDS OF AUDIENCES

To compare television and the stage as media for communicating ideas, you must first consider the two audiences because to sell an idea you must know the potential buyer. In the theater, the audience is seated and usually remains seated for the entire performance, having come to see a two-hour presentation. A member of the audience who becomes bored and walks out during the performance disturbs surrounding people and may even distract the performers on stage. The television audience, on the other hand, comes and goes at will, switching from channel to channel at any point during the program with no immediate effect on the performers. Viewers may tune in after the program is well underway; characters may have already died, or the opposing point of view may have already been presented. Viewers may talk to each other during the program.

Stand-up comedians performing on stage depend on the response of the audience, their laughter and applause. They soon learn that the Wednesday matinee crowd of shoppers will not react to the same gags that delight the Saturday night crowd. A television comedian often demands a studio audience, believing that the sound of laughter affects the home viewing audience. Recorded laugh tracks have been used for situation comedies, but most viewers can recognize "canned" laughter, and many directors favor a studio audience. Some acts are changed slightly for the benefit of this studio audience. Taped shows with studio audiences can be identified by the statement, "Recorded before a live audience."

Television and stage audiences differ in another respect: the circumstances that accompany their viewing situation. Students watch-

**FIGURE 2.2**

"The Oprah Winfrey Show," taped before a live studio audience, depends on audience participation. *Photo courtesy of Oprah Winfrey Productions, Chicago.*

ing *Hamlet* on a classroom television set with a teacher keep their eyes open and their faces turned toward the screen, regardless, of where their thoughts may wander. Those same students, watching *Hamlet* on portable sets at the foot of their beds, may doze off now and then.

A young person watching a football game alone on a seventeen-inch screen may remain quietly seated before the television set, except for occasional trips to the refrigerator. Two other people watching the same game on a wide screen may shout at each other and argue. A crowd watching the same game in Kansas City's Truman Sports Complex may cheer as wildly at the instant replay on the stadium's huge television screen as they do during the actual play on the field.

Another difference between the television and stage performance lies in the control of the viewer's attention. The theatergoer can look anywhere on the stage at any actor, regardless of where the playwright intended the center of attention to be. Television viewers see only what the director wants them to see; they cannot see a speaker unless the camera is focused on that speaker. In the theater, voices and action tend to direct attention to the actors, but the audience still has a full view of the stage and can look wherever they choose.

The theater audience, remaining in a fixed location, sees the entire show from the same viewpoint. During a television show, the camera controls what the viewer sees, and the director may show the action first from a great distance, then with a tight close-up. The director may decide the actors should be photographed from above the stage or from the far left side. The focus may be an actor's hands or right profile. While this selective view provided by the camera concentrates the viewer's attention on a specific area, it restricts the actors' freedom of movement. On stage, actors may vary their positions a step or two without seriously affecting the scene, but television actors must keep within camera range, or the audience will lose sight of them. For these reasons theater is often called the actor's medium and film the director's medium.

This need to keep an actor's movements within camera range is so important that occasionally even professional performers rely on chalk marks on the floor to indicate their correct positions in relation to the camera. John R., a student playing the role of the station-master in a television production of Arnold Ridley's mystery thriller,

*Ghost Train,* found it difficult to stay "in character" while remembering to adapt his stage crosses to the limits of camera range. During rehearsals, the director warned him, even threatened him, to move only as directed with no improvised sauntering around the stage. During the telecast, John followed instructions and stood exactly in front of the ticket office door. However, he kept twitching his left shoulder and jerking his body at three-second intervals. These weird movements, completely out of character, distracted the studio audience and the home viewers, and drove the director to the verge of delirium. Not until after the telecast did the director learn the explanation for John's strange behavior. The filament in the specially constructed scoop light was water-cooled. A leak in the covering lens allowed hot water to drip rhythmically on John's shoulder, causing him to jerk at the three-second intervals. However, he did stay within camera range, and the show went on!

> *Theater = actor's medium*
> *Film = director's medium*

Still another difference between television and the stage is provided by the television control room. The director of a play cannot communicate with the actors while they are on stage, so he or she must make all comments during rehearsals. The television director, however, can converse with the floor manager via the intercom; the manager, in turn, can give instructions to the actors throughout the show. Directors can determine at any moment which of the characters' reactions they wish the audience to see.

Even the setting in a television play is different from the stage presentation. Television directors can change scenes instantly by having the camera focus on a different part of the studio where a scene has been set up in advance. A thirty-second commercial allows adequate time to dolly the camera to another part of the set, a technique used on "Saturday Night Live." Of course, theaters have speeded up their set changes with lighting blackouts and skeleton set pieces—techniques adapted from films and television.

Then, too, settings can be "faked" in television productions more easily than on the stage. Because the camera sees with one eye at a time, the viewer cannot judge the size of objects. A two-foot model of a park, for instance, appears as a real full-size park until a life-size finger points to an inch-high tree. A head-and-shoulders shot of a hunter with tree branches visible at the curve of his shoulders suggests an entire forest. To the camera—and thus to the viewer—the only thing that is important is what is in the frame of the shot.

**FIGURE 2.3**

Newscasters and program hosts should avoid wearing the same shades of color as the background.

*All that counts is what's in the frame*

With the use of chroma key (an electronic process whereby a television performer stands in front of a blue or green background), film, videotape, or slides are inserted where the camera "sees" the blue or green in the original picture. This technique creates instant scenery. In television news, for example, a picture or videotape is often shown over the anchorperson's shoulder. Behind the performer is a blue background. Another camera scans a picture on an easel, or from another video source; where the blue appears on the original camera, the viewer sees the picture coming from the second source. Newscasters must be careful not to wear a blue coat or tie as the picture would also appear right through their clothing.

One of the most noticeable differences between stage and television production is the timing. The curtain rises on a school play at 8:15 Friday night. There are two ten-minute intermissions, and the final curtain falls at 10:20. On Saturday night, a snowstorm and a resulting traffic jam cause the opening curtain to be delayed five minutes while late arrivals are finding their seats. The Saturday night audience is the more responsive, applauding and laughing frequently. The final curtain comes down at 10:35, fifteen minutes later than on Friday night. A television program, on the other hand, is not interrupted by audience feedback. It begins at 8:31 (even if the audience hasn't tuned in yet), and the final commercial brings down the curtain at 8:59:30. Thus, the television actors have less freedom to ad-lib or to lengthen or shorten their pauses because of the exact timing required by the program schedule. An earthquake tremor in California which threw electric clocks off for only 30 seconds caused problems for network officials in New York as they waited half a minute for a program coming from the West Coast. Thirty seconds of silence and a blank screen are an eternity for a commercial network. The value of 30 seconds of commercial time—hundreds of thousands of dollars—is lost forever.

## CHOOSING THE MEDIUM FOR THE MESSAGE

The student who has a message to communicate needs to compare the audience, the setting, the time requirements, what can be seen and heard, and the movement required, in order to choose wisely between presenting his or her program on stage to a live audience or presenting it on television.

### Why Not Radio?

It may be that radio, rather than television or the stage, is the best medium for what you want to get across. Although radio programs are subject to the same strict time scheduling as television, the radio show can transport the listener back and forth in time and space. Certain sound effects suggest a scene in a factory: A few bars of music and a little imagination take the listener to the Far East in seven seconds. Radio is often called "theater of the mind" because listeners actually participate by creating the scene in their own minds. There are no props, no costumes, no makeup, and no scenery. The performer may use a script throughout the program. If the message can be conveyed through verbal clues alone, if it can be conveyed through words, sound effects, and music, then radio is an effective medium.

For example, many advertisers prefer radio to TV or newspapers because radio allows them to be more creative. TV can impose restraints on creativity because the message must be presented visually. Radio, on the other hand, allows listeners to create their own visualization. One advertising firm that relies on radio for product commercials is Dick Orkin's Radio Ranch in Los Angeles, which uses radio to sell products for advertisers. This firm has earned millions using humorous radio commercials to sell everything from Pepsi and AT&T to *Time* magazine and Southwest Airlines.

Although radio is effective, if you plan to convey part of your message through nonverbal clues, you will want to select television or the stage as your medium. If a comedian's facial expressions and clumsy movements are his or her stock in trade, television is the appropriate medium for that brand of humor.

In certain areas, radio appears to be a more effective medium. Teachers of young children often find that radio stories stimulate a child's imagination and develop creativity more than television programs, even those TV shows specifically designed for children. An eighty-five-year-old seamstress who had never seen a baseball game in her life became an avid fan and quite knowledgeable about the fine points of strategy by following Chicago Cubs games on the radio, assisted no doubt by the fact that radio sportscasters have to describe and explain more than television sportscasters.

Another factor that might affect your choice of a medium for your message is the widespread use of radio today. Far from collapsing after the invention of television, radio is still a powerful means of communication. Radio, however, has changed greatly to meet the demands of a new audience. FM, for example, was originally created for broadcasting classical music because of its high fidelity and static-free reception. Today, many rock stations crowd the FM band, while AM radio broadcasts many all-news or talk programs. Students carry their radios to the beach, to the picnic grounds, to the student union. The car radio has become indispensable to home-bound commuters, who listen to traffic directions and music while stuck on the expressway.

Not long ago, an eastern university received a complaint from students because the library was so quiet they could not study. They had gone through high school doing their homework to music selected by radio's popular disk jockeys and had become conditioned to the noise of today's popular music. So the university piped recorded music into one of the library's soundproof rooms for those who needed music along with their reference books.

Although many counted radio out when TV came into existence back in the late 1940s, today radio is as strong as ever because it differs from television. The two distinct media require different methods of communication and therefore attract two different audiences. Never discount the power of radio.

## Film and Videotape

No comparison or analysis of nonprint media is complete without reference to videotape or film. Before portable video equipment, television depended on film for most "on-the-spot" news stories outside the studio. Film was smaller than bulky video recorders and could record news events easily. Film is still the medium of choice for theatrical releases, TV dramas, and made-for-TV movies. We have grown accustomed to film's look, particularly in exterior shots and low-light situations. However, film is not without its disadvantages, which encouraged stations to use tape when video became smaller. One problem with film was that it had to be physically transported from the news event, and it often took up to an hour to get the film back to the TV station. Then, of course, the film had to be processed and developed before it could be edited and used on the air. This took time and prevented some good stories from getting onto the newscast.

Videotape has replaced film for television news departments. With portable ENG (Electronic News Gathering) video recorders and professional camcorders, news teams can record a story on videotape and send the signal back to the station via a microwave signal. Most TV newsrooms use a remote van for news footage. On top of the truck is a large microwave antenna. An engineer beams the signal back to the station directly from the truck. This also allows the remote news crew to report "live" during the actual newscast from anywhere in the city.

So if you choose television to put across your message, you are selecting a composite medium—one that combines techniques from theater, film, and radio; a highly technical medium used to produce artistic results; an impersonal, electronic instrument used by people to communicate in a personal way.

*TV news today depends on video-tape.*

Television, however, does not perform magic. What is boring in reality will not become exciting when videotaped. A dull band does not become interesting just because we see it on television. People are becoming accustomed to viewing TV to see action. With videotape's editing features, cut-ins, cutaways, and other film techniques can now be used to add many visual effects. The television medium carries the message from the sender to the receiver. With radio or television you may be heard by thousands of people at once, but it is important to remember that you are speaking to only one or two people in one place. This *one-to-one* communication makes television more personal than a live performance. With its focus of attention, its personal one-to-one relationship, its visual emotional impact, its immediacy, and its mass appeal, television has many strengths.

## THE COMMUNICATION PROCESS

In order for any communication to take place, three elements are necessary: a sender, a message, and a receiver (see Figure 2.4). Each element must be present for television communication to take place, and each element of the communication process is affected by various factors. The broadcaster's ability to send a message is affected by his or her skill and experience. The message, whether it is a commercial or a TV newscast, is affected by technical transmission and mechanical clarity. The impact of the message on the receiver is affected by the viewer's knowledge and attitude toward the broadcaster and toward the message itself.

**FIGURE 2.4**

**A Communication Model**

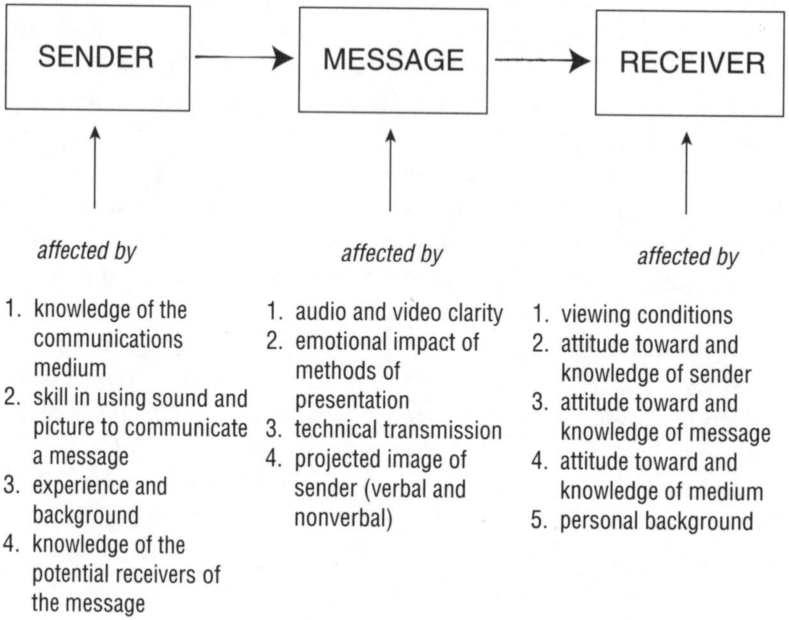

*affected by*

1. knowledge of the communications medium
2. skill in using sound and picture to communicate a message
3. experience and background
4. knowledge of the potential receivers of the message

*affected by*

1. audio and video clarity
2. emotional impact of methods of presentation
3. technical transmission
4. projected image of sender (verbal and nonverbal)

*affected by*

1. viewing conditions
2. attitude toward and knowledge of sender
3. attitude toward and knowledge of message
4. attitude toward and knowledge of medium
5. personal background

To communicate an idea effectively on television, you must respect the basic principles of communication. You must know your viewers: their attitudes, their viewing conditions, their prior knowledge. It is important to evaluate your message from the viewers' standpoint. What will your message mean to them? How will they decode it in terms of their own experience and feelings? Only when you reach an understanding of your audience can you send your television message with any hope of their understanding it.

## IT'S A WRAP

If you have a message that you wish to communicate to others, what is the best way? If you want to reach a large audience, would your message be more effective in print? Or do you want to reach your audience more quickly by communicating in person, by appearing before them on stage? In this chapter, you learned the difference between stage audiences and television audiences. Television audiences are affected by the camera range, the director, the setting and background; even the timing of the presentation is different in television communication.

Another medium for communicating your message is radio. Radio is as popular today as it was in the days before television. It can be more effective in some cases, as radio allows your audience to use its imagination. Other nonprint media to consider are film and videotape.

In order for any communication to take place, three elements are needed: a sender, a message, and a receiver. It is important to evaluate your message from the point of view of your receiver (your audience). If you understand your audience, your message, and the best method to send it, your message will be effective.

# 2

# Video Lab

1. Tune in any football or basketball game that is being broadcast on both radio and television. One quarter tune in the television broadcast. During another quarter turn down the sound from the television and turn on the radio. How does the sportscasters' play-by-play coverage differ from one medium to the other? Which do you think is more difficult to do? What kind of fill-in information, or "color," does each use? Did the radio announcer keep up with the action as you saw it on television? Compare and analyze the differences and similarities between the two.

2. Watch a football or basketball game on TV, turn off the sound, and see if you can talk fast enough to keep up with the action as it happens. Make a list of fill-in information you could use during time-outs, between quarters, and at halftime. How could you devise a method of keeping all the players straight? What statistics should be kept so the viewers can keep up with the action?

Try the same technique with a baseball game, which is slower. What is the difference in broadcasting a fast-paced event like football and a slower-paced one like baseball? How important is color information to a baseball game? Try to find information that could be used to fill dull moments such as the changing of pitchers.

3. Tape one of your school's basketball games play-by-play. Before the game, bring in background information on each team including records, injuries, last week's games, and styles of play. Plan a pregame show for about five minutes before tip-off. Then, cover the game by giving a play-by-play description, as well as any color information you can use during time-outs. Perhaps you could do an interview during halftime. After the game, plan to "recap" by giving percentages, free-throw attempts, fouls, and mistakes. Listen to the tape when finished to evaluate your performance on the air.

4. Videotape a school basketball game for public access cable presentation. You can do this simply with one camera situated in the stands with a microphone. The camera operator can record the game while the play-by-play announcer gives the audio account of the game. It is a good idea to coordinate with each other so that the camera is capturing the same picture the commentator is describing. This is easily accomplished, as most TV cameras used for recording offer an audio earphone jack that allows the camera operator to hear what is being said. Use an extension microphone, not the one located on the camera.

5. Plan a televised cooking or science demonstration that you can perform easily. List the ingredients or equipment needed and the steps in the process. Indicate which of these steps the viewer must see at close range in order to understand the process. At these points have the camera operator move in for a tight shot, or close-up (CU). As the class views the demonstration, evaluate the clarity of the explanations and offer suggestions for improvement. Now perform the same demonstration without the camera, explaining on the mike exactly how to follow the recipe or procedure. Discuss the major differences between the live and the televised versions.

6. Prepare a thirty-second radio commercial for one of these products.

a. a toothpaste     e. a video recorder
b. a soft drink     f. an airline
c. a safety tire     g. car company
d. a stereo set

Using a tape recorder or radio studio equipment, create a straight radio commercial (one using no sound effects or music). Here are some suggestions for creating an effective commercial:

- Keep your idea simple and to the point.
- Get your listeners' attention immediately.
- Remember that you are talking only to one person; imagine you are talking to someone you know.
- Develop your commercial around some emotional appeal such as economy, safety, status, pride, love, or guilt. A thirty-second commercial is approximately sixty-five words, depending on how fast you speak. Write and record the commercial to determine if you can "sell" your product. Remember to be enthusiastic and sincere.

7. Present the same commercial (developed in exercise 6) on television. Videotape the commercial to determine how your eye contact, gestures, and delivery help sell the product. For television, you probably will have to memorize the script because reading on camera is distracting and ineffective. How can you visualize your presentation for TV?

8. Create a short story on videotape. Use a single video camera for your production. Plan to have credits with a title and performers listed at the beginning. The story should not have to depend on sound. Include the following types of shots in the film:

a. a wide shot (when used early on, this is called an establishing shot)
b. a medium shot
c. a close-up (often used for showing emotion or detail)
d. a panning shot
e. a shot in which the camera moves (try to convey emotions through camera technique)

Here are some topics for your video:

- A student's day (best day, worst day, day something changes)
- Why you should take the bus to school rather than drive
- Working
- Washing a car or dog (warning: wet dogs smell really bad)
- Feelings (love, hate, happiness, or sadness)
- A humorous story (put a character in a situation and have funny things happen; then get the character out of that situation)

Remember that a film is not a one-shot wonder, but a series of scenes composed of shots that tell a story when they are put together. Plan your video completely before you start filming. Edit the video in the camera as you shoot. Remember that shooting with a single camera is different from using several cameras in a studio.

## Take Two

**1.** Select two or three of your favorite television shows and study them carefully the next few times you watch. Discuss with your class which of these programs would make good radio shows. Which shows depend on visual images? Could any of them be transferred successfully to the stage?

**2.** If any students recently have seen stage, club, or concert appearances by popular musicians, have them comment on the performance. Then discuss the differences between the live performances and the same musicians performing on television.

**3.** Television frequently utilizes both classic and contemporary literature for programming. Watch a television production of a book you have read recently. Discuss the differences and the similarities between the book and the program. Be prepared to offer examples.

**4.** Of the methods available for disseminating news (newspapers, radio, television), which do you prefer? What do you feel are the advantages and disadvantages of each medium?

**5.** Imagine you are a producer for a radio station. Check your local newspaper and find a story that you would follow up on during a local newscast. How would you change the story for your listeners to give them a perspective they couldn't gain by reading the newspaper? Keep in mind that radio is immediate. Always keep the story up to the minute. Who would you interview? Take this a step further. Imagine now you are a producer for a local TV station's news facility. Suppose you read the same story in the newspaper. Explain what you would do to put the story on your six o'clock news telecast. How would you "visualize" the same story? Create a one- or two-minute TV story.

## ADDITIONAL RESOURCES

Biagi, Shirley. *Media-Impact: An Introduction to Mass Media, second edition,* (Belmont, Calif., Wadsworth, 1992).

Biagi, Shirley. *Media-Reader: Perspectives on Mass Media Industries,* (Belmont, Calif., Wadsworth, 1989).

Stephens, Mitchell. *Broadcast News: Radio Journalism and an Introduction to Television, third edition,* (Ft. Worth, Tex., Harcourt Brace, 1993).

Whetmore, Edward Jay. *Mediamerica: Form, Content and Consequences of Mass Communication, fifth edition,* (Belmont, Calif., Wadsworth, 1993).

# 3

# Visualizing the Message

If you want to communicate effectively, you must clearly understand your message and how you want your audience to respond. If you want to communicate via television, you must also know what kind of visual images or pictures will make your message most meaningful to the viewer. As a telecommunicator, you must think of everything you want to say or do in terms of pictures; you select, devise, and compose television pictures that get your idea across without distracting the viewer's attention from the response you wish them to make to your message.

To achieve effective visual communication, you must know how to obtain television pictures that will tell the story, explain the idea, or sell the product. You should begin to think in terms of pictures rather than words to communicate your message. For example, imagine you are the director of a major league baseball game. It's the bottom of the ninth, with two outs. The clean-up man is up to bat. The score is tied, and it's all up to the batter. This is a tense situation, isn't it? How could you show the tension of the game, especially that of the pitcher and the batter, with the pictures you are televising to the viewers? What shots would you put on the screen from your cameras on the field?

You might get a close-up of the pitcher's face as he wipes the perspiration or shakes off the sign from the catcher, a medium shot as he uses the resin bag, a close-up of the batter's face as he stares down the pitcher, a close-up of the batter's hands as he fidgets with the bat, a long shot of the fans, a close-up of the dugout as everyone anticipates the first pitch. These pictures tell a story when they are put

**FIGURE 3.1**

The studio camera operator's job is to create a visual message.

together on the screen. That is your job—to create a visual impression that communicates your message. You also have the audio to help you, but it is the visual element that is important in television. Sometime, turn off the sound for a minute during a TV program and notice how much you know from just the pictures presented.

Remember, pictures must tell the whole story. The way you choose your shots determines what impression you leave with your viewers. If the director is doing a good job, the viewers will be unaware that someone has chosen the pictures for them; the choices will seem inevitable. Try it for yourself. Imagine you are directing a short TV sequence in which a small boy of four or five is listening at the keyhole of his parent's bedroom. He is standing there feeling frightened because his parents are arguing. What pictures would you show to not only give the viewers the idea of what is going on but also to convey the emotion of the situation? Plan this sequence for eight to ten different shots. Write down each shot. When everyone in class has attempted this, notice how each person has interpreted this scene.

The television camera is the vehicle that takes you on the journey of telling a good story. Whether you drive a Cadillac or a Jeep, certain common operating principles apply. In television, too, certain basic principles apply regardless of the type and sophistication of your camera equipment. You must be functionally familiar with (1) the television camera, its lenses and capabilities; (2) camera movement; (3) picture composition; (4) visuals, graphics, and props; (5) scenery and background; (6) lighting and color; and (7) special effects.

## THE TELEVISION CAMERA

The logical starting point as you begin to think with pictures is the television camera, which provides those pictures.

**FIGURE 3.2**

A television studio camera. *Photo courtesy of Ikegami Electronics (USA), Inc.*

## Types of Cameras

Early cameras were large and cumbersome, and the quality of the color signal was marginal at best. They often used three-and-one-half- or four-inch image orthicon pickup tubes, which made the cameras large. A smaller, less expensive camera tube was created for the industrial market and schools. The cameras were smaller, rugged, and less expensive, but the picture was not as clear, and the camera needed much more light.

Many kinds of cameras are in use today for consumer, industrial, cable, and commercial TV purposes. Nearly all modern cameras use a chip rather than a tube to convert the light source to electrical energy, which is the function of any TV camera. The major advantage of this type of camera is that it can be made much smaller and more portable than other Electronic News Gathering (ENG) cameras.

**FIGURE 3.3**

A portable color television camera. *Photo courtesy of Ikegami Electronics (USA), Inc.*

**FIGURE 3.4**

A portable video cassette recorder/color camera. *Photo courtesy of Panasonic Communications & Systems Company.*

## Setup

When you use a video camera, some setup is usually necessary to "teach" the camera what the proper colors should be under various lighting conditions. Our eyes and brains automatically know what the colors should be, and we see them correctly under any lighting. Unfortunately, the camera cannot.

The setup for most chip cameras used by schools and consumers is relatively simple. First, most cameras have an "indoor/outdoor" switch to tell the camera whether the lighting will be for indoor (3,200 Kelvin) or outdoor (5,500 Kelvin) use. Make sure this switch is set in the correct position.

The next procedure is to set the white balance. The theory is that if we teach the camera what white light is under the specific lighting conditions of a room or scene, then the other colors will appear natural. White light is a specific proportion of red, green, and blue light. Once the camera learns white light, it can produce any color. In most cases it is necessary to zoom in on a white card (a T-shirt works fine) until it fills at least 80 percent of the picture. Most cameras are now automatic, so when you push the white-balance button and hold it for about five seconds, the colors will be correct. Remember, most TV cameras do not have a color viewfinder, so you will not see the colors in the camera. If you are in a studio with a waveform monitor and a vector scope, you can use other means to adjust to the proper brightness and color balance.

## LENSES

Another important tool the director must work with is the camera lens. An understanding of TV lenses and their function is necessary for anyone who wants to communicate through the medium of television. What the viewer sees on the screen depends on what the lens picks up, so you must have a working knowledge of the effects achieved by different lenses and composition.

### Focal Length

Older television cameras had turrets in front that had four different lenses, ranging from a wide-angle lens for shots of large groups, to a long close-up lens for faraway shots. When a different lens was needed, the camera was taken off the air and the camera operator moved the turret so that a new lens was placed in front of the pick-up tube. This system was time-consuming and awkward. Now, all TV cameras use zoom lenses (often called variable-focal-length lenses).

The principle of a zoom lens and a single-focal-length lens is the same. A zoom lens can become a short-focal-length lens (wide angle) by zooming out, or it can become a long-focal-length lens (telephoto) by zooming in. To set the lens, simply crank in to the tightest shot and focus. (Of course, you should do this when you are not on the air.) When the director calls for your camera, the lens is ready for any zooming. Remember, you must set the lens each time you go to a new shot.

## Wide-angle lenses

The wide-angle (or zoomed-out position) lens has many advantages for creating composition and special effects in front of the camera. First, a wide-angle lens picks up a large field of view. If you have a large number of people in the shot, you need the wide-angle shot to get them all in the scene. If there is a lot of movement in the shot, you need a wide-angle lens. A wide-angle lens can make objects and people appear larger than normal.

Cars, for example, are usually shot fender-high at close range with a wide-angle lens to make even the smallest car appear much larger than it really is. When guests visit a TV studio for the first time, they often comment that the studio seems smaller than it looks on TV. This is because the wide-angle lens makes it look larger. Faces can become grotesque if they are moved close to the camera and shot with a wide-angle lens. A director might use this feature to show what people look like to a baby as they talk to him in the crib.

A wide-angle lens also makes movement appear faster. If you want to show the speed of a 100-yard dash, use a wide-angle lens at a close range at the end of the track. As the runners approach the camera, they will appear to be moving very rapidly. With a knowledge of lenses, a director can create the illusion of speed in the shot. Because a wide-angle lens has a great depth of field (discussed later in this chapter), it easily keeps people and objects in focus. A wide-angle lens helps track people in motion if they keep going out of focus; the camera operator can simply zoom out.

## Telephoto lenses

The telephoto (or zoomed-in position) lens has the opposite qualities of the wide-angle lens. It does not have a large field of view, but it does magnify the area you want the viewer to see. The camera operator will have more difficulty keeping objects in focus (see the discussion of depth of field), but an experienced director or camera operator can use the telephoto lens effectively. For example, if you are shooting several people in one scene and you want to emphasize certain individuals, the zoomed-in lens allows you to selectively have those people in focus and the others slightly out of focus.

The zoomed-in lens makes movements appear much slower. If you want those runners in the 100-yard dash to look as though they are running in slow motion, use a telephoto lens positioned farther back. The telephoto lens tends to flatten perspective and make distances hard to detect. Suppose you are a producer for a local newscast doing a story on a tremendous traffic jam. Using a telephoto lens as you shoot from an overpass will make the cars look much closer together than they really are; a wide-angle lens will make the cars look farther apart.

## f Stop

In addition to focal length, lenses are classified according to the amount of light they let into the camera. Because the amount of light entering the camera is the most important single element in taking the picture, this characteristic of the lens is an essential factor in the ultimate quality of the television picture. The iris diaphragm is the opening that can be made larger or smaller to regulate the amount of light admitted to the sensitive surface of the vidicon pickup tube. You adjust the iris opening, generally call the *f stop*, according to the amount of light you have on the set or on the object you are televising. The number of the f stop, marked on the lens ring, indicates the size of the iris opening. The lower the number, the wider the opening and the greater the amount of light entering the camera. In other words, the size of the f-stop number has an inverse relation to the size of the lens opening. An f/3.8 lens has a smaller opening than an f/2.5 lens. Lenses usually range from f/1.0 to f/22.0. A lens is considered "fast" when a great amount of light can enter even at a low f-stop number, it's "slow" when only a small amount of light can enter even with a high f-stop number (see Figure 3.5). It is important to practice adjusting the lenses with different amounts of light to determine the best opening for a clear picture. If you have to open the lens very wide to get enough light, it will be much harder to focus.

## Depth of Field

In addition to the focal length and the speed of the lens, a third factor affects the visual communication of your message: depth of

> *The lower the f-stop number, the wider the opening: MORE LIGHT.*

**FIGURE 3.5**

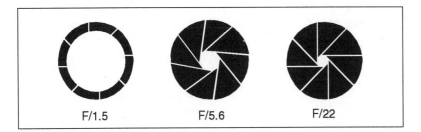

F/1.5          F/5.6          F/22

field, or the area in which all objects at different distances from the camera are in focus at a single lens setting.

The focal length of the lens, the size of the iris opening, and the distance between the camera and the object affect the depth of field. For instance, there is greater depth of field in a long shot than in a close-up; therefore, there is greater freedom to move the camera and still keep the object in focus. Increasing the amount of light on an object is a simple way to increase the depth of field because the iris opening does not have to be so wide.

The fact that objects not in the depth of field are out of focus can help or hinder communication of the idea you want to convey. Backgrounds out of focus help the viewer concentrate on objects in focus within the depth of field. This is called selective focus, when certain objects are in focus and others are out of focus. Sometimes a director may want to make the scene in focus go out of focus and bring the one in front of or behind the original scene into focus.

Imagine a television scene focused on a woman in the background, with a telephone in the foreground out of focus. Suddenly the telephone rings, the woman's image goes out of focus, and the phone becomes sharp and clear. This is accomplished by having a short depth of field. The television viewer can concentrate better on a shot of the coach and benchwarmers at the side of the gym floor if the background of fans in the bleachers is out of focus, and the coach and benchwarmers are in focus within the depth of field. The greater the depth of field, the fewer problems you will have in focusing on a subject quite close to the camera and in focusing when the camera or a performer moves. The greater depth of field

*The best way to learn depth of field is to practice with a camera.*

is easier for focusing and movement, but you will want to use a more shallow depth of field for variety and special effects (see Figure 3.7).

The depth of field is controlled by (1) the focal length of the lenses (short lenses provide greater depth of field), (2) the f-stop opening (smaller openings provide greater depth of field), and (3) camera movement (the greater the distance between object and camera, the greater the depth of field).

The most practical way to acquire a working knowledge of depth of field is to practice with the camera in a lighted studio or classroom—moving the camera back and forth, adjusting the focus for a clear picture at each distance. If the floor space is small, try using shorter lenses, or zooming out. Have another student walk beside your camera for the first few tries, adjusting the lens opening as you move the camera and focus. *Remember that the viewer will see only what your camera sees, not what you see as you look over the top of the camera.*

**FIGURE 3.6**

Short depth of field

Greater depth of field

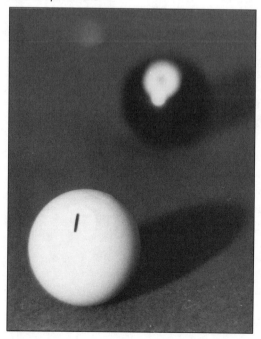

**FIGURE 3.7**

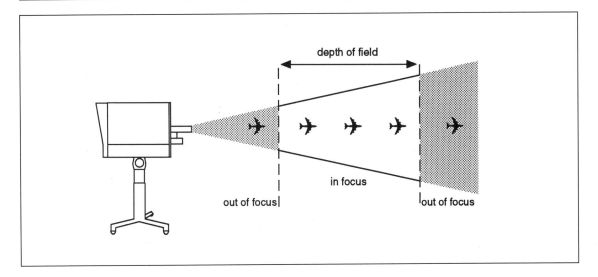

## CAMERA MOVEMENT

Another factor affecting visual communication is the movement of the camera. The support on which the camera is mounted is called a *tripod,* and the wheels are called *dollies.*

### Dollying

To *dolly in* means to move the camera and its mount closer to the subject; to *dolly out* means to move the camera away from the subject. Commercial studios sometimes have crane dollies that permit the cameras to be elevated. Most school studios have dollies that, if they can be raised at all, are lifted by hydraulic pressure at the turn of a wheel or by changing the length of the tripod legs. Often the director uses the cameras subjectively; the camera actually becomes a character. In a courtroom scene, for example, the defendant shouts, "Here he comes!" Everyone looks into the camera as it dollies down the aisle. Suddenly the camera becomes the central character, and we become the witness walking down the aisle to settle the court dispute.

**FIGURE 3.8**

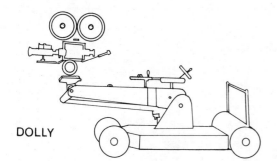

DOLLY

**FIGURE 3.9**

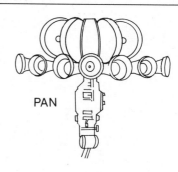

PAN

**FIGURE 3.10**

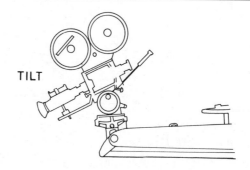

TILT

You would dolly in to concentrate on a person's facial expression or to follow a performer moving toward the rear of the set, from the general to the specific. A dolly-in would achieve that effect in the courtroom scene. In a dolly-out, you would be moving from the detail to the overall. Directors of horror films often use this "subjective shot" to heighten fright as a potential victim runs away from the villain.

## Pan

The horizontal movement of the camera from left to right or right to left while the pedestal or dolly remains stationary is called a *pan*. It corresponds to turning your head left and right without moving your body. This camera movement, a shortened form of the word "panorama," is the one you would use in shooting across a row of singers or a chorus line of dancers. It can be used to follow a moving object or to show the association of several objects that have something in common, such as the expressions on a row of students' faces when their teacher makes a startling statement. When you pan past several objects, be sure there is not too much space between them. While you are focusing on an object, pan slowly; while you are between objects, pan faster. Directors usually zoom out to pan uninteresting areas.

## Tilt

The up-and-down movement of the camera while the dolly remains stationary is called *tilt*. It is the same as panning up or down and can be used for dramatic effects, such as tilting *up* to make a person or object appear taller or higher, or tilting *down* to reveal the pot of gold at the base of the rainbow.

You have probably seen tilt used in a scene. Imagine someone escaping from a murderer. The hero is running through the bushes, usually in a subjective shot as we see the branches knocked out of the way. Suddenly our hero falls. As he looks up he sees the bottom of a pair of boots in front of him. The camera tilts up the boots to the face of the villain.

## Mounting Heads

There are two basic types of mounting heads that permit you to pan and tilt the camera. One, the *fluid head,* balances the camera on the dolly even when the camera is tilted at an extreme angle. It does not have to be locked into position to hold the camera safely, even if you have to walk away from the dolly. The *friction head* counterbalances the camera with a strong spring and has both a vertical and a horizontal locking device. This is the more commonly used head for small television cameras because it is less expensive.

## Truck

The lateral movement of the camera, tripod, and dolly to the left or right is called *truck.* It is an easy way to keep a laterally moving object in focus because the object is always the same distance from the camera. If you were televising a swim meet, for instance, a pan would be insufficient because as the swimmers moved past the camera, you would not be able to tell who was in the lead. But if you truck the camera as they swim, you can always determine who is in first place.

If you were chosen to direct a program at a local art museum and you wanted to show several paintings on a wall as the host walked from painting to painting, you would have to truck the camera to keep the same distance between each painting and the lens. If you panned the camera, the paintings would eventually "keystone," or have an angular look to them.

*Truck* and *dolly,* then, refer to movements of the camera and its dolly. *Tilt* and *pan* refer to movements of the camera while the dolly remains stationary. To make smooth transitions from one picture to another, so that the viewer can concentrate on the message without disturbing distractions, camera operators must practice these four basic movements until they can execute them perfectly.

## SWITCHING EQUIPMENT

In addition to the TV cameras used in a studio, a *switcher,* or *special effects generator,* is a necessity. This equipment allows the director to cut from one camera to another and perform transitions like wipes and dissolves between cameras. Generally, consumer-type cameras cannot be used in a TV studio because they do not allow you to cut from one camera to another during the production. Each of these inexpensive cameras has a built-in "sync generator" that allows a video recorder or TV screen to be locked into the picture the camera is sending. If you go to another camera, the video recorder or TV screen will roll until it becomes locked with the synchronizing generator of the second camera. This is extremely annoying to the audience, and a good director would never tolerate it.

Most studio cameras are designed to be integrated with a switcher, or special effects generator. Instead of using a built-in sync generator, these cameras receive sync (synchronizing signals) from a central source. All the cameras in the studio "read" the picture in exactly the same manner, so the director can go from one camera to another smoothly. Switching and special effects can now also be done

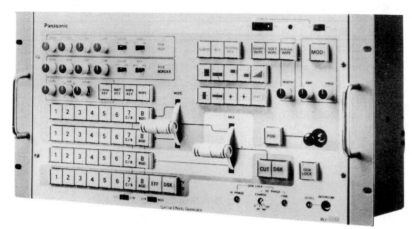

**FIGURE 3.11**

Special effects rack-mount generator. *Photo courtesy of Panasonic Industrial Company.*

through computer-based equipment. The signals are digitized and can be mixed and altered without their sources being in sync. The following paragraphs describe some of the most common effects created by a special effects generator.

## Scene Changes/Transitions Between Shots

### Cut

A cut is a rapid change from one camera to another. In a panel discussion, for example, the camera might be on a close-up of one guest. When another begins to talk, a camera with his or her close-up is on the air next. The switcher or technical director puts the new camera on the air by pushing a button on the special effects generator. Being humans with eyelids that blink, this seems the most natural transition to us.

### Dissolve

Another way of changing cameras is by using a dissolve. In this instance one camera slowly goes out, and the new camera slowly comes in over its picture. This is usually done with a fader handle; it is more dramatic than a cut. Later in this chapter, the rules of when to cut and when to dissolve will be examined.

## Fade

Rather than dissolving from one camera to another, a director can fade in from or out to black. This is especially common at the beginning and end of a production; usually the first shot fades in from black, and the final shot fades to black. This is the equivalent of a curtain opening at the beginning of a play and closing at the end. Fades in the middle of a show can also be used to show time passing.

## Corner wipe

Most special effects generators can begin a new picture in a corner of the screen. This allows the director to put a smaller picture from one camera in a shot from another camera. He or she may choose to gradually fill in the screen with the new camera.

**FIGURE 3.12**

Corner wipe

**FIGURE 3.13**

Split screen

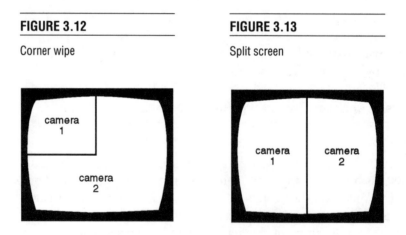

## Double Screen Effects

### Super

When a dissolve is stopped in the middle, both cameras are on the air at the same time in a *super* (short for superimposition). This allows some creative special effects during a production. Often during a song, shots of the singer from different angles are superimposed on the screen.

## Split screen

Most special effects generators allow the director to split the screen in various fashions to allow different shots from various cameras to be on the air at one time. For instance, an anchor in the studio may be on the air with a reporter in the field. The split screen shows that they are in different locations.

## Internal normal key

To place a name under the shot of a guest, the director could super a card with the name in white letters on a black background over the shot. But the intensity of the shot of the guest diminishes as the super is brought on. A key is a more effective method. The key (made possible with a key control on most special effects generators) allows the name to be cut into the shot without any degradation in the original picture (see Figures 3.14–3.16).

## External key

If the key camera is placed on a white circle, a picture from a third camera is placed on the circle using an external control. This works during a newscast, for example, to place a title over the shoulder of the newscaster. Be aware, however, that this ties up all three cameras for one effect.

## Chroma key

More advanced, expensive special effects generators have chroma keys. A color, usually blue or green, is selected to be the key source. Wherever the camera sees the blue or green in the original shot, a new picture is inserted in its place. The talent (performers) must remember not to wear blue—or the new picture will appear on their clothing.

## Digital video effects

Many digital effects generators that use a computer are being used by TV stations and the networks. These effects include page wipes (like turning a page of a book), echo effects (where the picture looks as if it were between two mirrors), and compression (where a director can shrink a picture from its full screen into a corner with-

*New digital effects are being created every day.*

out losing any of the picture). Other effects include mosaics and posterization, which makes the picture look like a drawing. The newer computer generators can create literally thousands of effects.

## PICTURE COMPOSITION

One of the best examples of effective framing and composition of a picture to communicate a message is the cartoon strip. Study the *Peanuts* cartoons, for instance, or *Wizard of Id,* or *Doonesbury,* and notice how each frame makes a picture statement. The following basic suggestions will help you arrange camera pictures to focus your viewers' attention on the message and communicate it without confusion.

1. Use an "establishing shot," which tells the viewers what the whole looks like before they see a part. For example, show a discussion group around a table before going to a head-and-shoulders shot of one speaker.

2. If you have two cameras and are shooting ad-lib (without a script), keep one camera on an establishing shot ready to show the entire situation. If you do not know who will be speaking next, cover the whole group until one individual begins speaking. If you are filming a basketball game, show the entire floor with one camera while the second follows a player down the court. This way, if you do not know what is going to happen next, you can always get a shot of the entire action with a wide-angle lens to be safe. This is called a *cover shot.* The general rule is, "When in trouble, go to cover."

3. Seat speakers so that their physical relationship represents their intellectual or emotional relationship. For example, have opposing political candidates sit on opposite sides of a table. Make sure the camera angle is such that the center of the picture framed by the camera is not a blank wall. Never separate people at opposite ends of the screen; keep them closer to the center of the shot.

4. A simple rule of thumb for framing two people during an interview is to have two or four shoulders visible, never three.

5. Try to frame your television pictures from a variety of angles instead of always shooting directly in front (see Figure 3.14).

**FIGURE 3.14**

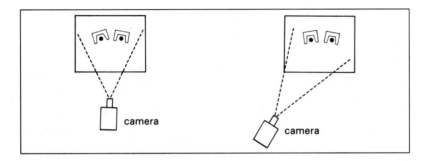

6. Another good rule: Normally the camera is at the eye level of the talent. Point the camera *down* on the subject to show weakness or inferiority. Shoot *upward* toward the subject to show strength or dominance. In the film *Citizen Kane,* every time the audience sees Kane, he is shown from a low angle to show his importance and power over people. The other characters are shot from high angles to make them appear less important. Often, a small child looking up at his or her parents requires a low-angle shot to make the parents look larger.

7. Avoid a camera shot that appears to cut off a performer's arms just below the elbows, and avoid a shot that appears to cut off a performer's legs at the ankles.

8. When framing a picture, notice how the set pieces in the background relate to the performer. Avoid the appearance of ferns growing from a person's head or a lampstand bisecting a handshake.

9. Try to change from one picture to another at the time when the viewer will want to see something different because of a thought change. In other words, compose a new picture at the end of a sentence, a paragraph, or one step in a demonstrated process.

10. The viewer should be able to see how each shot relates to the previous one. If in one shot a man is knocking at the door and the next he is seated in a chair, the viewer is distracted from the story by wondering if the man walked, skipped, or staggered from the door to the chair.

**FIGURE 3.15**

**FIGURE 3.16**

A combination of shots from different angles makes for good storytelling on television, as demonstrated by these students working on a video project.

11. The picture should show the viewer how the various props relate to the person using them. If a chef lifts a bottle of milk to measure out a cupful, the viewer needs to know where the bottle was when the chef picked it up and where he or she got the cup. Let the viewers see what they need to see to make the message clear, without distractions.

12. When two people are facing each other, a tight profile close-up should face the same direction the person faced in the preceding picture.

13. When framing a tight close-up of a head, allow enough space at the bottom of the picture for the person to look down without his or her chin disappearing from the picture.

14. Avoid a close-up that will distort an individual's appearance or emphasize physical defects.

15. In framing the picture for the camera, don't try to crowd too much into any one frame.

16. Try to use the same aesthetic principles of balance, emphasis, and composition that you would use in nontelevised pictures (see Figure 3.17).

17. When performers face to the right, place them a little to the left of the center of your picture. If they face left, place them a little to the right of center. Then they won't look as if they're facing the picture edge and ready to leave.

18. Two people in a frame should be placed slightly diagonal to the camera rather than directly in front of and parallel to the bottom line of the picture.

19. When performers cross from one place to another, keep the camera ahead of them as if pulling them in the direction they are going, rather than following them (see Figure 3.18).

> *Create the illusion of depth by having some things near the camera and some far away.*

## FIGURE 3.17

(1)

      This                           Not This

(2)

    This          Better than           This

**FIGURE 3.18**

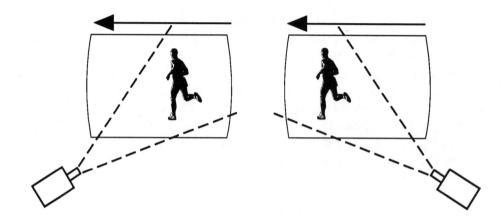

20. Always keep your camera on the same side of the action, or the action will appear to be reversed. In a football game, keep all the cameras on one side of the field. If you are following a runner toward a goal and suddenly cut to a camera on the other side of the field, the runner will appear to have reversed direction (see Figure 3.19).
21. Try a variety of camera locations for shooting two or three people at a table (see Figure 3.20).
22. During actual production, you will not have more than a few seconds to compose television pictures. So practice arranging props and people effectively until you have developed an "instant sensitivity" to which pictures will communicate your message clearly and without distraction.
23. Because the two-dimensional TV picture tends to be uninteresting, try to achieve a three-dimensional effect by giving attention to an object in the foreground and to the background of the picture.
    *Creating Three Dimensions or Depth on a Two-Dimensional TV Screen*
    a. Shoot your action from many angles, not just one front angle.

**FIGURE 3.19**

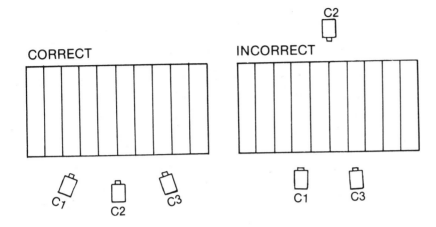

**FIGURE 3.20**

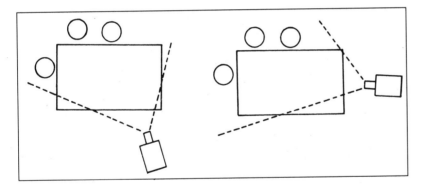

b. Make sure your performers move around. Have them walk to and from the camera.

c. Move your cameras. Dollying and trucking the cameras simulate depth.

d. Use short depth-of-field shots. If one subject is in focus and another out of focus, we can assume there must be some distance between them.

e. Use receding or gradient lines in your shots; shoot in the corners of the room or set, and take angle shots. All of these create the illusion of depth.

    f.  Place smaller objects—like plants—nearer the camera.

    g.  Use the three-point lighting mentioned later in this chapter, giving attention to back lighting.

24.  Just as the student of a foreign language must learn to think and dream in that language, so the television student must learn to think and dream in terms of picture messages. As you plan a program, compose pictures for ideas; frame them as a still photographer would with your hands. Don't think of the idea, think instead of pictures you can convey. For instance, don't think "environmental hazard,"; think "junk pile" (see Figure 3.21).

25.  Plan to set up a sequence of objects to be shot in the same location. For example, four weather forecasting cards should be arrange in sequence, so the camera can pan smoothly (see Figure 3.22).

26.  When shooting a host with two guests, it is not a good idea to place the host between the guests. When you go to a 2-shot of the host and one of the guests, the host will appear to jump from one side of the screen to the other, which will

**FIGURE 3.21**

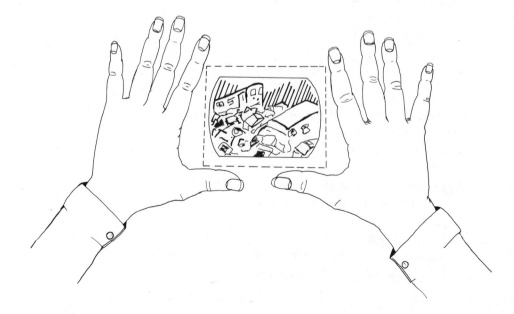

**FIGURE 3.22**

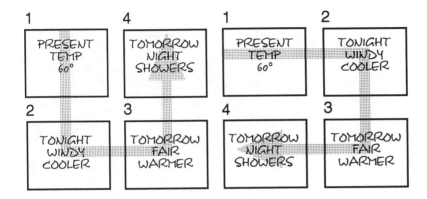

confuse the audience. It is better to place the host to the left of both guests. This allows for close-ups of each person, a 2-shot, or a 3-shot, as needed (see Figure 3.23).

27. Decide *how* to change your picture statements by changing from one camera to another. Cutting to another camera requires a reason: perhaps to show a new subject, or to emphasize a point. When changing to a new camera, here a few suggestions to follow.

*Suggestions for Cutting*
a. Good cutting goes unnoticed.
b. Do not cut blindly for variety.
c. Do not cut to a similar shot from another camera. There is no reason to cut if the other camera has essentially the same shot.
d. Do not cut on a pan.
e. Do not reverse the action in your cutting.
f. Do not cut abruptly from a long shot to a close-up. Go to a medium shot first.
g. Do not cut to extreme angles. A sudden cut to a person's profile may make that person look entirely different.

*When to Dissolve*
a. Dissolve to show that time has lapsed.
b. Dissolve to show a change in place.
c. Dissolve to things that are not anticipated. For example, dissolving to a woman wearing a unique hat during a baseball game surprises the audience.

**FIGURE 3.23**

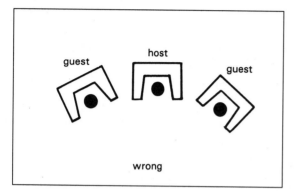

wrong

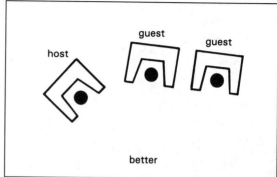

better

d. Dissolve when going to different media. For instance, dissolve when going from a slide to live studio or to a film, unless the slide or film has been given an oral introduction.

e. Dissolve to keep the flow of continuity. For example, during the performance of a ballad, go from a medium shot of the singer into a close-up. Some songs might require a cut at the end of each line; others might require a dissolve when the ideas are unclear.

*When to Cut*

a. Cut to a close-up when you know where the person or object is in the preceding shot. If the talent is holding an object, cut to a close-up instead of dissolving.

b. Cut to new objects or people when they are introduced orally.

c. Most of the time, use a cut. Remember that during a dissolve the audience is temporarily confused.

## VISUALS: TWO-DIMENSIONAL

Mastery of effective picture composition and correct camera work does not guarantee good television photography if the individual components of the picture are blurred, too bright, too crowded, too small, too large, too numerous, or too muddled. Therefore, one of the most obvious and frequently used "visuals" with which you must become familiar is the two-dimensional picture, photo, sign, poster, or label known as a "graphic."

## Aspect Ratio

The first principle you need to know is that television pictures are currently in a four (horizontal)-to-three (vertical) aspect ratio. That is, the ratio of the width to the height is always four to three. The camera tube picks up and the receiver presents this rectangular composition. If you try to frame a vertical picture whose proportions are three by six with a TV camera, for instance, you must either cut off the top and bottom or show parts of the studio at the sides of the picture. (See Figure 3.24).

If it is impossible to obtain pictures, graphs, charts, and so forth that are rectangular in a four-by-three ratio, mount them on a four-by-three card. It helps if all graphics in any one production are the same size, say sixteen by twelve inches, so that you can use one camera adjustment for all.

## Borders

A second important principle in preparing and using graphics is the "rule of six." About 10 percent of the picture you see on camera is lost in transmission to the receiver. It is important to compensate for this loss by leaving a border of unused space around the frame of each picture, sign, poster, or notice.

*Plan on losing 10 percent around the border of your shot.*

**FIGURE 3.24**

VERTICAL MATERIAL

...will appear like this        ... or this

**FIGURE 3.25**

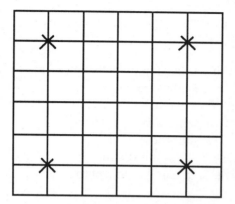 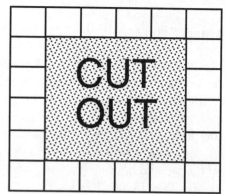

To determine the amount of space you should leave in the border, use the rule of six. Take a piece of cardboard the size of your graphics (sixteen by twelve inches, for instance). Divide this area into six equal parts thus:

At the intersections of the lines nearest the edges, mark an X, and join these *Xs* with a heavy line.

Cut out the part inside the heavy line. Use the remaining frame as a guide for any graphics you prepare. Lay it over a sign or other announcement, and keep all the letters within the cut-out area. Do the same with all pictures. Words or picture elements outside this center portion will not be visible on the television screen.

## Preparing Graphics

There are several other basic principles to guide you in the traditional preparation of graphics for visual communication on television. These techniques are not necessary for those studios that have computer graphics generators available.

1. Use dark cards and letter them with light colors, for keys or supers, rather than using light cards with black letters.
2. Bear in mind that dull textures televise better than shiny, glossy surfaces.
3. Don't try to crowd more than three lines of lettering onto one graphic.
4. Number graphics in the order in which you will use them.
5. Leave more space between letters and between lines than you would leave in an off-camera sign.

**FIGURE 3.26**

A key or super card consists of dark tag board with white lettering. During keying, the black background drops out.

**FIGURE 3.27**

An illustrated title card

**FIGURE 3.28**

A plain title card

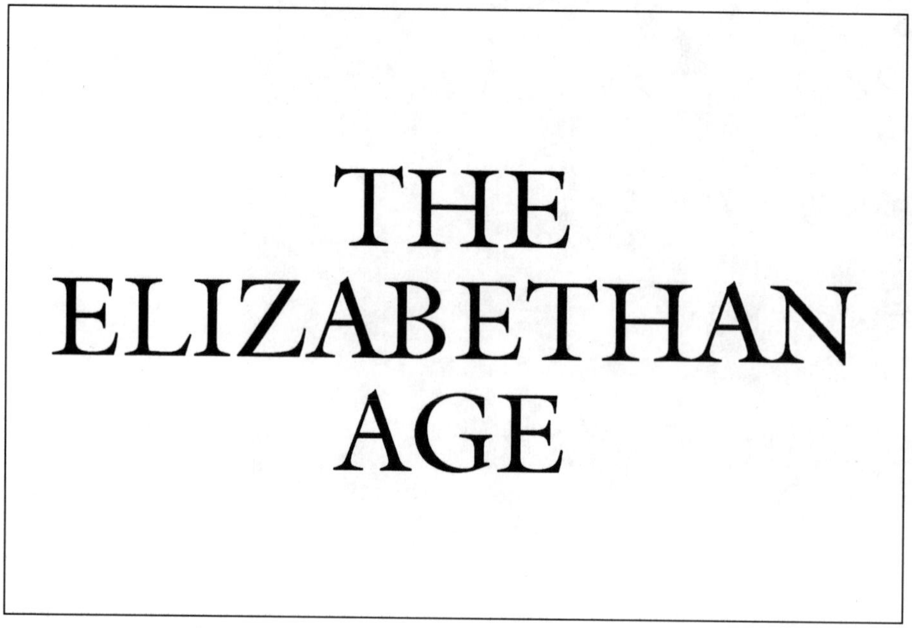

# THE ELIZABETHAN AGE

**FIGURE 3.29**

Chalkboard divided into 4 x 3 sections

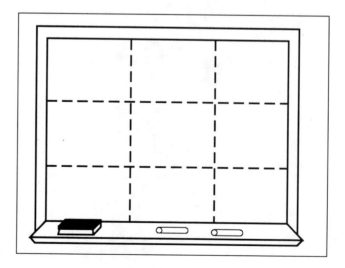

6. If the lettering or writing is to be done on a chalkboard, the four-by-three ratio still applies. Consider dividing the chalkboard into sections.

7. Yellow chalk on a green chalkboard televises better than white chalk on a blackboard. Television chalk, a special half-inch square chalk, is more legible than ordinary chalk.

8. You can do lettering quickly with a brush or speedball pen, tracing the shape of letters through a stencil. Don't use freehand lettering unless you are a skilled artist; amateurish lettering on graphics can ruin an otherwise superior presentation.

Most television stations now use a character generator, a keyboard that electronically inserts the letters on the TV screen. These can be incorporated into a computer and stored for retrieval during news broadcasts or sports events.

**FIGURE 3.30**

A student technician uses computer graphics technology to create special effects.

9. Commercially prepared maps are usually cluttered with too many small items to be clear. Trace important areas with a felt-tip flow pen to darken the boundaries; or trace your own map, including only the areas to be discussed.

10. Computer programs allow you to create titles, pictures, and artwork for the camera. These are easy to use and allow several type styles and pictures that can be printed on paper and shot in front of a camera.

11. Relatively inexpensive software/hardware combinations can provide graphics and effects that only a short time ago were impossible to produce at any cost.

## VISUALS: THREE-DIMENSIONAL

Properties and articles used in a telecast are also called visuals. (Some production centers use the word *visual* for both graphics and three-dimensional objects.) Obviously the selection, placement, and use of visuals are of utmost importance in television, a medium in which effective communication requires more than "radio with pictures." If a visual will hold viewers' attention and help them understand your message, use one—and use it correctly. If the visual is being included just to give viewers something to look at on the screen, don't use it.

The satisfactory use of visuals in televising a message depends on (1) the method of display, (2) the background against which the objects are seen, and (3) effective lighting. Each of these varies with the complexity of your equipment, but the principles are the same.

### Display

First, consider how to display the object. Show its size by placing it next to a human being or an article whose size is well known. If the object is to be operated or manipulated, try to have the camera face the object in the position of the operator. The importance of the camera position to the viewer is illustrated by imagining the difficulty you would encounter trying to show someone you were facing how to tie a tie.

It is important not to obstruct the viewer's vision. Use a pointer or pencil to indicate the different parts of the object. If it is a small article, hold it on a firm surface like a tabletop instead of waving it about where the camera can't focus on it. Any object is more readily identified when viewed against a contrasting background and correctly lighted. For example, dark liquids in a test tube should be displayed in front of a light background; light or clear liquids should have a dark background. One TV performer who uses numerous chemical visuals keeps a piece of cardboard that is dark gray on one side and light gray on the other; it enables him to display clearly all types of liquids in test tubes and beakers.

It is sometimes advisable to fasten a mirror directly over the object and focus the camera on the reflected image. This kind of overhead shot is especially helpful, for example, when the viewer needs to see the position of someone's hands on a keyboard or the consistency of the ingredients in a mixing bowl.

An imaginative setting can provide interesting display areas as well as a contrasting background. You can use "pole cats" to mount graphics on squares or rectangles of colorful materials and textures that contrast with the draperies or flat wall surfaces. Extension poles used for lamps and bathroom towels make good pole cats if your studio ceilings are not too high (see Figure 3.31).

To provide these two essential visual elements—contrast with the background and an unobstructed view—certain set pieces, such as furniture, can be helpful. Furniture used by performers should be placed at least six feet away from the wall to permit the kind of backlighting that outlines the performer and the visuals, separating them from the background. Specially shaped tables and counters make it easier for cameras and lights to get close to the subjects for a clearer view.

With some types of pictures, it may be necessary to use duplicate objects—one in a shot that shows a person handling the object; the other, properly displayed outside the playing area, in a tight close-up by a second camera. Such duplication is especially helpful in televising coins, stamps, musical notes, library cards, footnotes, and the like.

A word of warning: Any unobstructed, well-lighted interior shot may reveal sloppy production efforts: unpressed clothes, dirty surfaces, dusty tabletops, wrinkled draperies, scaly paint, or daubs of dried paste. These betray the amateur and distract the viewer.

**FIGURE 3.31**

Extension poles that are used for lamps and towels can make good "pole cats" if your studio ceilings are not too high.

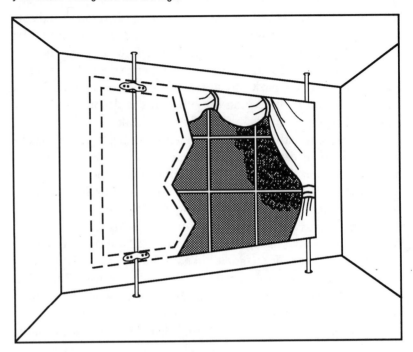

## Backgrounds

Settings do not have to be elaborate to be effective. Heavy, rough-textured draperies can be hung at the corner of a classroom to provide an interesting background and at the same time improve the acoustics by covering some of the hard reflecting surface of the wall.

Although networks can spend millions of dollars on the sets of programs such as "The Tonight Show" or the network news, it is not necessary to spend any money for your sets. The theater department can be the source for most of the sets and props used for television programming. Donations from parents or other supporters can provide chairs, tables, lamps, couches, and other large items.

Backgrounds are easy to make as well. First, explore some of the sets from the theater department. Perhaps a fake brick wall was designed for a theatrical production. This could be used for the set of a panel discussion. A *flat* in theater is a piece of muslin stretched between a frame of one-by-three-inch lumber. You can construct flats for your TV productions as well. The name of the program can be painted on a four-by-eight foot flat. Flats are light enough to be stored out of the way with little effort.

Many wallpaper stores sell large murals of scenes such as skylines, forests, seashores, and clouds designed for creating a "mood wall" in a room. These make perfect backgrounds for your TV productions as well. Don't forget inexpensive wallpaper as a design for the back of a set. You can also make an interesting background from window shades on which you have pasted photomurals or pictures. Raise or lower these shades to reveals settings appropriate for an individual speaker, newscaster, or commentator.

A library scene using bookcases is easy to create. One high school teacher created his own set of bookcases by obtaining the jackets of older books from a library. He built a flat of half-inch plywood on a one-by-three-foot frame. His shelves consisted of one-by-two-inch wood nailed to the plywood. The end jackets of the books were cut and glued to styrofoam, then glued to the plywood. This made them look like books placed on the shelves. These bookcases are light and easily moved and can be stored for any TV production.

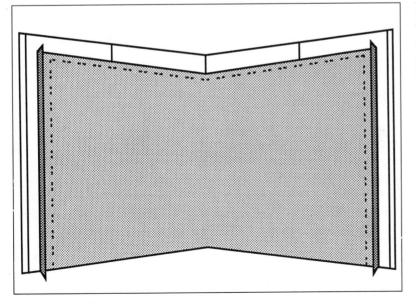

**FIGURE 3.32**

An inexpensive backdrop can be made by stapling seamless paper to a theatre flat.

A visit to a lumber or hardware store may also provide ideas for your productions. Inexpensive four-by-eight-foot sheets of panels can create a set. Simply create a frame using one-by-three-inch lumber, and nail the panels to it. Cut corner braces from plywood and attach them, using glue and nails (see Figure 3.33). Simply spring vise grips will help hold the sets together (see Figure 3.34). A triangle frame on the rear of the set will hold the frame up.

At the hardware store you may find simple Plexiglass set pieces that may also be used for backgrounds. You can obtain seamless photo paper in many colors from most good photo supply houses. Colors such as blue, red, and black make good backgrounds. Some TV supply houses (such as Comprehensive Video and Universal Video) also sell seamless paper for TV sets. These outlets also sell complete sets that are ready to use for your production. But be prepared; completed sets are expensive.

Set pieces like lamps, plants, pictures on a wall, fireplaces, and sculptures add to the decor of any TV set. Secondhand stores can provide these, or you might be allowed to borrow them from the faculty lounge or office.

### Floor plans

It is a good idea to create a floor plan for your TV production. The floor plan will help you design the set and create the best plan for your shots. A good floor plan includes the backgrounds used, your set pieces, graphics areas, camera angles, and talent locations.

Figure 3.35 is a sample of a floor plan for a three-camera production.

### Lighting

A general understanding of television lighting is important to any director. Lighting is often overlooked in the harried process of putting together a TV production. TV lighting is important for several reasons. First, lighting is necessary to get the best picture from your camera. If there is not enough light, the picture will look grainy and flat and will lack vibrant colors. The video engineer will demand enough base light to get the best picture from the cameras.

**FIGURE 3.33**

Back view of a flat

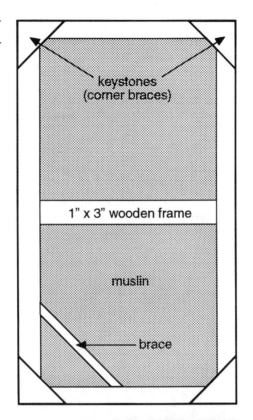

keystones
(corner braces)

1" x 3" wooden frame

muslin

brace

**FIGURE 3.34**

Inexpensive vise grips hold flats together.

**FIGURE 3.35**

Sample floor plan

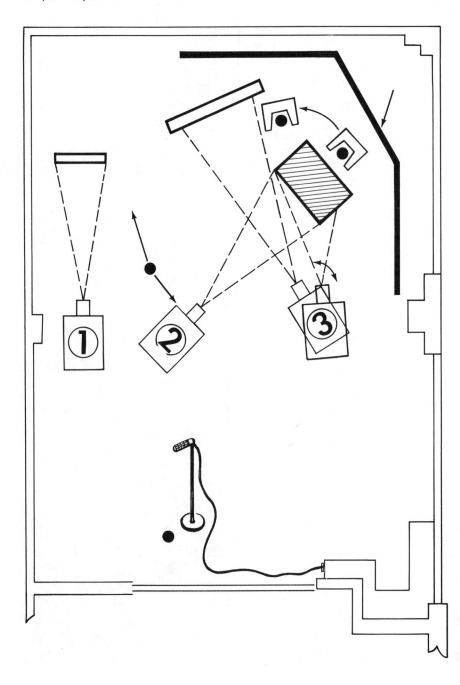

Good lighting also helps create a three-dimensional picture. Remember, TV is only two dimensions: height and width. However, good three-point lighting creates some shadows to suggest dimension. Lighting also separates the performers from the set and makes them appear more lifelike. Lighting can inspire the entire mood of the production. Low-key, dark lighting was used effectively in *Citizen Kane* to show the somber mood of that film. To soften or diffuse light for special effects, a *scrim* is used. This is a spun-glass material, a gauze-like curtain, that is put in front of a lighting instrument to diffuse light. When lighted from the front, the curtain appears opaque. If light is brought up from behind the scrim, it becomes transparent.

All sorts of unexpected things can affect lighting. The glare from the chalk dust in the eraser tray can cause a distracting line across the screen. The shy slats of a Venetian blind can cause streaking across the picture. The glare of lights reflected from a glossy photo print can cause "hot spots," or white light. Fluorescent lights may flicker and produce horizontal lines across the television picture. The color temperature may also give the picture a greenish appearance. Silk dresses or houndstooth patterned suits can reflect light and create what looks like heat waves shimmering upward from the bottom of the television screen. A person's nose can make a dark mustache-like shadow on the upper lip. The shoulders can reflect a bib-like shadow across the chest.

Cameras have their own idiosyncrasies in reacting to varying degrees of light. A commercial studio discovered this while televising a style show, when its camera #2 mysteriously transformed a black skirt with a white blouse into a white skirt with a black blouse. It is always wise to check everything with your own cameras and your lights. Have the auditorium director or someone familiar with stage lights suggest what you can do with available equipment. No camera and no performer can achieve visual clarity, much less effective communication, if the lighting is inadequate.

Bright lights are not the simple answer to lighting problems. A lighted area will appear bright only when there are dark tones present to contrast with it. If the faces of the performers do not appear bright enough (no pun intended!), merely adding more light may not help. The additional light will flatten out their facial features and force the camera operator to "stop down" the lenses (close them to shut out light). A better solution may be to provide more contrast between the area behind the performer and the area in which he or she is standing by simply reducing the background illumination. Conversely, too little light on a scene may obscure the picture with snowy specks called "noise."

Having the correct kind of light in the correct place is as important as having the proper amount of light. The amount, or intensity, of light is measured in footcandles or lumens. Some light meters used by photographers are calibrated in footcandles—that is, units for measuring light or illumination—just as sound is measured in decibels and weight in pounds. Classrooms are usually lighted at levels varying from 40 to 75 footcandles. Remember to check the cameras in your studio or classroom to determine the amount of light required by the peculiarities of your particular system.

### FIGURE 3.36

Use light from different angles to achieve visual clarity without distortion. The basic kinds of light are distinguished by the source or angle from which they illuminate the TV picture.

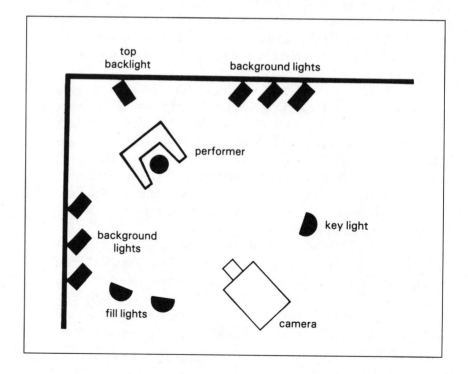

**FIGURE 3.37**

A portable light used by cable companies and TV stations for remote telecasts.

A portable lighting source may be necessary for a "remote shoot" (away from a studio). Often lights are located in the ceiling, and faces seem dull and two-dimensional. A light about face-high, usually from one side of the camera, adds dimension and highlights the face. It is a good idea always to take small portable lights, usually available from any video store, to any remote location.

The source of light is as important as its intensity, whether at a remote shoot or in the studio. If all the light comes from directly above a person's head, for instance, the frontal bones at the eyebrows will cast shadows on the eyes, the nose will cast shadows on the upper lip, and the chin will cast shadows on the neck. If all the light comes from below, equally distorting shadows will result. If the source of light is all at the front, people and objects tend to flatten into the background, and you lose the three-dimensional effect. You are familiar with the silhouette effect created by having all the light behind an object.

*Never use an open-faced lighting instrument without a scrim.*

## Studio Lighting Instruments

Most TV studios have different kinds of lighting instruments hanging from the ceiling. These are usually suspended from a grid or pipes that allow these lights to be placed in exact spots where needed. In almost all TV studios, ranging from school TV studios to cable TV or broadcast studios, quartz or tungsten-halogen lights are used. They allow the cameras to pick up the correct colors and are set for the 3200° Kelvin most TV cameras today require. The advantage of these lights is that the white light they produce remains constant even when they grow older or are dimmed. Regular incandescent lights tend to turn yellow as they grow older or are dimmed.

### The Fresnel spotlight

Perhaps the most popular spotlight used in TV studios is the Fresnel. This light ranges from 300 watts to over 2,000 watts and produces a bright light source. You can adjust the Fresnel to produce a narrow beam of light for highlighting a person or scene or a wide beam to reduce shadows.

There is usually a focusing spindle in the rear of the light that allows the lighting director to adjust the beam to the exact position needed. In addition, "barn doors" help keep the light out of areas where it is not needed. Adjust the beam very carefully, as these lights get extremely hot. It is usually necessary to wear gloves to keep from being burned by them. Also oils from your fingers burn hotter on the lamp, possibly causing those points you touch to weaken, resulting in the lamp exploding. Exercise caution.

*Never touch a lamp with bare fingers.*

**FIGURE 3.38**

Fresnel

For back or key light

Scoop
for base light

*Photos courtesy of Arriflex Corp. and
Mole-Richardson.*

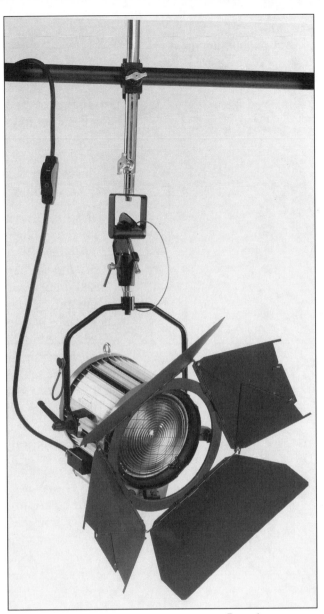

Fresnel

## Scoops or floodlights

Instead of producing a sharp beam of light like a spotlight, the scoops or floodlights produce a very diffused light with little shadow. They are used to eliminate shadows or light a large area on a TV set. These lights usually are used as a base light. Some scoops have an adjustable focus to spread or tighten the beam of light.

## Broads

A broad light acts like several scoop lights and will light a large area of a scene with diffused light for general illumination of the set. It lets the director raise the overall level of the lighting and still use key and back lighting.

It is important to use light from different angles to achieve visual clarity without distortion. The basic kinds of light, distinguished by the source or angle from which they illuminate the television picture, are as follows:

1. *Base light:* Overall illumination of the area by instruments that spread the light, such as scoops.
2. *Back light:* Illumination from back and above to form a rim around the head and shoulders of performers, making them stand out from the scenery in a three-dimensional effect, usually provided by spotlights.
3. *Front* or *key light:* Aimed from the same direction as camera to produce highlights and shadows on the face of a performer, outlining the bridge of the nose and creating high spots on the forehead, cheekbones, and chin.
4. *Fill light:* Used to reduce the extreme shadows caused by front lighting.
5. *Eye light:* A tiny spot mounted on or near the camera to throw light specifically on the face of the performer.

Use just enough light to do the job. Adding more light to eliminate shadows may not work as well as adjusting the light. Arrange the light on a performer so it is coming from above, to keep the person's shadows from falling directly behind him or her. Placing the performer several feet away from the set or walls will also help get rid of annoying shadows.

This is the result of the difference between the perception of the human eye and the pickup capabilities of the television camera. The human eye can distinguish hundreds of shades between black and white; the television camera can differentiate among about ten. These contrasting degrees of color that the camera can pick up and the receiver can reproduce are called the "gray scale"; engineers use a chart of ten steps from television white to television black.

To provide appropriate contrast for visual clarity, the color of a performer's clothes should not be too near the color of his or her skin. Makeup that makes the face slightly darker than street makeup can be used to accentuate this difference. The basic purposes of stage makeup—to cover perspiration sheen, to hide wrinkles, to

## FIGURE 3.39

To have the correct *kind* of light in the correct place is as important as having the proper *amount* of light.

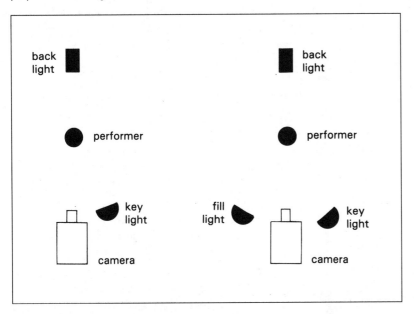

highlight bone structure, to mask the blotchy appearance of a dark beard, and to frame the eyes for emphasis—apply in television as well. During the 1968 presidential debate, the first televised, candidate Richard Nixon had handkerchiefs soaked in witch hazel, ready to absorb the shiny perspiration from his face whenever the camera was turned away from him. On the other hand, according to author Joe McGinnis in his book *The Selling of the President, 1968,* candidate John F. Kennedy's makeup was more effectively done and achieved a "cooler" appearance during the debate.

In the early days of television, all performers used a whitish pancake makeup and a dark liner on eyes and lips, to provide adequate contrast for a satisfactory camera pickup. With modern cameras heavy makeup is not necessary, and most performers need little if any. True, some people with dark skins may require highlights of tinted makeup, and men may occasionally need to hide shiny bald spots or to darken skin that photographs lighter. Most women when appearing on television use makeup a little heavier and darker than the kind they normally wear.

## SPECIAL EFFECTS

The foregoing principles of visualizing the message have practical applications in various special effects that you can achieve with film and certain types of equipment available in most schools.

### Films and Slides

1. The four-to-three ratio applies to any films or slides you may want to show in your televised presentation.
2. In slides, especially color slides, the contrasts must be sharp and clear.
3. Most sixteen millimeter film was not made for the TV screen. When it is reduced from a projected nine-foot image to a twenty-inch image, much of the definition is lost.
4. You must get specific permission to broadcast films or video-tapes, or parts thereof, on television. It is not sufficient that your school has rented a film to be shown on a projector in classrooms. Most films are copyrighted and require permission to televise. This is true even if you own the print of the film; televising the film requires a special license from the film producer.
5. You can use sound film only if the film itself was shot at sound speed. However, you can show it as a silent film and add your own commentary.
6. Using slides requires little special equipment. With slides you can take the production out of the studio without having to take the cameras to remote locations. Most video stores sell inexpensive film chain units that allow home videophiles to transfer their home movies and slides to a videotape. You can then film these videotapes with your studio cameras to show films and slides in your productions.

Remember: Television is a *visual* medium. You cannot expect your viewers, accustomed as they are to watching commercial television, to accept uncritically a series of ill-conceived, inadequately lighted, poorly composed television pictures simply because they are being picked up by a school camera and transmitted by a student crew. If television is worth doing at all, the picture must be good!

## IT'S A WRAP

In order to get a message across via television, you must learn to use a visual medium, where pictures tell the entire story, explain the idea, or sell the product. Thus you must become familiar with the various components of this visual medium.

This means you must learn about: (1) the television camera and its setup, as well as the types of camera lenses; (2) camera movement and the terminology for the many directions in which the camera is able to move; (3) switching equipment that allows using more than one camera; (4) the many elements of picture composition; (5) visuals, which include aspect ratio, borders, and preparing graphics; (6) scenery and background, as well as knowing the type of lighting to use; (7) how special effects can augment your message.

Learning about these technical elements and how to effectively use them will help your audience respond meaningfully to your message.

# 3

# Video Lab

Four projects typify the problems and techniques of visual communication: still picture music video, commercial, demonstration, and musical production. Although only one project is suggested, it will be helpful to televise as many as you can.

## Still Picture Music Video

What are you trying to learn?

1. How to begin with picture statements.
2. How to communicate with television.

### Instructions:

1. Pick a modern song with lyrics that are easily understood. Bring in a good recording of the song.
2. Write a script for each line of the song so that you can follow the separate ideas contained in each line.
3. Find pictures that illustrate each idea in each line of the song. Mount them on cardboard or tagboard. Check for aspect ratio, and make certain they are large enough.
4. Divide the pictures and place them in front of two cameras.

5. Play the music for the audio, and match the pictures in front of the camera with each line of the song.
6. If the song is fast-paced, cut from one picture to another. If it is slower, dissolve from one picture to another.
7. Videotape the project. The audio will come from the recording, and the video will reflect the ideas in each line.
8. Use your imagination. Let the viewers see your interpretation of the song through your use of visuals.

## Commercials

What are you trying to learn?

1. How to communicate ideas using a camera.
2. How to use persuasive appeals to influence the actions of others.

*Length:* Thirty seconds
*Visuals:* Use a minimum of two. One must be a graphic (two-dimensional sign).
*Subject:* Do *not* copy a television commercial. You may use the same ideas or methods, but you must change the product. What you are

selling may be real or fictitious. You may exaggerate the methods of used-car sales; the circus-type barker; the consumer testifying to the wonders of soap, fruit juice, or hair spray; the buyer who has suddenly become popular because of his or her chewing gum, hair color, shaving lotion, or toothpaste. Be as creative as you wish, as long as you show good taste and do not offend anyone.

*Content:* Make sure your message includes the fundamental human appeals—to self-preservation, property, power, guilt, duty, reputation, affection, physical attraction, love for family, and taste. Check a speech textbook if you need to learn more about how a salesperson appeals to the fundamental drives that motivate people to act.

*Effectiveness:* Have other students in the class assess your effectiveness and suggest buyers to whom your presentation would appeal.

### Production principles

1. If you use brand-name products, cover the name with a label bearing a fictitious name in letters large enough to be clear and neat enough to look professional.
2. If you use food, check it on camera. Raw meat often looks more appetizing than cooked meat. Onions need a little food coloring. Real poached eggs may not look as appetizing as half a peach inverted on a crustless slice of bread. Don't forget that food can be difficult and messy to use in a TV studio.
3. Hold the product still long enough for the camera to focus clearly on it.
4. Check the lighting on your product. The *product* must look good!

5. Display the product against a contrasting background, so the viewer can easily distinguish its shape. (How will a frisbee look against your plaid shirt?)
6. Information that is easy to forget (advertisers' phone numbers, prices, addresses) should be lettered neatly on a graphic even though you plan to give it orally too.
7. Time is a problem. Which is worse, to have time run out before you tell us where we can buy the product, or to stand there with "egg on your face," in silent terror, for the final fifteen seconds? Solution: Have a cushion of music, or signs, or object displays that you can put in or leave out to adjust time variations. You might have a logo or a nice display of the product ready to dissolve to. This would serve as a pad at the end of the commercial.
8. Use your imagination. Be creative. Don't let viewers turn to another channel while you are selling your product. One clever student demonstrated the effectiveness of a liquid plant food by pouring a few drops on a wilted vine, which immediately shot up 24 inches (via an invisible wire pulled by an accomplice hidden behind drapes).
9. Check your own effectiveness. Would you buy this product if all you knew about it was what the viewer will see on your television presentation?

### Demonstration

What are you trying to learn?

1. How to organize for clear understanding.
2. How to communicate ideas using a camera.

*Length:* Three minutes

*Visuals:* One required

*Subject:* Select a process that you can demonstrate in three minutes. It should not be as complicated as a steam engine or have as many parts as a chess set. The process should be one you know thoroughly and one you expect your classmates will find interesting. The following are only suggestions and are not meant to limit your imagination:

- How to throw a football (or baseball)
- How to pack for a short vacation
- How to kick a soccer ball
- How to build a birdhouse
- How to serve in tennis
- How to tie a half-hitch knot
- How to play a chord on a guitar
- How to peel an orange
- How to put on makeup
- How to make dreadlocks
- How to put on a lifejacket
- How to do a card trick or magic trick
- How to perform wrestling, boxing, or karate moves

## Production Principles

1. Remember to check every prop and every movement on camera for lighting, contrast, focus, and placement.

2. If you are making something, have the finished product on hand. You can hide a birdhouse in the file cabinet and pull it out to finish your demonstration of birdhouse making.

3. Do not let your hands hide what the audience needs to see. Turn articles toward the camera. Point with a pencil or finger if your hands get in the way.

4. Keep display surfaces clear of extra objects or background objects that will detract from a clear view of your process.

5. Plan carefully where the camera will be. If you are showing stances for golf, will the camera have to tilt up to your face, pan over to a chart, tilt down to your grip, up to your face, down to your feet? What order is best?

6. If you have to move objects, move them slowly enough so that the camera can stay in focus.

7. If you are cooking, have you checked *on camera* the articles you will use? Do you have extra food for retakes? Will materials change (meat for example) under hot studio lights?

8. If you must lift an object, brace your hand or arm on a table or counter. Otherwise you may tremble, or the object may be too heavy to stay in focus.

9. Plan what you will do if things do not work. Always be ready with an alternative—just in case.

10. Have a running commentary ready for any lengthy process. While you open the can or container, say something.

11. Plan carefully a logical order for the demonstration. Do not confuse the viewer by inserting, "Oh I should have told you…"

There is an old saying "An order that *can* be misunderstood *will* be misunderstood—by somebody." Is your demonstration so clear that it cannot be misunderstood?

## Musical Production

What are you trying to learn?

1. How picture statements help clarify meaning and mood.

2. How cuts, dissolves, and other special effects help create an effective production.

*Length:* Length of one short song

*Subject:* Often during late night talk shows, the director is asked to direct a song sung by one of the guests. It is the director's job to create the best pictures possible to show the singer and the mood of the song. Watch how directors bring out the best of the song with camera shots. Now imagine you have been asked to televise a singer or musical performer (perhaps a guitarist) for a local cable TV production. How would you divide the song into several shots? You might work in teams of two. One could perform and the other direct the production. If the performer is not a good singer, he or she could lip sync. The two of you should plan this song very carefully and decide if you wish to show the performance or show the story of the song.

## Production principles

1. Write the lyrics down to help you decide where in the song the picture statements should change. Identify each idea in the song, and change the picture statement when the idea changes.
2. Use cuts where the pace of the song is fast. Use dissolves for slower-paced songs.
3. Remember the importance of lighting to mood.
4. Consider using a slide or videotape insert in the song.
5. It would be helpful to prepare a script for the production.

## TAKE TWO

**1.** What is meant by a "picture statement?" Why is it important to think in terms of picture statements? Think of several situations for a short video production—for example, two Western gunfighters in the street. How would you divide the shots? Pick a short sequence and create a shooting script for it. Try to make it as detailed as possible so anyone could shoot the sequence using your script.

**2.** List three characteristics of the wide-angle lens of the TV camera. Think of a situation where this lens would be beneficial in the shot. Do the same for the telephoto lens.

**3.** Name two situations in which television directors would want a shallow depth of field in a shot. Explain what they could do to achieve it.

**4.** Give an example of a situation when a director would use a subjective shot in a TV production.

**5.** Why is it important to keep the camera at the eye level of the performer? Discuss situations when you might want the camera higher than the performer.

**6.** Why is it important to know about aspect ratio for television?

**7.** Name the functions of the following types of lights on a television set:
   **a.** key light
   **b.** fill light
   **c.** back light
   **d.** base light

## ADDITIONAL RESOURCES

Compesi, Ronald J., and Ronald E. Sherrifs. *Small Format Television Production,* (Boston, Mass., Allyn and Bacon, 1990).

Johnson, Ron, and Jan Bone. *Understanding the Film,* (Lincolnwood, Ill., NTC Publishing Group, 1993).

Mathias, Harry, and Richard Patterson. *Electronic Cinematography,* (Belmont, Calif., Wadsworth Publishing, 1985).

Millerson, Gerald. *Techniques of Television Production, twelfth edition,* (Stoneham, Mass., Focal Press, 1989).

Millerson, Gerald. *TV Scenic Design Handbook, third edition,* (Stoneham, Mass., Focal Press, 1989).

Oakey, Virginia. *Dictionary of Film and Television Terms,* (New York: Barnes and Noble Books, 1983).

Schroeppel, Tom. *The Bare Bones Camera Course for Film and Video, second revised edition,* (Tampa, Fla., Schroeppel, 1992).

Utz, Peter. *Today's Video Equipment: Setup and Production, second edition,* (Englewood Cliffs, N.J., Prentice-Hall, Inc., 1992).

Wurtzel, Alan, and Stephen Acker. *Television Production,* (New York: McGraw-Hill, 1989).

Zettl, Herbert. *Sight-Sound Motion, second edition,* (Belmont, Calif., Wadsworth Publishing, 1990).

Zettl, Herbert. *Television Production Handbook, fifth edition,* (Belmont, Calif., Wadsworth Publishing, 1992).

# Sounding the Message

The next time you watch a rerun of your favorite television program, turn off the sound and see how much of the show you can understand and enjoy. If that doesn't confuse you, try watching any commercial during the late movie with the sound turned off. Can you imagine watching a music video without sound?

## SOUND SOURCES

In television, as in radio, the sound consists of speech, music, and sound effects. However, the sound source in television is often in motion; the singer or speaker moves about the stage or across the studio floor; whereas in radio, the sound source is positioned at a stationary microphone, even for special effects. Moreover, in radio the performer "addresses" (that is, directs his or her words toward) the microphone, but in television the performer addresses the camera. Microphones in television move about the studio to keep up with the action and remain out of camera range. Microphones in radio stay in their positions, but the performers move on and off mike.

> _Know the capabilities_
> _of your microphone._

## CHARACTERISTICS OF MICROPHONES

In both radio and television, it is necessary to know the characteristics and capabilities of the microphones available to you. One obvious difference that you can see without understanding the technical characteristics is the way the microphone is "mounted."

## Mounting

### On a floor stand

Use the *floor stand mike* only when it is appropriate for the mike to be seen, never during a dramatic presentation. You cannot use it during a dance number or any other activity in which floor vibrations could interfere with good pickup. It is often used for featuring sections of an orchestra.

**FIGURE 4.1**

A floor stand mike is appropriate for taping or broadcasting live performances.

Inexperienced performers tend to kick the base of a floor stand or grip the center shaft and rock the entire instrument back and forth. If you are recording country music in Nashville, using special electronic effects, you may want to grab the microphone, but such a grip is not standard procedure in a television studio.

## On a table stand

The *table stand mike* is convenient for panelists or other speakers seated around a table. A disadvantage is that it picks up the sound of drumming fingers or pencils on the tabletop. It is not effective when it must be passed around or shoved back and forth along the top of the table. It provides a good way to mask notes or a script, but the rattling of cards or sheets of paper against its base can be quite distracting. A felt table covering can prevent some of the disturbing noises usually picked up by this type of microphone.

**FIGURE 4.2**

The table stand mike is convenient for panel discussions and similar types of programs.

### On a lavaliere cord

The *lavaliere mike* has a cord (named after a necklace) that permits users to wear the mike around their necks, freeing both their hands and giving them more flexibility of movement on the set. It can be hidden easily, but it is likely to pick up noise by rubbing against buttons or tie clasps. Users must avoid being too close to it when they bow their heads to read something or look down at something they are demonstrating.

### On the lapel

This mike is clamped to the lapel of your coat. It is easily hidden from view and has the same advantages and problems as the lavaliere mike. Hiding the lapel mike underneath clothing tends to muffle the sound.

Both lavaliere and lapel mikes give the user more freedom of movement than the floor stand or table mikes, but at the same time they present a problem—the dangling mike cord that the performer must avoid tripping over, twisting in the camera dolly, or entangling in set furniture.

## FIGURE 4.3

Two micro-mini lapel mikes are shown in this illustration. The mike in the lapel clip is a unidirectional model. The model in the foreground is an omnidirectional mike. *Photo courtesy of Telex Communications, Inc.*

**FIGURE 4.4**

The hand mike is especially good for on-the-spot interviews and demonstrations.
*Photo courtesy of Nady Systems, Inc.*

## In the hand

The *hand mike* is especially good for outdoor programs like person-in-the-street interviews. The interviewer can hold the mike close enough to the mouth of the speaker for a good pickup, in spite of street or other extraneous noises. The hand mike has the disadvantage of keeping one of the performer's hands tied up, and it is thus unsuitable for a demonstration. A hand mike can also be clamped into a floor stand. Thus, it can be lifted out of the clamp when performers wish to move about with the mike in their hands, and it can become stationary again during another part of their presentation, such as a musical number.

Inexperienced performers are likely to wave a hand mike around like a baton, swinging it to and from their mouth. This can drive audio engineers to distraction, as they try to "ride gain" on volume that varies from one extreme to the other. To achieve a fairly even volume level during a telecast, the engineer must constantly manipulate the controls to allow approximately the same amount of sound to pass through at all times. These volume controls are called *faders, mixers, gain controls,* or *pots,* and the process of controlling the volume is called *riding gain.*

### On a pipe or extension pole from the ceiling

A microphone suspended from the ceiling, hanging straight down over a group of performers, is sometimes called a *pool mike* because it simply picks up the pool of sound underneath it. You can use a pool mike in a small studio that does not have a boom mike.

A mike hung from overhead has several advantages. There are no mike cables on the floor, no shadows cast by the boom, no need for an operator to move it about; it is easier to keep out of the picture, as the camera operator is not likely to be shooting upward. Also, the absence of a floor cable makes moving the camera much easier. The disadvantage of a pool mike is that it must be kept high to remain out of the picture, and it may be too far away to pick up well, without extraneous noise. If the mounting is too high, the pool mike is likely to pick up reverberations from studio or classroom walls.

### On an extension rod overhead

The so-called *boom mike* is one of the most flexible of all microphones used in television, but it does require more floor space and one more studio crew member to move it about and adjust it as needed. The operator of the boom mike can raise, lower, pan, retract, extend, or rotate the microphone to keep it just above and in front of the performer. He or she must be careful to keep the boom mike in front of the sound source. Commercial studios usually have space for four-wheeled boom platforms that give the entire assembly a steadier base and more flexibility to move the mike 360 degrees. Most school studios, however, have to be satisfied with the "giraffe" boom, a tripod frame with a narrower wheel base, moving on three casters.

The boom mike creates problems for the camera operator because of its shadows. It can also be a problem for performers, who must telegraph their anticipated movements to the boom operator in order to avoid getting hit in the head with the mike when they stand up. Some camera operators tie a two-inch-long white ribbon to the bottom of the mike to warn that the mike is beginning to be visible at the top of their picture frame. Then they can tilt down in time to avoid getting the boom mike in the picture.

**FIGURE 4.5**

The boom mike can be raised, lowered, panned, retracted, extended, or rotated in order to keep the mike in front of the sound source.

**FIGURE 4.6**

A closeup of a boom mike. *Photo courtesy of Nady Systems, Inc.*

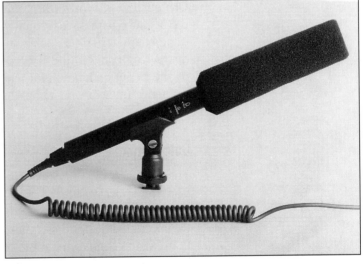

## On the body

The *wireless mike* is really a small transmitting station concealed on the wearer's body. Although it is expensive, it is especially desirable in musicals or outdoor presentations where stringing long cables is impractical. In many television newsrooms, anchors wear wireless microphones so they can walk over to the weather reporters or feature reporters. The microphones are attached to small FM transmitters on the anchors, so they are not tied down to desks by microphone cables. Receivers in the control room process the signals into the audio control boards.

## Pickup

You can refer to a microphone, then, by the way it is mounted: boom mike, lavaliere mike, hand mike, and so on. Microphones are also classified according to the direction from which they pick up sound. These differences are not always visible. There are four common types.

## Omnidirectional

The *omnidirectional mike* picks up the sound from any and all sides in a circular pattern around the mike. Usually its pickup range has a limit and the main sound source must be within 10 to 12 inches. Obviously, it is a convenient mike to use with a group of several people because it picks up equally well from all sides. However, this same characteristic makes it susceptible to picking up all kinds of distracting background noises. It would not make a good microphone to put on a boom for television because it might pick up unwanted sounds of camera operators and the rest of the stage crew as well.

## Unidirectional

The *unidirectional mike* picks up sound from only one side. Sounds from the opposite side are de-emphasized; sounds from the sides of the mike are virtually wiped out. A performer using a unidirectional mike can stand as much as fourteen or fifteen inches away from it, but cannot stand off to one side. This is the microphone used most frequently in radio stations because unwanted noises are kept to a minimum.

## Bidirectional

The *bidirectional mike*, as its name implies, has two live, or pickup, sides and two dead sides. It has been standard equipment for radio's dramatic shows, but is not very practical for the television studio. If two actors face each other from the live sides of a bidirectional mike, one of them must have his or her back to the camera. Furthermore, the mike will be visible.

## Cardioid

Most new microphones utilize a *cardioid*, or heart-shaped, pattern. These microphones can be used for more than one person. They have eliminated much of the feedback problems (when a microphone is near a speaker, and emits a high-pitched squeal).

**FIGURE 4.7**

A cardioid or heart-shaped pattern

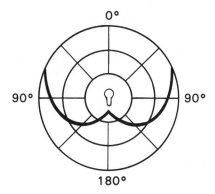

## Frequency Range

You have been introduced to two characteristics of microphones: mounting and pickup pattern. The third characteristic, and one of the most important, is the range of frequencies (high and low tones) that a mike can pick up. Because television sound is broadcast by the frequency modulation method, you need equipment of high fidelity that will respond to and reproduce sounds of widely differing pitch. *Frequency modulation* (FM) refers to a technical change in the radio wave carrying the sound. Broadcasting that uses FM is free from static and more faithfully reproduces sound.

## TYPES OF MICROPHONES

The basic function of a microphone is to change sound into electrical impulses. Most microphones have two elements: a diaphragm, which vibrates in accordance with pressure changes in sound; and a generating element, which changes these sounds into electrical energy. In broadcasting, several types of microphones are used, but the effect is essentially the same.

### Dynamic Microphone

*Dynamic mikes are rugged, but are not good for recording music.*

The dynamic type is perhaps the most popular microphone used in broadcasting. This mike has a diaphragm attached to a metal coil located near a magnet. When a person speaks, the diaphragm vibrates. As it moves to and from the metal coil, a voltage is produced and varies as the diaphragm moves.

The dynamic mike is rugged, which suits it for outdoor "remote" programs, and it resists distortion. Although the frequency response is not as good in some music recording studios, it meets the needs of radio and television stations that do not broadcast live music.

### Ribbon Microphone

Ribbon, or velocity, microphones are very similar to dynamic microphones except that a very thin metal foil serves as the diaphragm and coil. The ribbon microphone is more sensitive and has a slightly higher frequency response. It is suitable for musical recordings and good also for voice, but is confined to studio use as pickup range drops off after three feet.

The ribbon mike does have disadvantages for radio and television productions, however. You cannot use it outdoors because the slightest wind will sound like a tornado. It doesn't work as a boom

**FIGURE 4.8**

This wireless microphone system is designed for camcorders and video cameras. *Photo courtesy of Nady Systems, Inc.*

for television because it sounds like wind when the boom is moved. You must also take great care not to misuse or drop the microphone.

## Condensor Microphone

The condensor microphone works on the same principle as the dynamic microphone, except that the backplate is fixed. An electric current, supplied by a separate power supply (usually a battery), changes the capacitance. When using these mikes in remote locations, you must check the batteries. As the diaphragm moves with changes in air pressure, the voltage changes. Many television stations use this type of microphone as lavaliere mikes for newspeople. Music recording studios often use condensor microphones because of their excellent frequency response.

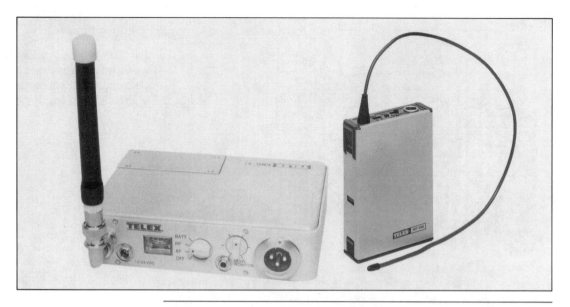

**FIGURE 4.9**

A compact wireless microphone system makes it easy to broadcast from remote locations. *Photo courtesy of Telex Communications, Inc.*

## Pressure Zone Microphone®

A unique microphone created by Crown International Inc. is called a *Pressure Zone Microphone* (PZM). It is a miniature condensor mike mounted face down next to a sound-reflecting metal plate. This plate traps the sound waves and builds up a pressure in front of the diaphragm where sound waves hit at the same time. This microphone is especially useful for large groups of people or musical instruments. For example, instead of several desk mikes for people at a table in radio or TV, one PZM mike located in the center could pick up all the guests from one source. It makes an excellent microphone for picking up bands or orchestras at a distance. When using this mike for guests seated at a table, be careful because it tends to pick up the rustling of papers as well as the sounds of any bumps into the table.

The frequency range of microphones may seem like a problem only for engineers, and this is true in some studios with large staffs. However, in other television setups, student crews are responsible for selecting and setting up mikes for a program. If a script calls for both speech and music to be picked up by one microphone, you need to know which mike has a wide range of frequencies, to obtain the best pickup. If a mike will be used only by an announcer in a separate room called an "announce-booth," you will want the mike that is best for a voice pickup coming from only one direction. Even expensive, sophisticated recording equipment cannot produce good music from a pickup by a cheap mike with a low-frequency range.

## ACOUSTICS

Another factor affecting the sound of your televised message is the acoustics of the studio or classroom in which your program originates. In other words, how clearly can sounds be heard or transmitted in it? Some sound waves pass directly into the microphones; others are reflected off walls, floor, ceiling, windows, chalkboard, and other flat surfaces (such as counters with formica tops). When the walls are far away from the mike, sometimes there is an echo effect. To control the length of time it takes any sound to bounce off the wall and back into the mike, studios have irregular wall surfaces, draperies, and wood or composition panels. The most flexible studios have both live (reflecting-sound) areas and dead (absorbing-sound) areas, which can be adjusted to regulate the amount of reverberation. A practical student once explained live and dead areas by saying that studios need to sound both "zing" and "ker-plunk."

Outdoors sound, because there is no restraining space, is "dead." A room with considerable reverberation of sound bouncing from one hard surface to another is "live," or "zing." A studio is deadened by heavy draperies and carpeting. It is made live by exposing plaster walls and hard, shiny surfaces. In a classroom, a wood floor, plaster walls, and large window and chalkboard areas cause the sound to have a hollow or echolike tone. The brilliance and timbre of music and speech tones would be removed, however, if all the walls, floor, and ceiling were covered with absorbent surfaces. So you need to experiment with window shades, rugs, drop cloths, felt cloths, and screens until you achieve the best balance. You do not expect an interview recorded in the locker room to sound like a concert in the auditorium, but neither do you expect an oboe solo to sound like a leaky showerhead.

The number of people in the studio can affect the amount of sound that is absorbed. Each person represents the acoustical equivalent of about 4.6 square feet of absorbent material. Make at least one check of the sound quality with the people, the flats, and the material the studio will have during the telecast. If you rehearse in a classroom full of students and then record the program after school in an empty room, do not expect the same tones to be picked up by the microphone.

This acoustical problem can be illustrated by the story of a broadcast series by a famous symphony orchestra. At dress rehearsals, the studio engineer and the conductor were both pleased with the tone quality. Yet invariably, the actual broadcasts were less satisfactory, although all the audio controls and mikes were adjusted the same way. No explanation could be found until someone recalled that during the actual broadcast there was a studio audience. The front rows were filled with wealthy old men with starched dress shirts and shiny bald heads, which provided sound-reflecting surfaces the engineers had not taken into account.

## THE PERFORMER'S USE OF THE MICROPHONE

*Talk into the mike as if you're talking to one person.*

The final and most variable factor affecting the sound of a television program is the performer. The public address mike in the auditorium, gym, or stadium is used to project the speaker's voice to large groups of people sitting together and reacting as a group, an audience. The microphone in the television studio carries the speaker's voice to large numbers of people, too, but they are listening in small groups or individually, usually at home. The ability to speak directly, as if talking with one individual, is as necessary for a successful television performer as the ability to look "through" the camera lens to the viewer sitting in an easy chair in front of his or her television set.

Furthermore, microphones do not transform sloppy articulation into clearly enunciated speech, nor do they add variety and vitality to monotonous, deadly voice patterns. However, microphones do call attention to *s, ch, sh,* and similar sibilant sounds. To avoid

**FIGURE 4.10**

A "combo-operator" is responsible for checking audio levels as well as announcing.

these and other hazards, the inexperienced performer may find the following suggestions helpful.

1. When you are testing a microphone to get the proper level for the audio engineer, never tap or blow into it. If you are using a ribbon microphone, you can damage the metal ribbon by tapping it. Never test the mike by saying, "Testing 1-2-3." Test it by reading the first lines of the script. Then there won't be any surprises for the engineer when you start.

2. Practice "swallowing" *s*, *ch*, and *sh* sounds and concentrating on the vowel that follows each one, to avoid sending a narrow stream of air from your lips into the microphone. Concentrate on the *gra* in *grass*, the *all* in *shall*, and the *ne* in *happiness*. Pronounce *statistics* "stay-TIH-sticks."

3. Check with the technicians on the correct distance between you and the specific mike being used. Then stay there; do not be a creeper (edging to and from the mike) or a weaver (rocking from side to side). If you get too far away, the technician will have to turn the volume up. Then, in addition to your

voice, the listener may hear the piano pedals or the rumble of the camera dolly trucking across the floor.

4. Do not rattle script pages against the mike stand or on a table-top. Remember that rattling paper is used to simulate the sound of a forest fire or rain on the roof.

5. Do not hit the mike stand with your feet or bang it against the top with your hand.

6. *Never* whisper a cue or direction or question to another performer. You cannot hide anything from a mike that is turned on.

7. Do not hold the mike too close to your mouth. It will pick up little puffs of air when you pronounce words beginning with *p* and make them sound like shots from a BB gun. A whistle will sound like a mild explosion and can actually injure some sensitive mikes. A mike held too close will pick up breathiness, lip smacking, tongue clacking, swallowing, and occasionally even a heart flutter.

   Generally, it is a good idea to keep a script's length away from a desk or floor microphone. The best distance to keep from "popping" consonants into the mike is eight to ten inches away. Also keep in mind that lavaliere or clip-on mikes are meant to be talked over, not into, so do not pick up a lavaliere mike and talk directly into the top.

8. Be ever aware of the sound of your total presentation. It is as important as the picture. Don't ignore that microphone!

> *If you want to prove you're an amateur, the best way to do it is blowing into the mike during a sound check.*

## THE AUDIO BOARD

Several microphones are necessary during a typical TV production. Perhaps you want to use a theme song for the beginning and end of the program. For this you will need an audio mixer or console. A typical radio mixer can mix many microphones as well as tape recorders, turntables, cart recorders (mentioned later), and facilities for receiving programming from remote locations. At first a radio mixer or "board" looks complicated, but it is really not. And, once you have learned to operate one, it is easy to operate any other at another station because the principle remains the same. There are several volume controls or "pots" (short for potentiometer) that control the volume for mikes and other equipment. These pots are round on most older boards and sliding on the newer ones. A switch above the pots turns the mikes on and off.

**FIGURE 4.11**

A television production director adjusts volume with a *pot,* one of several round control knobs common on audio consules.

**FIGURE 4.12**

Demonstrating a new audio console system, a technician adjusts sound using one of the sliding volume control levers.

Another important element of any audio board is the "cue" feature. This allows the audio operator the chance to get the record going in exactly the right position so there is no dead air until the record finds the opening groove. A VU (volume unit) meter shows exactly how loud the signal is going on the air no matter at what volume the monitor speaker is set. The monitor speaker is usually set low in a control room so the director can issue commands. The VU meter should generally read between 85 and 100 percent. If it is too low, or "in the mud," the sound may not be loud enough for the signal to be recorded. If it is too loud, or "pinning the needle," the sound will be distorted as it is recorded. Each audio board is different, so the audio operator must become accustomed to the board and its operation.

**FIGURE 4.13**

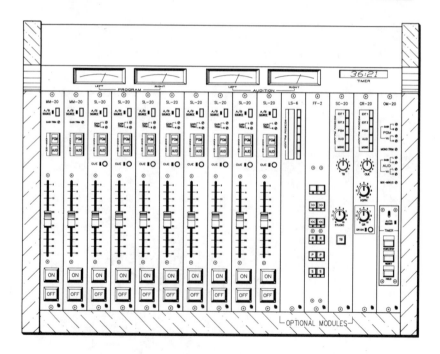

A diagram of an audio board. *Courtesy of Wheatstone Corporation.*

## COMMUNICATING BY SOUND ALONE

You can get the clearest impression of the images sound can convey by studying radio programs—how they are presented and what techniques enable them to excite the imagination and translate auditory impulses into characters and situations as definite and real as any you see on television. You may be familiar with radio news, music programs, and an occasional weather report or emergency message, but most of you are less knowledgeable about radio drama and the old-time comedy and variety shows your grandparents enjoyed.

### Voice of the Radio Performer

Radio performers have to do with their voices alone what television performers do with the assistance of settings, costumes, properties, makeup, graphics, visuals, and observable movements. The radio actor, for instance, has to put his or her mood (not visible in a frown) and various bits of stage business (stroking the chin thoughtfully) into the lines. If these are not conveyed by the words, by the way the lines are spoken, they do not exist. The audience cannot see the performer listening to another character. The performer can indicate that he or she has been listening only by the response to the other person's lines. When someone being interviewed on radio concludes an anecdote by saying, "It was the most frightening experience of my life," we are a bit suspicious of the concentration of the interviewer who merely answers, "Is that so! And when did you become interested in the migrations of birds?" However, if the interviewer follows up with a question like, "After such a terrifying experience, did you ever go back again?" we feel the interviewer has been listening attentively and reacting to the guest's comments.

### Positions at the Mike

Radio actors do have a mike and a script, and they must know how to use the mike from five basic positions: (1) on mike, (2) off mike, (3) fading in, (4) fading out, and (5) behind a door, wall, or other obstruction. In general, when speaking on mike, an actor stands eight to ten inches away from it and uses enough volume to address a person four feet away. If an angry mob is moving into the scene, their shouts should become louder as the group steps closer and closer to the mike. Fading in and out are as important as going on and off mike.

The cast of a radio play usually gathers around two or three standing microphones, but a small cast of two or three may be seated at a table. Usually, actors prefer to stand to "get in the mood" by performing actions suited to the words. Because the body responds as a whole, performers know their voices will sound more excited if their bodies are tense and they are moving their legs up and down as if pacing with impatience. A radio director once had trouble getting the lovers in a tender scene to use the proper tone of voice. After he moved them to the same microphone, where they stood physically close together, it was easier for them to sound affectionate. Helen Hayes, playing the role of nurse Florence Nightingale in a radio show, held the script in her left hand while she stroked her left arm as if she were caressing a wounded soldier. In a radio presentation, action and feeling must be readily discernible in the tone of voice. The audience, seeing nothing, must hear all.

## Reading the Script

These special techniques for using the voice effectively to communicate meaning and feeling in radio are complemented by equally important techniques for using the script to advantage. The fact that radio performers can read the script and do not have to memorize it is an important aid. However, it is also the downfall of inexperienced performers who sound as if they are reading and keep their eyes so "glued" to the script that they miss helpful cues from the director or the technicians.

Experienced, skilled radio speakers memorize the script almost as completely as if they were going to deliver it from memory. At rehearsals they mark their scripts, circling or underlining each of their cues. They mark time cues in the margins so they will know where they should be reading one minute before the close of the show. Descriptive comments (such as "as if frightened at the thought") are added to help actors interpret meanings for the listener. Radio speakers slide each page of the script quietly beneath the others after reading them and are careful not to hold the script as a sound barrier between themselves and the mike. They watch for cues from the director and follow directions for special effects produced by the technical and sound effects crew.

## NONVERBAL CUES FOR RADIO AND TELEVISION DIRECTION

Although each director creates his or her own nonverbal cues for communicating with radio performers, certain cues have become so standardized that they are used in both radio and television.

### Stand by

The signal to stand by consists of raising the arm above the head with the forefinger pointing upward. It warns the participants that it is almost time for a cue to be given, alerting them to be ready to perform on cue.

### Cue to start

This is the go-ahead signal that tells actors to execute whatever is supposed to be done or said at a particular time. It consists of pointing the finger at the person who is supposed to perform the action. It must be a clear, direct movement. When the arm is already upraised in the "stand by" position, the director merely lowers it to a horizontal position, with the finger pointing directly at the person being cued. Curved fingers, waving limply back and forth, only serve to confuse the performer.

**FIGURE 4.14**

Cue for performer to start.

## Speed up

Rotating the index finger clockwise is an indication that the director wishes the performer to speed up the tempo. If the director rotates the finger slowly, speakers are to increase the speed just a little. If the finger rotates quickly, speakers know time is running out fast, and they must deliver their lines much faster.

## Slow down

Directors move their hands from a together position to an apart position, as if stretching rubber bands or elastic, to tell the performer to "stretch it out."

### FIGURE 4.15

Cue to slow down.

## FIGURE 4.16

Cue for time—four minutes are left.

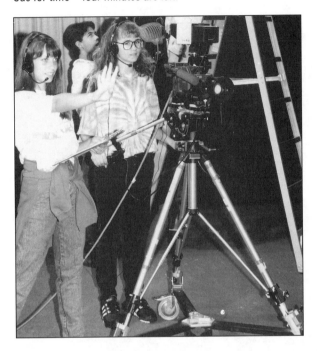

### More volume or less volume

Directors request more volume by extending their arms with the palm upward and raising their hand slowly or quickly to indicate how much more volume is needed. Less volume is indicated by extending the arm with the palm turned down and dropping the hand quickly or slowly.

### Move closer or move back

To request speakers to move in relation to the mike, directors place their hands in front of their faces. The palm is turned inward to indicate moving closer to the mike and outward to indicate moving away from it.

### Time cue

The director holds up fingers to indicate the number of minutes remaining.

---

**FIGURE 4.17**

Cue to wrap it up—close discussion.

### Wrap it up

An upraised fist with fingers toward the talent is a signal to close the discussion as quickly as possible.

### Cut

Drawing the index finger slowly across the throat is the signal to stop.

As you will learn in Chapter 5, "Verbalizing the Message," the television director relays the directions for the speaker, via an intercom system, to the studio floor manager, who in turn signals the performer in a variety of ways. In radio, the director signals the performer with hand signals, such as the nine just described, and with facial expressions and other nonverbal cues. In television, the sound must be consistent with what appears on camera. In radio, however, the sound must be sufficiently effective to create a visual image in the mind of the listener.

**FIGURE 4.18**

Cue to stop or cut.

## IT'S A WRAP

Television brings beautiful music and fascinating conversation into our homes. When we laugh at a comedian's jokes or learn from an insightful interview, we owe a debt to skillful sound technicians. We benefit from their knowledge of microphones, acoustics, and audio mixers. Together with talented directors and performers, they add the words and music to the pictures we enjoy on television.

As good sound technicians know, one of the secrets to providing the proper sound is to be sure the microphone suits the situation. The two key characteristics of a microphone are the way it's mounted and the direction from which it picks up sound. Sound technicians may select a floor or table stand mike, a lavaliere, lapel, or hand mike, or a boom mike, depending on the situation. They may require omnidirectional, unidirectional, bidirectional, or cardioid sound pickup. Their best option may be a dynamic, ribbon, condensor, or Pressure Zone microphone. It takes experience and knowledge to select the right microphone for the setting and the performers involved.

Performers also have a role to play in ensuring quality sound production. They must understand how to use the microphone properly, their enunciation must be clear, and their vocal delivery expressive, especially if they are performing on radio. Finally, they must be alert and able to follow the director's cues and hand signals to achieve the exact timing required in radio and television.

So when you like what you hear on radio or television, remember that it took a skilled group of media professionals to create those sounds for you.

# Video Lab

## 1. Sound effects

You can purchase sound-effects recorded on tape or CD, or create sound effects with your own equipment and record them on tapes and cassettes. Or, you can produce sound effects manually—a method that requires greater effort and imagination, but enables you to cue more accurately and blend the sounds more realistically into the script. Before you begin presenting a program, try to reproduce the following sound effects, record them on audiotape, and then play them back to check how real they sound.

a. *Raindrops*—Drop rice on the head of a drum.
b. *Tap dancing*—Beat out the time with drumsticks on a folded newspaper, or hold shoes in your hands and tap them on a board near the mike.
c. *Roar of a plane*—Hold a stiff blotter against electric fan blades, or hold an electric toothbrush against the palm of your hand.
d. *Fire*—Crackle cellophane or crush onionskin paper near the mike.
e. *Breaking bones*—Chew candy mints or celery close to the mike.
f. *Gunshots*—Snap a ruler against the side of a cardboard box.
g. *Telephone voice*—Hold the open end of a drinking glass to the side of your mouth while talking. (Normally this is done with a filter microphone.)
h. *Monkeys*—Rub wet cork against bottle.

## 2. Recordings

For music in a show, compare the advantages and disadvantages of using cassettes, reels of audiotape, CDs, and broadcast cartridge machines.

**ECONOMY NOTE:** If your school has no filter mikes or echo chambers, try some of these inexpensive makeshifts to achieve special effects like ghosts, or telephone voices. Hold the open end of a large drinking glass at the mike in such a way that you direct your words into the top of the glass and the mike at the same time. Or cover your head and the mike with a large metal wastebasket. Or speak into the big end of a megaphone with the small end toward the mike.

**FIGURE 4.19**

Audio "carts" will automatically cue taped music and commercials. The Ampex model at the right, known as a "cart machine," allows up to 72 hours of pre-programmed video to be fully automated—from commercials to prime time programming. *Photo courtesy of Ampex.* On a smaller scale, in the photo below three carts are used to cue music at a school broadcasting station.

Most radio and TV stations today rely on broadcast cartridge recorders for music, sound effects, and commercials. A cartridge recorder uses a "cart" with a continuous loop of tape in predetermined lengths (five seconds, ten seconds, twenty seconds, etc.). The advantage of a cartridge recorder is that the tape or cart is cued to a precise spot by way of a thousand hertz Hz tone put on at the beginning of the program material. The recorder automatically stops when it reaches that tone and is ready for the next play. The tapes do not warp or become scratched, and this eliminates the need for cueing.

Most TV stations now "cart" the introductions and closings to newscasts or any TV production. Both the music and the announcer can be put on the same tape to be ready for the start of the program. Both the open and close of the program can be put on the same cart and will be cued for the right time.

If you do not need to start the recording at an exact spot or cue, you can take the easy way out and simply slide a cassette into the playback. If you have an inexperienced sound crew, with one member who is always pushing the wrong button and erasing the tape, you will be grateful for one ingenious feature of the cassette. On the back of each cassette are two cavities covered by plastic tabs. If you break off those tabs, you cannot record or erase the tapes until you tape over the hole again.

Put a CD and CD player, a reel of tape and a recorder, a cassette and a cassette playback out on a table. Now see which one you can load and bring up to correct volume the fastest. Check how long it takes you to find an exact spot on each of the three. Which seems best for a disk jockey? As background music for a story? For theme music that will be repeated at the beginning and end of each show for a week? or cue a cassette or audiotape, relying on the counter-numbering system of the playback machine. Finding a single measure of music on an audiotape can be a challenge because the amount of leader tape wound around the take-up reel varies as much as an inch or more each time the tape is rewound. Marking the reel tape with a colored wax pencil will show you when the "spot" approaches the playback head, but it takes experience to get the timing down right. One tape editor was so proficient in locating words that she was even able to add "ing" to the final syllable of each "goin'," "thinkin'," and "hopin'" in the speech of her somewhat inarticulate employer.

### 3. Radio shows

With the ability to put sound effects and music on tape and cassettes, with music on CDs and tapes, with live, manually operated instruments ready, try a radio show of your own. Have another student record your three-minute presentation of one of the following and play it back for you.

a. *A disk jockey show.* Limit the recordings to one minute so that you will have time for a two-minute introduction. Plan carefully how the music will be played. Do you want it to fade out under your voice? To stop abruptly? What will be your transition between records? Will you have an opening and closing theme? Will all recordings be by one group or one composer? Will all be on one theme? Will you interview one of the recording artists? Will you "plug" (promote) one of the recordings?

b. *A news-weather-sports presentation.* An important part of your preparation is to determine the answers to these questions: What can you do in three minutes? What portion of the time will be news? Will the intended audience determine how much time will be devoted to sports? Will you have a musical theme? How will you make the transition between the parts of the show? Will you use the sound of a teletype? Will your speech tempo and tone of voice be the same for news, weather, and sports? Will you want the reports recorded elsewhere by another voice? If so, how will you play that tape and cue it in? Will you use a recorded interview for part of the sports segment? How can you make these recorded passages clear and distinct for the listener? How much local news will you include?

If you are near a radio station, ask for some "copy" from a wire service such as AP or Reuters. This copy (news) is designed for radio performers. If you must get copy from the newspaper, you will have to rewrite the story for radio. For example, a newspaper story might start, "Mr. John Jones, 57,...." Now, who talks like that? No one. You would change the beginning: "Fifty-seven-year-old John Jones...." Always speak in the present tense. Read some good books on broadcast journalism to understand the style of writing for broadcast.

c. *Editorial comment.* Pretend you are the radio station manager giving an editorial comment on such topics as freedom of the press, the construction of a new highway through the city, the vandalism of shopping malls, or some other matter of local concern. How will you command attention and keep your script from sounding as if you were reading it? If listeners turn to another station, your cause is lost!

d. *Play-by-play.* Give your imagination a workout by presenting an on-the-spot play-by-play of a baseball game, a stock car race, a hundred-yard dash, or some other sports event. How much background sound should you include for atmosphere? Will you include a remote recording of an interview with a participant? Will someone introduce you? From what vantage point will you watch the event?

Before attempting one of the following group experiences in communicating by sound alone, you will find it helpful to listen to a daytime radio serial, a radio play, or a variety show. Because one person can play several parts in a radio show by changing his or her voice and manner, a group of four or five students can present a radio play requiring a sizable cast.

a. For your first radio group presentation, do not try to use an original script. Use a collection like *Plays from Radio* (see Additional Resources on page 000.). Some libraries have collections of radio scripts. Let members of your group take turns being responsible for creating sound effects, making the opening and closing announcements, and directing the show by giving the cues.

b. Write a fifteen-minute radio drama adapted from any short story. Perhaps you could write an original drama called "Night-Life in the City," which might present lives of people who work at night. Short stories from anthologies also make good radio dramas. You will soon read a radio script adapted from two of Edgar Allan Poe's famous short stories. A great horror story works well on radio because of the sound effects and the audience's imagination. You can easily see how, in 1938, Orson Welles used an already famous story to convince the nation that martians were invading Earth in "War of the Worlds."

## 4. Commercials

Commercials play an important part in the broadcast industry. Sometimes as much money is spent on the commercial itself as on the program it sponsors. There are basically three types of commercials you may want to produce: straight, voiceovers, and situations.

**Straight commercials.** The easiest to produce is a one-minute straight commercial using no sound effects or music. A thirty-second commercial is approximately sixty-five words.

Try to make your commercial as sincere and conversational as possible. It is a good idea to plan around one of the universal appeals that will hold the listeners' attention. Some of the appeals used by advertisers are love for your family, guilt, physical attraction, pride, and saving money. Pick a product, decide what appeal you will use to capture and hold attention, write the script, and deliver the commercial on tape. Listen to the tape to determine how effective you were in selling the product. Did *you* believe in what you were saying? Did it sound natural, or like words from a sheet of paper?

**Voiceover commercials.** Music plays an important part in many radio commercials. It sets the mood for the entire piece. A fast-paced commercial will use fast-paced music. Usually instrumental music is used rather than a vocal arrangement, unless the vocal is a jingle written for that product. The music is background, and it should not be something everyone will recognize. If you used "The Power of Love" from the movie *Back to the Future,* your listeners might be tempted to listen to the music rather than the commercial. Bring the music up at the beginning, hold it, then fade it under your voice during the delivery (check the levels), fade it up at the end, and fade it out. Listen to the finished production. How effective was the music? Did it add to the effect or detract from your presentation?

**Situation commercials.** Many advertising agencies use humorous situations to capture

REPUTATION    :30 TV    "CALVIN GRAPEVINE"    1 of 2

CALVIN:   YEP, I'M PART
OF THE MANAGEMENT TEAM
NOW.

MAMA:   OH BABY, I'M SO
PROUD OF...

CALVIN:   IT'S ONLY THE
          AFTER-SCHOOL SHIFT.
MAMA:     BUT STILL IT'S...
CALVIN:   GOT TO GET BACK
          TO WORK.

MAMA:       THAT'S RIGHT,
(ON PHONE)  ANNA.

ANNA:       CALVIN'S THE
(TO HER SON) NEW MANAGER
            AT MCDONALD'S.
TEEN:   YO, STRAIGHT UP?!!

TEEN:       CAL'S BEEN
(TO A FRIEND) ON IT AT
MICKEY D'S, SO THEY GAVE
HIM HIS PROPERS.

## FIGURE 4.20

A commercial done for television starts off as a storyboard, a kind of outline of visuals and audio. *This storyboard is provided courtesy of McDonald's Corporation and Burrell Communications Group, Chicago, Illinois.*

and hold the attention of the listeners. They use characterizations, sound effects, and music to sell the product. This is the most difficult commercial to produce because it uses all aspects of radio production: voice, music, and sound effects. (See Figure 4-21 as an example.)

Write and produce a commercial utilizing a situation. For this commercial you should include an announcer, two actors, music, and at least one sound effect. Ask your classmates to help you create a situation commercial.

**5. From radio to television**

Your group is now ready to experience sound for radio as compared to sound for television. Imagine you are a video disk jockey for a local version of MTV, and you are going to introduce the newest music videos. How can you put a disk jockey program on a medium like TV? How will you change the format? What will the audience see? Will viewers see the technician or you rolling the tape? Will the source of the sound ever be seen? Will viewers see dancers, or musicians, or still pictures? Will they see the group that made the recording? How much will you have to change the script to make it suitable for television?

Suppose you have been made public relations/publicity chair of the United Fund drive, the new band-uniform drive, the muscular dystrophy fund drive, the prom, or some other worthwhile project for which you have been given a one-minute spot on both radio and television. You have "one minute of sound" to promote or sell your project to the radio listener. Do not waste a second of it with a trite beginning like "Thank you for letting us come into your living room tonight." Make every second count.

After you have heard and criticized the playback of your radio promotion, try a one-minute television plug for your campaign. Again, make every sound—and sight—count. What visuals will be most convincing in persuading viewers to contribute to your cause? Which is more effective, a few visuals shown long enough to affect their emotions, or a bombardment of many pictures that blasts away at their consciousness? Use a storyboard format to outline your approach.

Music and sound effects as a background to establish the mood for words can have an emotional impact. The sound track on a movie sometimes becomes as famous as the movie—for example, *The Bodyguard* or *Singles*. Have two or three students from an oral interpretation or English class read aloud brief selections from either poetry or prose that describe a setting or a mood. Provide appropriate mood music and sounds as background. Does the sound help the reader create the mood? Or is it distracting? Is it too loud or too soft? Repeat the reading, and observe the reader through the viewfinder of a television camera. Does seeing the reader help you sense the mood, or is it distracting?

Familiarity with all kinds of music is one of the most sought-after qualifications for both radio and television personnel. Recordings of "mood music" are helpful, but they cannot provide the enormous variety needed as background for a wide range of programs.

Figure 4.22 is an example of a script that adapts a short story to radio. Notice the use of music and sound effects to make this story effective for radio. Produce this program on radio to see how the elements mix to create effective use of radio as a storytelling medium. After reading and discussing the chapter on writing for TV, try rewriting this radio drama as a teleplay, allowing for the visual elements found in TV.

## FIGURE 4.21

## Commercial Created by a High School Student

**Music:**       **Up, hold, and under**

ANNCR:    Now let's visit Ralph and Marge in their home discussing business.
RALPH:     I'd better get that upstairs heating system fixed, not to mention those basement steps.
MARGE:    Yeah, you should. Someone could freeze on the second floor and fall through those stairs.

**Sound:**       **Knock on door, opens, then closes**

INSPCTR:   I'm the building inspector. Do you have a building permit for your home remodeling?
RALPH:     Well, I uh . . . .
INSPCTR:   Just as I thought. I'll have to look upstairs to see if everything is in order.
RALPH:     I wouldn't do that if I were you.
INSPCTR:   Nobody tells me what to do. I'll open that door if I want to.

**Sound:**       **Door opens, blizzard is heard, then a scream and door shuts**

INSPCTR:   AHHHHHHHH! That's cold. You've got a heating violation coming, and I'm not even to the basement yet.
RALPH:     Please don't go down there, I'm begging you.
INSPCTR:   What's the matter? You got something to hide?
MARGE:    No, he doesn't, but you'll be sorry if you go down there.
INSPCTR:   Hah, you're trying to scare me, but it won't work. I'm opening this door.

**Sound:**       **Door opens, body falls down steps, then a scream**

MARGE:    At least he didn't land in the sewer drain.

**Sound:**       **Splash followed by a scream**

INSPCTR:   (OFF MIKE) I'll sue you for everything you've got. You won't have a thing left.
MARGE:    Big deal. We can always get a loan from Helpful Finance.
RALPH:     That's right. We can always count on getting some help from the friendly people at Helpful Finance for a remodeling loan or an emergency loan. They'll listen to our problems, and we can pay back in forty-eight easy installments.
INSPCTR:   (OFF MIKE) Yeah, all right. But could you do something about those crocodiles?

BOTH:    (IN UNISON) Crocodiles?

ANNCR:    Every one of our fifty-seven Helpful Finance offices has nice, friendly people that you would really like to take home with you, but you can't because we make them stay here so they can solve your money problems faster. Some can even get rid of your crocodiles, too.

**Music:**    **Up, hold, under**

by ERIC SZAMBARIS, student at THORNTON TOWNSHIP HIGH SCHOOL, Harvey, Illinois

---

**FIGURE 4.22**

RADIO DRAMA
*adapted from a radio script originally produced at*
*Thornton Township High School, Harvey, Illinois.*

Edgar Allan Poe's
"Cask of Amontillado"
"Tell-Tale Heart"

**TALES OF TERROR**

**Sound:**    **Sound of nitre—Footsteps (hollow)**

Narrator:    You hear that dripping? That's the sound of the nitre *oozing* from the walls and ceiling of the catacombs. These are the burial vaults of the Montresors. Here, under the riverbed, repose the last remains of my proud ancestors. They have not been disturbed these fifty years. Nothing, not a bone. (FOOTSTEPS AND NITRE) Notice the white clammy surface. It increases as we go deeper into the vaults. Nitre—everything is encrusted with it, the passageways, the arches, or here in the wine room. These old casks are the pride of the Montresors. That pile of bones over there? A special tomb! Let me tell you about it. I was a young man, young and poor with a family name centuries old, poor and despised by the Fortunatos, Lord and Lady, whose house faced mine. Lord Fortunato used to snub me publicly to jest at the tattered remnants of the proud Montresors. It all started with a cask of Amontillado, (LAUGH) yes, that's it, (FADING) a cask of Amontillado.

| | |
|---|---|
| **Music:** | **Eerie theme** |
| Announcer: | The Radio-Television Production class of Thornton Township High School presents "The Cask of Amontillado" by Edgar Allan Poe, on *Tales of Terror.* |
| **Music:** | **Eerie theme (Up, hold, under)** |
| Narrator: | Ha, ha, the thousand injuries of Fortunato I had borne as best I could, but when he ventured upon insult, I vowed revenge. He had a weak point. He prided himself on his taste in wine. It was about dusk one evening, in the supreme madness of the carnival season, that I encountered my friend. I was so pleased to see him that I thought I should never stop wringing his hand. He greeted me with excessive warmth, for he had been drinking much. |
| FORTUNATO: | (DRUNK) Montresor, Montresor, my friend. |
| MONTRESOR: | My dear Fortunato, you are luckily met. How remarkably well you are looking today. |
| FORTUNATO: | Yes, the carnival is magnificent this year. |
| MONTRESOR: | Fortunato, I have received a cask that passes for Amontillado, and I have my doubts. |
| FORTUNATO: | Amontillado, a cask? Ah! Impossible; and in the middle of carnival season too. |
| MONTRESOR: | Well, I have my doubts, and I was silly enough to pay the full price without consulting you in the matter. You were not to be found. I was fearful of losing the bargain. |
| FORTUNATO: | Ah! Amontillado! |
| MONTRESOR: | I have my doubts, and I must satisfy them. As you are engaged, I am on my way to Luchese. If anyone knows good wine, it is he. He would tell me.... |
| FORTUNATO: | Luchese cannot tell Amontillado from Sherry. |
| MONTRESOR: | And yet some fools will have it that his taste is a match for your own. |
| FORTUNATO: | Come, let us go. |
| MONTRESOR: | Where? |
| FORTUNATO: | To your wine vault. |
| MONTRESOR: | My friend, no! I will not impose upon your good nature. Your mask, your costume, I perceive you have an engagement. Luchese will.... |
| FORTUNATO: | I have no engagement! Come on. |
| MONTRESOR: | My friend, no! It is not the engagement but the severe cold with which I see you are afflicted. The vaults are insufferably damp. They're encrusted with nitre. |
| FORTUNATO: | Let us go nevertheless. The cold is a mere nothing. Amontillado, you've been imposed upon. And as for Luchese, ah, he cannot distinguish Amontillado from Sherry. Come, come, we go! |

| | |
|---|---|
| **Music:** | **Eerie theme** |

Narrator: Thus speaking, Fortunato possessed himself of my arm and led me off to my house. I took from their sconces two torches, and giving one to Fortunato, followed him through several suites of rooms to the archway that lead to the vaults. I passed down a long, winding staircase, requesting him to be cautious as he followed. We came at length to the foot of the descent, and stood together on the damp ground of the catacombs of the Montresors. The walk of my friend was unsteady, and the bells on his cap jingled as we walked.

FORTUNATO: The Amontillado?

MONTRESOR: It is further on, but observe the white webwork that gleams from these cavern walls.

FORTUNATO: Nitre? (COUGHING)

MONTRESOR: Nitre! How long have you had that cough?

FORTUNATO: (COUGHING) It is nothing!

MONTRESOR: Come, we will go back! Your health is precious. You are rich, respected, and admired. You are happy as once I was. You are a man to be missed. For me, it is no matter. We will go back! You will be ill, and I will not be responsible. Besides, there is Luchese....

FORTUNATO: Enough! The cough is a mere nothing. It will not kill me. I shall not die of a cough.

MONTRESOR: True! And indeed I had no intention of alarming you unnecessarily; but you should use all proper caution. Ah, a drink of this wine will defend us from the damp. Here, drink.

| | |
|---|---|
| **Sound:** | **Cork from bottle** |

FORTUNATO: I drink to the dead who repose around us.

MONTRESOR: And I, to your long life!

FORTUNATO: Ah! These vaults are extensive!

MONTRESOR: The Montresors were a great and numerous family.

FORTUNATO: What's your coat of arms?

MONTRESOR: A huge human foot of gold in a field of blue. The foot crushes a serpent whose fangs are embedded in the heel.

FORTUNATO: And the motto?

MONTRESOR: "No one injures me without punishment!"

FORTUNATO: Oh? Good! Ah, come, the Amontillado!

| | |
|---|---|
| **Sound:** | **Footsteps** |

| | |
|---|---|
| **Music:** | **Eerie theme** |

Narrator: The wine sparkled in his eyes, and the bells jingled. My own fancy grew warm with the wine. We passed through walls of piled bones with casks and barrels intermingling into the innermost recesses of the catacomb. I paused again, and this time I made a bold gesture to seize Fortunato by the arm. He recoiled a few paces.

FORTUNATO: Your grip is strong.

MONTRESOR: The nitre! See? It increases and hangs like moss above the vaults. We're below the river's bed.

FORTUNATO: (COUGHS)

MONTRESOR: The drops of moisture trickle on the bones. Come, we will go back before it is too late. Your cough?

FORTUNATO: It is nothing. Come, let us go on!

MONTRESOR: If you insist! As for Luchese....

FORTUNATO: Ah! He is an ignoramous.

| | |
|---|---|
| **Sound:** | **Footsteps** |

| | |
|---|---|
| **Music:** | **Eerie theme** |

Narrator: We continued our route in search of the Amontillado. We passed through a series of low arches, descended and passed on and arrived at a deep crypt. The feeble light did not enable us to see further than the end of the niche. Fortunato stood stupidly before it. I urged him forward.

MONTRESOR: Here, proceed. Herein is the Amontillado.

| | |
|---|---|
| **Sound:** | **Footsteps and chains** |

Narrator: My friend stepped forward unsteadily, while I followed immediately at his heels. In an instant, he had reached the extremity of the niche, and finding his progress arrested by the rocks, he stood stupidly bewildered. A moment more and I had him fettered to the granite. (CHAINS) Throwing the chains around his waist it was but the work of a few seconds to secure them. He was much too astonished to resist. (PADLOCK CLOSING). Withdrawing the key, I stepped back from the recess.

MONTRESOR: Pass your hands over the walls. You cannot help feeling the nitre. Indeed, it is very damp. Once more let me implore you to return. No? Then I must positively leave you. But I must first render you all the attentions in my power.

FORTUNATO: The Amontillado?

MONTRESOR:     True! The Amontillado!

Narrator:     As I said these words, I busied myself among the piles of bones, throwing them aside. I uncovered a quantity of mortar and building stone. With these materials and the aid of my trowel, I began vigorously to wall up the entrance of the niche. It was about midnight and my task, although difficult, was drawing to a close. I completed the fifth, the sixth, and the seventh tier when suddenly....

FORTUNATO:     (CHAINS SHAKING) Umm! Ah!

Narrator:     I discovered the intoxication of Fortunato had in great measure worn off. This was not the cry of a drunken man. His cries were followed by the curious vibrations of the chains. The noise lasted for several minutes during which my heart fluttered with great satisfaction. I ceased my labors and sat down upon the bones. After a time, I rose and held my torch over the mason work, throwing a feeble few rays upon the figure within. (CRIES FROM WITHIN) His cries seemed to crush me violently back. For a moment I hesitated. I trembled, frightened that he might free himself. I placed my hand on the solid fabric of the catacomb, and a touch of the granite reassured me. I was satisfied. I replied to Fortunato, I re-echoed, I surpassed him in volume and strength. Finally, the clamor grew still. (PAUSE) I then completed the eighth, ninth, and tenth tiers. I had finished a portion of the last, the eleventh. There remained but a single stone to be fitted and plastered in. I struggled with its weight. I placed it partially in its destined position. But now there came from out that niche.

FORTUNATO:     (WEAKLY) Ha-ha-ha! A very good joke, indeed. An excellent jest. We will have many a rich laugh about it at the carnival! Ha—over the wine.

MONTRESOR:     Over the Amontillado!

FORTUNATO:     Yes, the Amontillado. But is it not getting late? Will they not be waiting for us at the carnival? The Lady Fortunato and the rest? Let us be gone!

**Sound:**     **Footsteps and chains**

MONTRESOR:     Fortunato? Fortunato? May he rest in peace.

**Music:**     **Throbbing, eerie**

**Sound:**     **Footsteps**

Narrator:     Against the new masonry, I reerected this old rampart of bones. For the half century, no mortal has disturbed them.

**Music:**     **Up, hold**

MAN:    You, there! Don't turn away. Come back here a moment. Yes, there, that's better. Place your hand here on my chest.

**Sound:**    **Heartbeat**

MAN:    You hear it? A heartbeat! Simple, isn't it? Yet that hideous sound has put me in this place of terror. It was unjust in the extreme. You look at me with strange eyes. You believe what they say about me. True, nervous, very, very nervous I have been and I am, but why do you say I am mad? Listen and observe how sanely, how calmly I can tell you the whole story. You must remember always, it was the heartbeat of the old man that was my undoing. His cursed telltale heart.

**Sound:**    **Heartbeat**

**Music:**    **Eerie theme**

Narrator:    The Radio-Television Production class of Thornton Township High School presents the "Tell-Tale Heart," by Edgar Allan Poe, on *Tales of Terror*.

**Music:**    **Theme, up, hold, under**

Man:    You ask me why I did it? It is impossible to say how first the idea entered my brain. But once conceived, it haunted me day and night. Motive? There was none. Passion? There was none. I loved the old man. He had never wronged me. He had never given me insult. For his gold I had no desire. I think it was his eye. Yes, it was this, one of his eyes resembled that of a vulture. A pale, blue eye with a film over it. Whenever it fell upon me, my blood ran cold. And so by degrees, very gradually, I made up my mind to take the life of the old man; and thus rid myself of the eye forever. Now this is the point. You fancy me mad. Madmen know nothing! You should have seen how wisely I proceeded, with what caution, with what foresight I went to work. I was never kinder to the old man than during the whole week before I killed him. Every night about midnight, I turned the latch of his door and opened it. Oh, so gently. And then when I had made an opening sufficient for my head, I put in a dark lantern all closed; closed so that no light shined out. And then I thrust in my head. Oh, you would have laughed to see how cunningly I placed it in. I moved slowly, very, very slowly, so that I might not disturb the old man's sleep. It took me an hour to place my whole head in the opening so far that I could see him lying upon the bed. Ha, would a madman have been so wise as this? And then when my head was well in the room, I undid the lantern cautiously, oh so cautiously. I undid it just so much that a single thin ray fell upon the vulture eye. And this I did for seven long nights. Every night, just at midnight, but I found the eye always closed. I felt it would be impossible to do the work, for it was not the old man who vexed me, but his evil eye. And every morning, when the day broke, I went boldly into the chamber (FADING) and spoke courageously to him. "Good morning, sir. Did you have a sound night's sleep?"

OLD MAN:      Sound? Yes, my boy, sound as a dollar.

MAN:      That's wonderful, sir, wonderful. It shows you are healthy and free of care.

OLD MAN:      Thank you, my boy, that's very kind of you, very kind.

---

**Music:**      **Eerie theme**

---

MAN:      Upon the eighth night, I was more than usually cautious in opening the door. The watch's minute hand moved more quickly than did mine. I had my head in, and was about to open the lantern, when my thumb slipped from the fastener, and the old man sprang up in the bed.

OLD MAN:      Who's there? (OFF)

MAN:      I was quite still and said nothing. For a whole hour I did not move a muscle. And in the meantime, I did not hear him lie down. He was still sitting up in the bed, listening. I wondered what the old man felt, hearkening in the darkness to the deathwatch in the night.

OLD MAN:      It is nothing but the wind in the chimney. It is only a mouse crossing the floor. But what is that other sound? Some single cricket has awakened me, and I found myself trembling. I am an old fool to be frightened by shadows. It must be about midnight. All the world is asleep. Why do these terrors shake me? Night! Forever night. Will it never be morning? All dark! Black as death. Death! What is that shadow over there? Is that the door? No, it couldn't be! I am a fool. There is no shadow, only darkness, only night, only death. (Oh. Oh.)

---

**Music:**      **Up, hold, under**

---

MAN:      When I had waited for a long time, very patiently, without hearing him lie down, I resolved to open a little, a very little, crevice in the lantern. So I opened it, you could not imagine how slowly—until at length a single thin ray, like a thread of a spider, shot out from the crevice and fell upon the vulture eye. It was open. Wide, wide open, and I grew furious as I gazed upon it. I saw it with perfect distinctness. It was blue with a hideous veil over it. It chilled the very marrow in my bones. But I could see nothing of the old man's face or person. For I had directed the light, as if by instinct, precisely on the damned spot. And now, have I not told you that what you mistake for madness is that over-acuteness of senses? Now I say there came to my ears a low, dull, quick sound such as a watch makes when enveloped in cotton. I knew that sound well, too. It was the beating of the old man's heart. It increased my fury as the beating of a drum stimulates a soldier into battle.

| | |
|---|---|
| **Sound:** | **Heartbeat** |

MAN:        Do you mark me well? I have told you that I am nervous. So I am. And now at that hour of the night, amid the dreadful silence of that old house, those strange noises excited me to uncontrolled terror. Yet, for some minutes longer, I kept still. But the beating grew louder. *Louder.* I felt the heart must burst.

| | |
|---|---|
| **Sound:** | **Heartbeat** |

MAN:        Now I was afraid the sound might be heard by a neighbor. The hour had come. I made my decision with lightning quickness. I flung open the door.

OLD MAN:   HELP! How's that? No, keep away from me! Keep your hands off me! Let me live another hour. No. No.

MAN:        No you don't, you old fool. You can't get away from me. Your neck. Give me your neck. There, I have you. Now…Now…More…More…Hold…Hold….

| | |
|---|---|
| **Sound:** | **Heartbeat and stop!** |

MAN:        I removed my hands and examined the old man. Yes, he was stone, stone dead. I placed my hand upon the heart, and held it there for many minutes. There was no pulsation. He was stone dead. His eyes would trouble me no more. If you still think me mad, you will think so no longer when I describe the wise precautions I took for the concealment of the body. The night wancd, and I worked hastily but in silence. I took up three planks from the floor of the chamber and deposited the body within. I then replaced the boards so cleverly, so cunningly, that no human eye, not even his, could have detected anything wrong. There was nothing to wash out. No stain of any kind. I had been too clever for that. When I had finished, it was four o' clock. Still dark as midnight. Suddenly, there came a knocking at the street door.

| | |
|---|---|
| **Sound:** | **Door knocking from distance** |

MAN:        I went down to open it with a light heart. For what had I now to fear?

| | |
|---|---|
| **Sound:** | **Walking, opening of door** |

| | |
|---|---|
| SERGEANT DRAYTON: | Good morning, sir. Excuse us for this interruption at such an hour. I am Sergeant Drayton. This is Officer Shennally.... |
| MAN: | Ah, yes, the police. What can I do for you? |
| DRAYTON: | The neighbors heard a shriek during the night and were afraid there might be some trouble here. |
| MAN: | Oh, do come in, gentlemen. |

| | |
|---|---|
| **Sound:** | **Footsteps** |

| | |
|---|---|
| MAN: | There now, about the screams. No wonder it was heard; it was quite embarrassing. You see the shriek was my own, during a nightmare. |
| DRAYTON: | Oh, I see. Well, these things were reported to the police, so we thought we'd better investigate. |
| MAN: | Yes, of course. I understand. |
| DRAYTON: | So, if you don't mind, we'd like to take a look around. May we? Here's a search warrant we were given. |
| MAN: | Oh, by all means. You needn't bother with a warrant. Actually, I am the only one at home this weekend. The old gentleman, ah, my employer, is away in the country. Come with me. |

Before long I thought I heard a low, dull, quick sound. Such a sound as a watch makes when enveloped in cotton. (HEART SOUND) I gasped for breath. Yet the officers heard it not. I talked more quickly, more vehemently, but the noise steadily increased. I rose and argued about trifles in a high key and with violent gestures. The noise steadily increased. Why would they not be gone? I paced the floor to and fro with heavy strides, as if excited to fury by the sight of the men. But the noise steadily increased. Oh, God! What could I do? I fumed! I raved! I swore! I swung the chair upon which I had been sitting! But the noise arose over all and continually increased. (HEART) It grew louder, louder, louder. And still the men chattered pleasantly and smiled. Was it possible they heard not? No, no, they knew. Almighty God, they suspected. They were making a mockery of my horror. This I thought, and this I think. But anything was better than this agony. Anything was more tolerable than this. I could bear those hypocritical smiles no longer. I felt I must scream or die! (HEART) And now again, HARK! (HEART) Villains, pretend no more. I admit the deed. Tear up the planks. There! Here! There, I can stand no more. It is the beating of this hideous heart! (HEART)

| Music: | Up, hold, under |
|---|---|

Announcer:    You have been listening to *Tales of Terror* by Edgar Allan Poe. Heard in today's cast were:

_____  _____

_____  _____

_____  _____

_____  _____

_____  _____

_____  _____

Sound and music by: _____

Engineer was: _____

This program was directed by: _____

This is _____ speaking.

| Music: | Up, hold, under |
|---|---|

## TAKE TWO

**1.** In 1948 it was said that radio would die with the advent of television. One NBC executive said at that time that they would consider selling all radio stations and concentrate on TV. We all know that radio does exist in the "world of TV." Why? How did radio change to compete with TV? How does radio differ from TV?

**2.** Decide what microphone mounting would be most appropriate for the situations listed below. Be prepared to discuss the reasons for your choices.

   **a.** a kitchen demonstration of carving a turkey

   **b.** a panel of politicians and environmentalists discussing conservation

   **c.** a podium address given by a corporation president to a large audience of employees

   **d.** an on-the-street opinion poll

   **e.** a large choir concert given in a small auditorium

   **f.** on-the-scene commentary and description of a slalom ski competition

**3.** If you were the producer of a radio or TV program, you might be responsible for deciding which microphone to use. Examine the following situations. Decide which type of microphone would be best for each situation, and defend your choice.

   **a.** a panel discussion consisting of four guests at a table

   **b.** an on-the-street remote interview program where the interviewer uses a hand mike

   **c.** a newscaster at a desk

   **d.** pickup of a musical group

   **e.** two actors creating a radio commercial

   **f.** four actors doing a live TV drama

**4.** Analyze the acoustical features of your gymnasium, auditorium, and library.

**5.** Why is it important for radio or TV performers to imagine that they are talking to someone even though there is nothing but a microphone to pick up their words? Why is it equally important for a performer to imagine that he or she is talking to only one person at a time?

## ADDITIONAL RESOURCES

Holsopple, Curtis R. *Skills for Radio Broadcasters, third edition,* (Blue Ridge Summit, Pa., TAB Books, 1988).

Zettl, Herbert. *Television Production Handbook, fifth edition,* (Belmont, Calif., Wadsworth Publishing, 1992).

*Cassettes:*
National Recording Co.
P.O. Box 395
Glenview, IL 60025

*Recordings:*
"Golden Memories of Radio"
"I Remember Radio"

Longines Symphonette Society
Longines Square
Larchmont, NY 10538

Mar Bren Sound Company
420 Pelham Road
Rochester, NY 14610

National Center for Audiotapes
Stadium Building
University of Colorado
Boulder, CO 80302

Radio Yesteryear
Box H
Croton-on-Hudson, NY 10520

# 5
# Verbalizing the Message

It is the challenge of future generations to maintain a firm sense of morality and human understanding as the world around us rushes into the twenty-first century. This is probably the most important function of stories. Stories provide us with the wisdom of past generations. They make us laugh, make us think, arouse our emotions, and educate us. No matter what kind of television program or video you are making—from a news or documentary segment to a comedy skit to a complex drama—you are basically telling a story. The technology of TV and video will continue to change quickly, but the basic rules of storytelling will always remain the same.

## TELLING THE STORY

Audiences, especially in the United States, are used to a clear and strict structure for their films, television movies, novels, and stories. Even the most avant-garde works follow most or all of the basic rules of structure. As a writer or producer, you need to know these rules thoroughly before you can successfully break any of them. If you decide to tell a story in an unconventional way, you have to make up for what structural rule(s) you ignore by doing an excellent job at using a new approach.

Stories have a beginning, middle, and end. A story is carried by emotional tension. The audience gets involved emotionally and wants to know what will happen in the end. This tension is very important because it keeps the audience interested. It also gives them a sense of time in the story—a sense of building toward a conclusion. We are conditioned to expect this structure in a story from hours of watching TV, seeing movies, and reading books. If we do not feel the story is building up to something, we get distracted or bored.

Generally this tension comes in the form of a question. The audience waits through the beginning and middle for the question to be answered, and it is answered in the end. For example, the question in *The Wizard of Oz* is: Will Dorothy make it back home from Oz safely? A story can raise many other questions, but the main one keeps the audience watching until the end. In the beginning of the story, the question is introduced. If the writer takes too long to introduce the question, the story seems to be going nowhere. The question is often referred to as the *objective*. A good way to test whether your story will interest the audience is to identify the question or objective. Would you be interested in watching a video for ten, fifteen, or twenty minutes to find out the answer to this question?

Writers often begin a story in the middle of something to get the audience's attention. This is called starting *in media res* (in the middle of things). Later, the writer has to give background information to explain what is happening, usually by using dialogue or flashbacks. The last episode of the television series "Star Trek: The Next Generation" is an example of this technique of storytelling.

It is easier to create a story when you break it down into scenes. Like the story itself, each scene has a goal or objective that the emotional tension is building towards. This is true of very small scenes (Bob must leave his house to go to work) and very large ones (Laura Dern must get to the circuit breaker of Jurassic Park and turn the power on without the dinosaurs eating her). If you stray too far from the objective of a scene, you risk losing the tension and boring the audience. This would happen in *Jurassic Park* if Laura Dern were to change her mind and go jogging along the beach for exercise. If you keep the goal of the scene in mind at all times, the audience should remain engaged.

The objective does not have to be the most important question raised in the audience's mind. The relationship between the characters can raise questions that interest the audience. People like stories about people, and they will be interested in relationships. The main objective can give structure to the story but also raise more intriguing questions and objectives as it develops. This is most obvious in romantic thrillers. The objective usually has something to do with a villain who wants to destroy the world. But the audience is more concerned about whether the male and female leads will fall in love. However, the main objective is the one that gives the story its structure and sets up when the story will end. Usually romantic thrillers are structured so that the villain is destroyed and the two main characters fall in love at the same time. Hence, both questions are answered at once. This is why there are so many B-grade thrillers where the leading lady is captured by the villain and must wait for the hero to save her. Relationships between characters commonly develop as subplots to the main story.

## Developing a Main Character

Once you have a main objective, you can deal with developing the character. Generally, though not always, the audience is meant to sympathize with this person. If they don't, they may not care what happens. In the film *Silence of the Lambs*, the audience identifies with the character played by Jodie Foster. She is the most likable character and seems to have the best intentions. Often the main character is presented as a bit of an underdog, to gain our sympathies. As a female FBI agent in *Silence*, Foster is seen being ridiculed and harassed by her chauvinistic male peers. The audience develops sympathy for her, wants to see her prove herself to them. This becomes a personal goal for the character and acts as an underlying subplot. If the film were seen through the eyes of Hannibal Lechter, the cannibalistic psychopath she comes into contact with, it would be a much different film because few people would like the main character. Viewers or readers generally want to identify with a main character. The main character is often an outsider to the situation, just like the audience. Audiences naturally identify with whomever is the outsider in a scene. Using an outsider as a main character is a great way to provide a lot of necessary background material because it can be explained to the main character.

> *Viewers generally want to identify with a main character.*

## Genre

Often in television and video production, students like to work within the frame of a particular genre. It has been said that there are only fifteen or so basic types of stories. These are called *genres*. The movie industry is very concerned about genres because genres have expected target audiences (i.e., teens are expected to go to action films, children like cartoons, the twenty-something and thirty-something generations favor romantic comedies). It is unfortunate, but in Hollywood it is very hard to get a film produced if it doesn't fit easily into a particular genre. Producers think that if people have no preconceived notions they won't go see a film.

Still, the framework of a genre can be very helpful to writers because it gives them parameters—a field to play in. There have been some very interesting experiments with genres. The film *Something Wild* begins as a romantic comedy and turns quite unexpectedly into a suspenseful thriller halfway through. Students enjoy working with genres because it takes part of the pressure off in creating a story. If you have seen a lot of "NYPD Blue" episodes on television, you may be interested in making a cop thriller or a parody of a cop thriller. The one thing to remember is that a genre story is only interesting if you add something different—your own twist. There are already too many formula books and films out there to interest an audience. Try to challenge yourself as a writer. Here is a list of some of the basic film and television movie genres.

> *Many television programs and movies fall into familiar types or genres.*

### The Police Drama

This can be a lot of fun for students because most enjoy filming action scenes. However, it is important to note that when using toy guns in a public place—even the ones with bright red tips—you run the risk of alarming someone and having the police called in. This is no small offense, so be very careful and make sure you have approval of your instructor.

### The Gangster Film

Similar to the police drama, except we focus on the villains. Traditionally in Hollywood gangster films, the main character, usually a man, turns to crime because he has to—because he is poor or disadvantaged—whereas rich people turn to crime because it's easy. That is how the main character is made sympathetic by comparison, despite the fact that he's a criminal. He still, traditionally, gets punished in the end. Hollywood's fascination with gangster films is part of a nationwide fetish with guns that dates back to the Old West. Gangster films exist, essentially, to romanticize the gun. Next time you see a gangster film, think about how many times a shooting or killing is made to look glamourous.

## The Comedy

Comedy can be anything from a "Saturday Night Live" type skit to a parody of some type of genre. Though you shouldn't be discouraged to make any type of video, comedies are often easier for students to pull off. The average audience member—your classmates, friends, relatives—generally has less trouble dealing with the amateurish level of student videos when they intend to be funny. In comedy, for some reason, mistakes seem less important. The basic structure for comedy skits is: Create a situation, create three complications, then get out of it. The reason most bad skits fail is that the writer was unable to think of a satisfying conclusion, which is always the hardest part.

## The Horror Film

This can be difficult to pull off, but also a lot of fun. When making a horror film, pay close attention to the way you shoot a sequence—camera angles, lighting—to heighten the suspense. Some "classic" horror films famous for their techniques are *Alien, The Birds, Jaws, Night of the Living Dead, Evil Dead II: Dead by Dawn*, and *The Texas Chainsaw Massacre*. Remember that horror moviemaking is not simply blood and guts on the screen. It is the most craft-oriented genre in film, and the most dependent on film tradition. The blockbuster film *Jurassic Park* crams practically every horror movie convention into one scene—the first tyrannosaurus rex attack:

1. Darkness
2. Apocalyptic weather (thunder and lightning)
3. Children in jeopardy
4. Animals in jeopardy
5. Less important characters to kill off
6. Music leading—and misleading—the audience (builds to a point and then nothing happens...and THEN it happens)
7. We hear the villain before we see him (remember the impact tremors shaking the glass of water?)
8. We don't see the villain until the big scene (same method as in *E.T.*, different purpose)
9. Frightened people doing stupid things
10. Frightened people performing heroic, self-sacrificing acts

11.  The entire universe is working against the characters (the electric fence doesn't work, their vehicles don't work, and there's a storm)
12.  Humor to break up the suspense (this actually works to sustain it longer)
13.  And, most importantly, waiting! That is all suspense really is: waiting.

## The Sci-Fi Film

Similar to the horror film, the sci-fi film is even more difficult for a student to pull off. Still, it's possible to create a science fiction film as long as you develop a script that doesn't require many complicated special effects.

## The Biographical Film

A video about the life of a student can be very interesting and funny as well. Most of the films about high school that come out of Hollywood are written by people over the age of 30. You have the benefit of a student's perspective on student life. This could definitely be worth exploring, and it hasn't really been done much. Also, if you intend to be a serious writer, it is a valuable exercise to develop your perception of the world around you. Most stories are in one way or another autobiographical.

## A Visual Medium

The final bit of advice for you to remember is that you are working in a visual medium. At least 70 percent of the message should be in the visuals. A familiar phrase of screenwriters is "Show it, don't say it." Amateur writers frequently attempt to convey way too much in the dialogue of a scene. Think about how you could show the following things without any dialogue: that someone is a cop, that a couple is fighting, that someone is very lonely; that a man has just seen a murder, that someone is being followed, that two people are attracted to each other.

These are basic guidelines that should help and inspire you in making a short video. Video making can be a lot of fun, although unfortunately most high schools do not recognize the full potential of the resources they have in their broadcasting department. The only difference in making a bigger, more complex video is planning, which is the most important element in making a video. The more you plan, the fewer problems you will have, and you *will* have problems. It's part of the game. But if you plan carefully, problems won't hurt your product. The fact is, it takes people to make a video—people behind the camera and people in front of it. You will learn that as more people become involved in something, it becomes harder to control. That's basically all a director does on the set; he or she tells everyone else what to do. The more you tell each individual about what he or she is doing ahead of time, the less chance for mistakes. This is the purpose of storyboards, shot lists, and scripts.

You are working in a visual medium, so you must picture the action ahead of time and know how you are going to shoot it. Make a list of shots, and keep it on the set so that you don't forget to shoot any. On the set, with all the confusion, it is easy to forget things, but one missing shot can ruin a video. Storyboards are used to communicate exactly how the director wants each shot to look. Brief sketches can help to clarify a lot when you are on the set. In a chase scene you could have ten shots described as "John runs." Storyboards help you recall the angles you wanted. Video is cheap, and the more footage you take the easier it will be to edit the original into something watchable.

Making videos well has a lot to do with being able to work with people. You learn how to inspire a group of people to work toward the same goal. This skill is helpful no matter what you do in life.

## USING THE SCRIPT

Is a script necessary? Obviously a sportscaster can not prepare in advance a total script for the play-by-play account of a basketball game. On the other hand, a stand-up comedian can use memorized material, or a cue sheet, for opening jokes. Talk show host David Letterman, for instance, needs a large staff of writers who keep his material topical and appropriate to the locale and situation where he is performing. Does a host need a script to interview the guests on a talk show? Is the extempore (or unmemorized) style or ad-libbing more suitable for a comedian, and a scripted, memorized style more suitable for an actor or serious performer? Can you communicate better with or without a script? Why have a script at all?

## Why Scripts are Needed

Actors must follow the script of the drama they are portraying. If they come to television from live theater, they are accustomed to giving exact word cues to other performers and, therefore, to following a script verbatim. In the interests of national security, federal officials often use prepared scripts to ensure the accuracy and correct documentation of everything they say during a press conference. There are, however, three additional reasons for having script, and these are important not only for the professional performer but also for the student working in a laboratory situation in a television studio. In television production, scripts are used to:

1. provide a smooth, attention-getting beginning and an effective wrap-up or conclusion,
2. facilitate accurate, precise timing; and
3. provide the technical staff with the information they need to supply the right pictures and sound at the right time.

## Introduction and Conclusion

A script provides a performer with a polished introduction and conclusion. Without a script, inexperienced performers tend to sound awkward. The most awkward introduction an inexperienced, scriptless performer can use is simply, "Uh-h-h!" Another uninteresting ad-lib beginning is the dull "Well-uh, I'd like to start with...." Scriptless conclusions can be equally ineffective, such as "Well, I guess that's about all."

## Timing

For experienced professional performers, timing is less of a problem than it is for you. They know how much they can say in thirty seconds. They sense how fast they must talk to maintain a rate of 150 words a minute. They know about how long it takes to relate a certain anecdote and can add or subtract a minute by regulating the amount of detail they give. Yet you, who are learning to judge timing, may find yourself concluding lamely, "As I said before...," or "And so, let me say again...." "Egg on the face" describes your pained facial expression as you stare helplessly into a camera still focused on you when you have one minute left and nothing more to say.

**FIGURE 5.1**
Rehearsing with a script before production begins, these students discuss timing.

Equally disconcerting is the plight of the inexperienced demonstrator who sees the final wrap-up time cue just as he or she comes to the most important step in assembling a model helicopter. You've probably heard talk-show host thanking guests in a rush, with an apologetic "We're a little late tonight, folks." The hurried remarks are followed by a full 30-second commercial, time you may feel could have been better shared with the host. However, for every word of a commercial that is paid for but not used, the network must give a cash refund to the sponsor on a prorated basis. Money talks; so the show's host must not!

Because of the importance of precise timing in television, your script will need to provide *if-cuts* and *cushions*. An "if-cut" is a part of the script that you can omit when time is running out. For example, suppose your script for a public access TV program includes five successful community programs for pollution control. The entire fourth example has been bracketed in the margin of the script and marked "if-cut." If the floor manager signals you to speed up, you can omit example four and proceed to example five, the most impressive of all. A "cushion" is material that can be used to stretch a program that is too short. It may be words, or music, or a sound effect. It may consist of alternative conclusions, varying in length, the appropriate one to be selected according to the time cues. Obviously, if-cuts and cushions are extremely difficult to handle without a script.

## A Guide for the Crew

> *With a script, time is your friend. The if-cuts and cushions in a good script help you adjust to time variations.*

To an even greater extent, the script is a lifesaver for the technical staff. If you have ever taken a long auto trip through new territory, you know how much help a road map can provide. If you have ever tried to assemble a child's toy without printed directions, you know the frustration of wondering which end you fold in first or how far the rod extends. The director and camera operators need the same kind of help in moving the mikes and the camera. After you have directed an ad-lib show, you will appreciate even more the road map and directions a script provides.

Some experienced, skillful directors *can* "wing it" or "fly by the seat of their pants," as they say. They have learned to make split-second decisions, to judge precisely what a camera operator can do, to estimate accurately the amount of picture that any size lens can shoot, and to keep three shots ahead of the action. Until you reach their level of expertise, however, it is more sensible and more relaxing to work from a script.

## Completely Scripted Shows

Some types of television programs that always require a complete script are the following:

### Drama/Comedy

These shows demand close-ups of actors' faces, stage business and movement essential to the plot, and reaction shots of one performer while the mike picks up the lines of another performer.

### Political talks

In these shows, critical, or controversial issues must be discussed in exact terminology and with carefully chosen phrases.

### Commercials

Claims for the product must use the limited time as effectively as possible. Commercials must use the best video images to "sell" the product. Every shot must match perfectly with the accompanying audio. Line-by-line attention is given to details.

**FIGURE 5.2**

A camera operator who has seen the script knows what shot to take—and when to take it.

### Sports reviews

Accuracy of scores, players' names, and important features of many sports events must be crowded into the brief time allotted to these programs.

### News

Events must be reported in sequence to correlate with pictures, and in language that lends authenticity to the presentation. In addition to making sure accuracy is maintained, the director must insert videotape cuts and electronic visuals at precisely the right moment to coordinate with the words the anchor is saying.

### Music videos

Producers of music videos must make sure every idea in every line of the song is carefully represented in the video portion as well.

## Partially Scripted Shows

In partially scripted shows, such as the following, the introduction and conclusion have been prepared and certain transitions have been written into a script. However, large portions are left to be ad-libbed or improvised.

> *A well-planned script gives you the power to control your crew.*

## Interviews

The introduction, conclusion, and a list of provocative questions can be prepared in advance. When you are interviewing somebody, however, many of your most interesting questions will probably be ad-libbed in response to the answers. If you are being interviewed, your answers should sound spontaneous, but you may think about them ahead of time without selecting the exact words. You can plan to tell about shooting the rapids on the Colorado River—how you made up your mind to go, what you took with you, the most exciting moment, and what you saw—without composing the sentences you will use. For example, late-night talk show host David Letterman must read the exact introduction to a commercial from a teleprompter so that the start of the film or tape is precisely timed. He often reads his guests' introductions as well, but most of the program is not fully scripted, allowing for his ability to ad-lib.

## Demonstrations

In this type of program, a scripted introduction, conclusion, and rundown of the sequence of events will help both the performer and the technical staff. For instance, if you are going to demonstrate how to make a kite, the script might include (*a*) the introduction—about the fun of flying a kite along the lakefront on a windy day; (*b*) a list of parts needed to make the kite—paper, balsa wood, scissors, glue, string, pattern; (*c*) the order in which you will assemble the parts—lay paper on the table, lay pattern on the paper, and cut paper on outside pattern lines; (*d*) the conclusion—during which you plan to show the completed kite with a still photo of a similar kite in flight.

## Play-by-play sportscasts

Sportscasters always have with them certain details about each athlete. If an eligible end receives a forward pass for a gain that may make a first down, the sportscaster pulls out background material on both the quarterback and the end, which can be used while the officials are bringing the chain in from the sidelines to measure the yardage. Fill-ins for every time-out, narration for half-time activities, questions for interviews, lead-ins for every commercial and every station break can all be scripted in advance.

If you think a sportscaster needs no script, pay a visit to the booth where the play-by-play is done, and you'll see how he or she manages simultaneously to watch the field, watch three or four monitors, read notes from the spotters, shuffle cards telling about the players' background, and follow instructions from the director!

## Game shows

The M.C. (literally, master of ceremonies) or the announcer always has a script, with an introduction, a conclusion, a lead-in for each commercial, a specific introduction for each player who has been selected in advance, and questions to ask players chosen on the spot. The nature of the game determines whether or not there are cards with questions and answers, scoring regulations, comments to be made to winners, comments to be made to losers, activities or stunts to be performed, or equipment to be manipulated. Much of the content of a game show must be ad-libbed, but there is usually a sequence that you will become aware of if you watch the show regularly.

Which parts of your show should be scripted in advance depend on the difficulty of the camera work and the skill of the camera operators, the ad-libbing experience of the performers, and the nature of the message to be conveyed.

## How to Prepare the Script

Whether the script is a verbatim account of what is to be said or an outline of the sequence of events with some dialogue, follow certain practices in preparing it.

1. The script should be double-spaced on standard size paper. Use one side only.
2. If the script will be visible to viewers, use pale-colored paper (blue or green), not white.
3. Number pages in the upper righthand corner. It is a good idea to number the lines too. It save valuable rehearsal time if everyone can quickly locate a spot by referring to "line 12 on page 4."
4. Sentences should be completed on the same page on which they begin. Carryovers require turning or sliding pages in the middle of a sentence.

5. Type dialogue in upper- and lower-case letters.

6. Type all audio cues (other than speech) and music cues in capital letters. For additional ease of identification, you may underline them.

7. Directions to performers (e.g., WALK TO THE DOOR) are usually in capital letters and enclosed in parentheses.

8. Video instructions usually indicate shots by capital letters (e.g., LS, CU, TCU) contrasting with lower-case letters for directions (e.g., dolly in).

9. Pages should be clipped together in such a way that you can separate them easily during rehearsal if you so desire. Avoid stapling the script.

10. During rehearsals, copies of the script should be available to the talent (the performers), the director, production assistants, audio technician, technical director, switcher, floor manager, and engineer, even though not all these staff members will need or want copies during the performance.

11. Have two or three extra copies for the files.

12. Computer word processing programs, such as PowerScript from Comprehensive Video Corporation in Northvale, New Jersey, help TV producers write scripts easily. Most word processing programs are not suited to the special needs of the TV script. However, programs such as this one help the scriptwriter create TV scripts as well as screenplays.

Figure 5.3 is a page from a typical script for a television interview program. The original versions do not have to be written in this format. The handwritten instructions were added by the director during rehearsal, in preparation for the final production.

## Variations in Script Form

The form of the script varies according to the kind of studio in which you are working. In a television laboratory course, where the director is another student, you may need to insert in your script notes about the kind of shot you want at a certain point. Then the director can decide which camera will get that shot. For production class projects, you may want to use a script similar to the one in Figure 5.4 for a student demonstration of microphones.

**FIGURE 5.3**

**A Partial Script from a TV Program**

Ready to fade up #1
Ready to open anncr mike
Ready to cue anncr
Stand by -- 5 sec

fade up #1
open mike
Cue anncr
Ready to cue music

Cue music

Ready to fade under
Ready to cue anncr

fade under

Ready to cut to #2
Cue anncr

CU of ANNCR - #2

Ready to cut to #1
Ready to flip card

flip card
Cut to #1

CU flip #1 - CONGRESS

etc #1

Camera #2 DOLLY OUT
To MS of Joe WMS

Ready to cut to #2
Cut to #2

MS - Joe WMS

Camera #1

| # | | |
|---|---|---|
| 1. | ANNCR: | TITLE CARD "BIG TEN ROUNDTABLE" |
| 2. | | |
| 3. | MUSIC: | THEME (COLLEGE SONGS, |
| 4. | | DECCA 1567, SIDE 1, CUT 3, |
| 5. | | UP AND FADE UNDER AND OUT) |
| 6. | ANNCR: | This afternoon Big Ten |
| 7. | | Roundtable brings you |
| 8. | | four debaters from Ohio |
| 9. | | State University and |
| 10. | | Northwestern University. |
| 11. | | They will discuss a proposal |
| 12. | | currently being considered |
| 13. | | by the U.S. Senate. The |
| 14. | | proposal, a plan for a guaranteed |
| 15. | | annual wage, is being discussed |
| 16. | | by not only Congressmen, |
| 17. | | welfare workers, and taxpayers, |
| 18. | | but college students as well. |
| 19. | | We wonder why students are so |
| 20. | | concerned over an issue that |
| 21. | | only indirectly concerns them. |
| 22. | | Joe Williams, as a member of the |
| 23. | | Ohio State debate squad, would you |
| 24. | | mind telling us why you are so |
| 25. | | concerned over this particular issue |
| 26. | | at this time in your life? |

**FIGURE 5.4**

**Audio/Visual Script**

| Video | Audio |
|---|---|
| MS of Nina wearing lavaliere mike | NINA: Description of the lavaliere mike and when it is used. |
| CU of lavaliere showing on/off switch | NINA: "…some lavalieres have on/off switches, which the talent can turn on and off at will if he or she wishes to engage in some vigorous physical activity." |
| Back to MS shot of Nina | |

Note that the script is divided into two columns. The left, or video, column describes what the audience will see; the right, or audio, column describes what the audience will hear. The video column describes the camera shot in the usual abbreviated form: MS—a medium or waist-up shot of the talent; CU—a close-up shot of the lavaliere mike switch; and HS—a head-and-shoulders shot of the performer. In this same column, the director writes the number of the camera he or she wants to use for each of these three shots.

In the audio column, note the general summary of what the talent will say. The underlined words and arrow leading from the audio column to the video indicate that, as the speaker says, "have on/off switches," the director will switch to a close-up shot of the lavaliere mike switch. The arrow at the end of the quotation indicates that after the word "activity" the director will go to a head-and-shoulders shot of the speaker, Nina.

## A Newsbreak Script

One of the first TV programs you might wish to produce with a full crew is a newsbreak. Often during the evening the local station or network presents a one-minute news capsule. These are carefully planned and written. Figure 5.5 is an example of a newsbreak script that might be written by personnel in your school's television studio. Notice that the video information is on the left side of the script and the audio on the right side. Let's examine the format of the program, using the script as a guide.

The program starts in black, with nothing on the screen. A logo showing Channel 3 Newsbreak comes on the screen as we hear music. A booth announcer (whom we hear but do not see) gives the opening tag as the picture dissolves to another picture. This time it is a graphic—the logo for the school district, accompanied by music, which then fades out. The announcer introduces the anchor, and the picture dissolves to a medium shot of the anchor as he begins. We briefly see his name keyed under him. We see a picture (PIX) of the football team as the anchor reads the first story. Then we go back to the MS (medium shot) of the anchor as he introduces the second story. We then see a picture (PIX) of the speech team as the anchor reads the story about them. As the anchor wraps up, we see a medium shot of him. As he finishes, we see a picture of the Channel 3 logo as the announcer gives the closing tag. The camera dissolves to district logo as the music comes up and is held briefly. Both the audio and the video fade to black for the end.

Notice how the script on page 152 is written to give the director and anchor the exact words for the timing necessary. The director relays the instructions to the crew so that the program runs smoothly. The abbreviations used are MS (medium shot) and pix (picture). For convenience in storyboard preparation, abbreviations are very useful.

## The Storyboard

A script can also be outlined by using the storyboard technique, by drawing pictures of what should be on the screen as we hear the audio. Figure 5.6 is a storyboard of a promo—a corporate promotional video—designed for an animation and production studio. Most TV commercials are storyboarded in this fashion. Every new camera shot and angle is drawn to show what the effect will look like when the commercial is shot. This works only with shorter programs; it is not likely that the director of "The Tonight Show" would storyboard every shot during the one-hour telecast!

Figure 5.7 is a reproduction of another storyboard, a sequence of visuals ("thumbnails") for production of a PSA—public service announcement. The audio portion was prepared separately. Included is the audio script for each of the five panels of the storyboard. Note that VO stands for voiceover.

## FIGURE 5.5

### Newscast Script

*created by students from Thornton Township High School, Harvey, Illinois.*

| VIDEO | AUDIO |
|---|---|
| BLACK | |
| FADE IN NEWSBREAK LOGO | MUSIC: UP, HOLD, UNDER |
| | BOOTH: It's time for "Newsbreak," a brief look at the top stories from our |
| DISSOLVE TO DISTRICT 205 LOGO | Channel 3 Newsroom. Here is our Channel 3 anchor, Ken Small. |
| | MUSIC: UP, HOLD, OUT |
| DISSOLVE MS ANCHOR | ANCHOR: Good morning, here are our top stories from the District 205 |
| | schools. Our three football teams are continuing their winning ways |
| KEY: KEN SMALL | this year. All three teams have a combined record of six wins with only |
| | three losses. Thornton High School's record went to three and 0 with |
| LOSE KEY | an impressive win against Blue Island last Saturday. Thornridge |
| | defeated Argo, while Thornwood advanced its record to two and one |
| PIX: FOOTBALL | by defeating Bloom High School. All three teams will be in action this |
| | weekend. Thornton and Thornwood are at home, while Thornridge |
| | travels to Lincolnway. |
| MS ANCHOR | There are other activities going on in District 205 besides football. |
| | Our speech teams are competing against area teams as they prepare |
| PIX: SPEECH TEAM | for the District Finals coming up. Thornton's Speech Team— |
| | consisting of John Hendricks, Nancy Jenkins, Joe Handley, and |
| | Becky Jones—will be in competition this weekend as they travel |
| | to Homewood Flossmoor High School. |
| MS ANCHOR | That's the news for now. Join us on Channel 3 Tuesday for a |
| | complete look at our school's news. |
| CHANNEL 3 LOGO | BOOTH: This is Channel 3 "Newsbreak." You are always on top of the news |
| | when you watch Channel 3. |
| DISTRICT 205 LOGO | MUSIC: UP, HOLD |
| FADE | FADE AUDIO |

## FIGURE 5.6
## Storyboard for a Commercial

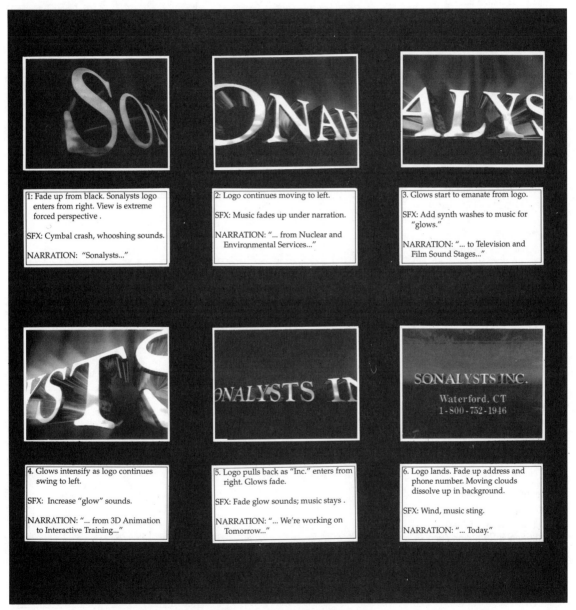

1: Fade up from black. Sonalysts logo enters from right. View is extreme forced perspective .

SFX: Cymbal crash, whooshing sounds.

NARRATION: "Sonalysts..."

2: Logo continues moving to left.

SFX: Music fades up under narration.

NARRATION: "... from Nuclear and Environmental Services..."

3. Glows start to emanate from logo.

SFX: Add synth washes to music for "glows."

NARRATION: "... to Television and Film Sound Stages..."

4. Glows intensify as logo continues swing to left.

SFX: Increase "glow" sounds.

NARRATION: "... from 3D Animation to Interactive Training..."

5. Logo pulls back as "Inc." enters from right. Glows fade.

SFX: Fade glow sounds; music stays .

NARRATION: "... We're working on Tomorrow..."

6. Logo lands. Fade up address and phone number. Moving clouds dissolve up in background.

SFX: Wind, music sting.

NARRATION: "... Today."

Courtesy of Sonalysts Studios, Waterford, Connecticut; Jay Nilsen, Senior Animator, ©1994 Sonalysts Studios, Inc.

## FIGURE 5.7  Storyboard for a PSA

1. VO: The computerized card catalog is a data base or listing of all or most of the Library Media Center's (LMC) holdings. Books, audiovisual materials, periodicals, and vertical file folders are listed here.

2. VO: To find out if the LMC has materials on a topic, or has a particular title or author, simply type in a topic like dinosaurs, or the author's name, or the title of the material. This information is typed on the main screen.

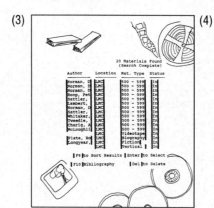

3. (Video text scrolls up over field of library materials) VO: The call number, title, author, location and information on the availability of the item in the LMC is given for each entry.

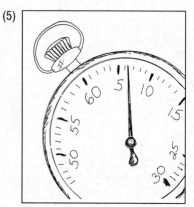

4. (Reporter appears on camera): Each entry also has a detailed screen giving additional information such as the publisher and a summary of the material.

Courtesy of John Holmes, Video Instructor, Communications Media/Broadcasting Department, John Marshall High School, Milwaukee, Wisconsin.

5. VO: The computerized card catalog presents the student with the LMC's holdings in a matter of seconds which takes the drudgery out of research.

## Timing

Television program scripts indicate timing. "*Front timing*" gives the hours, minutes, and seconds from the beginning of the show to the point indicated at the end of either a segment or a page. (1:15:00 in timing segments or length of program means 1 hour, 15 minutes, 0 seconds; in clock or schedule timing it means "at exactly 15 seconds after one o'clock.") At any time during the show, therefore, one can tell at a glance if it is running too fast or getting behind. Timing may be recorded at the left or at the right, according the director's preference.

For instance, if you are televising a commencement program that begins at 8:00 P.M. and is due to conclude within two hours, your front timing run-down sheet might look like Figure 5.8.

---

**FIGURE 5.8**

**Front Timing Run-down Sheet**

| Video | Audio | Timing | TRT* |
|---|---|---|---|
| LS of seniors entering Field House; CU of a few seniors; pan across row of parents in balcony; CU of more seniors, LS of Dr. Jones, CU of Dr. Jones, etc. | Orchestra: *Pomp and Circumstances* | 8:00 | 35.00 |
| | Dr. Jones: Invocation | 8:20 | |
| | *Star Spangled Banner* | 8:23 | |
| | Introduction of Platform Guests | 8:26 | |
| | Special Number by A Cappella Choir | 8:30 | |
| | Introduction of Senior Officers | 8:35 | |

| This column would include a variety of camera shots, such as the above. | This column shows at what time each event should begin if all is running on schedule. |
|---|---|

*TRT is total running time.

The processional should be over and the seniors in their places by 8:20. The invocation and *The Star Spangled Banner* should have concluded by 8:26. If the processional is still going on at 8:25, you know some kind of time adjustment will have to be made later in the program if you are to get off the air in time for the 10:00 news. (If you live on the East or West Coast, you will have an hour's cushion before the 11:00 news.)

Front timing may also be applied to the total amount of time allotted to the program rather than just to the 8:00–10:00 P.M. slot. If, for example, that same commencement program is being taped for use later, or if you have all the time you want, the timing column might read like Figure 5.9.

If you have been holding a stopwatch on these proceedings, you will know that when the choir begins to sing, the program has already been going on for thirty minutes.

"*Back timing*" means timing the program from the end to the beginning. The back-timing column indicates the amount of time remaining until the end of the show. Suppose, for instance, you have one and a half hours allotted for this same commencement program. The back-timing column would look something like Figure 5.10.

**FIGURE 5.9**
**Run-Down Sheet**

| Video | Audio | Timing | TRT |
|---|---|---|---|
| | Orchestra Processional | 00:00 | 35 |
| | Dr. Jones: Invocation | 00:20 | |
| | *Star Spangled Banner* | 00:23 | |
| | Introduction of Platform Guests | 00:26 | |
| | Special Number by A Cappella Choir | 00:30 | |
| | Introduction of Senior Officers | 00:35 | |

(This column shows how much time has been used up to the point indicated.)

**FIGURE 5.10**

**Back-Timing Sheet**

| Video | Audio | Timing | |
|---|---|---|---|
| | Orchestra Processional | 1:30 | |
| | Dr. Jones: Invocation | 1:15 | |
| | *Star Spangled Banner* | 1:13 | This column shows how much time you have left in your 1½ hours. |
| | Introduction of Platform Guests | 1:10 | |
| | Special Number by A Cappella Choir | 1:05 | |
| | Introduction of Senior Officers | 1:00 | |
| | Welcome by Senior President | 0:55 | |
| | Address by Prof. Einstein | 0:50 | |

**FIGURE 5.11**

**Segment Time Sheet**

| Video | Audio | Segment time | Running time |
|---|---|---|---|
| | Band | 2:00 | 2:00 |
| | Introduction of Coach and Players | 5:00 | 7:00 |
| | Interview with Coach | 3:00 | 10:00 |
| | Cheers | 3:00 | 13:00 |
| | Announcements re Game Tickets | 1:30 | 14:30 |
| | Credits, Sign-off Station I.D. | 0:30 | 15:00 |

If Professor Einstein begins his address with only fifty minutes of time remaining, you know that you will probably have to fade out during the recessional or even before the professor has completed his remarks.

In a partially scripted show, with only the introduction and conclusion written out, the segments can be timed and recorded on the script. Figure 5.11 gives the rundown of a pep rally to be televised that includes known time segments. The unknown must be estimated.

The segment time is the amount of time each section is expected to take; the running time is cumulative. By the end of the cheering, for example, you should have used up thirteen minutes. Most fifteen-minute programs are timed at 14:30 to allow time for station breaks.

Students in school are often conditioned to follow classroom clocks, even if the sweep second hand jerks sporadically. So it may be more helpful to prepare a timing schedule like Figure 5.12 for a show beginning at 9:25 A.M.

**FIGURE 5.12**

**Time Schedule**

| Video | Audio | Segment time | Clock |
|-------|-------|--------------|-------|
| | Band | 2:00 | 9:25–9:27 |
| | Introduction of Coach and Players | 5:00 | 9:27–9:32 |
| | Interview with Coach | 3:00 | 9:32–9:35 |
| | Cheers | 3:00 | 9:35–9:38 |

Sometimes, in class laboratory productions, there is a tendency to be lax about timing, but this is a bad habit to form. In any station that is actually broadcasting, the timing of the programs, station breaks, commercials, and sign-offs is strictly adhered to. So begin by becoming time-conscious. You can soon learn to judge how long a paragraph will take, or a sentence, or a scene. In television, there is no such thing as an excused tardiness, an early dismissal, or an overtime period. Write with the clock in mind.

## CLEARANCE AND COPYRIGHT

If you are preparing your script for a classroom studio presentation within your school building, the problems of clearance (that is, permission to use copyrighted material) will be minimal. Even so, you must obtain permission to distribute, via closed circuit, a film that your school has rented or purchased to project in the auditorium.

Familiarity with some of the basic regulations for clearance of copyright material may help you avoid trouble.

Reproductions of copyrighted pictures, and published literary selections are also protected by copyright laws. You must obtain permission to use these materials for most radio or television broadcasts.

Most commercial stations have contracts with the major organizations that hold music copyrights; BMI (Broadcast Music Incorporated), ASCAP (American Society of Composers, Authors, and Publishers), and SESAC (Society of European Stage Authors and Composers). Public access TV programs present problems for schools using this channel. It would be great to present your production of your school's fall play, *Grease.* However, royalties have to be paid to the writer of this play for each public performance. You would be in clear violation of the copyright law if you were to show the film *Grease* on your school cable system without making arrangements with the agency handling the rights. It is useful to know that cable rights are being granted to schools for a nominal fee, and these can be negotiated.

Music played as theme songs for your programs on the public access channel is also copyrighted. However, negotiations are currently being conducted to exempt music used on an access channel only, from paying royalties. The music used in music videos produced by your staff, and shown on the access channel, is also protected by copyright. Check with your local cable company to see if playing music is acceptable.

The stations agree by contract to pay a lump sum for the presentation of copyrighted music. Your responsibility is to submit to the station, in advance, the titles, composers, arrangers, and publishers of all musical numbers to be included in your program. If you plan to quote poetry or sing a song as you crown the homecoming queen during the telecast of a football game, or if your school plans a special halftime program of copyrighted music, avoid any possible difficulties by giving the station advance notice. Do not place your school or the cooperating station in an embarrassing situation by failing to comply with copyright regulations.

Being completely honest about the use of restricted material is a good habit to get into if you plan to do any programs on a commercial station. Even though your script may seem to be limited by the need for clearing copyrighted material, even though you may feel

**FIGURE 5.13**

A sample release/clearance form (Maine Township High School South, broadcasting department)

<u>RELEASE/CLEARANCE FORM</u>

I, _____ , hereby
(Print name of party granting release here)

grant permission to _____ to use and/or

present my services, performance, appearance, statements, creative

work, music, lyrics et cetera, on the television program entitled:

_____for unrestricted use

and/or distribution by television (to include cable TV and in-

structional TV), home video playback devices, and audio visual

library services.  I agree that my name, likeness, and biography

(or biographical information) may be used for the purpose of promoting

the program covered by this agreement.  These rights are granted to

_____ and apply throughout the world.


_____

(signature of party granting release here)



_____

(Date)

that your basic freedom of speech is being restricted, you are really just asking permission to use something that belongs to another person. It is a wise policy to obtain permission for taping or broadcasting any original works. (See Figure 5.13).

## TELEVISION GUIDELINES

A few guidelines for checking script for content include the following:

1. Profanity, obscenity, smut, and vulgarity are forbidden, even when likely to be understood only by part of the audience. From time to time, words that have been acceptable acquire undesirable meanings, and telecasters should be alert to eliminate such words.
2. Words (especially slang) derisive of any race, color, creed, nationality or national derivation, except wherein such usage would be for the specific purpose of effective dramatization, such as combating prejudice, are forbidden.
3. The presentation of techniques of crime in such detail as to invite imitation shall be avoided.
4. The creation of a state of hypnosis by act or demonstration on the air is prohibited, and hypnosis as an aspect of "parlor game" antics to create humorous situations within comedy situations cannot be used.

Other content areas that can be covered by guidelines include attacks on religion and religious faiths; reference to physical or mental afflictions and deformities; law enforcement; legal, medical, and other professional advice, diagnosis, and treatment; use of animals; use of gambling devices; on-the-scene betting at sports events; quiz shows; horror shows; lottery contests; and such expletives as "flash" or "bulletin" (to avoid a repetition of the famous Orson Welles radio show "War of the Worlds," which listeners thought was an actual newscast reporting an invasion of Earth by Martians); treatment of news and special public events; controversial public issues; and political telecasts.

The station and its cooperating advertisers, through television, visit most of the homes in America, where people of all ages, backgrounds, beliefs, and standards of conduct live. The revenue from advertising enables the American system of broadcasting to provide the finest programs of information and entertainment—as well as programs of lower quality. If you occasionally become disillusioned with the quality of a program or the taste of its advertisements, you have a responsibility to express your views and make constructive suggestions. Here are a few of the organizations you might wish to contact:

American Broadcasting Company
1330 Ave. of the Americas
New York, NY 10019

Columbia Broadcasting System
51 West 52nd St.
New York, NY 10019

National Broadcasting Company
30 Rockefeller Plaza
New York, NY 10020

Public Broadcasting Service
485 L'Enfante Plaza West, SW
Washington, DC 20024

If you complain about a specific program, include the time and date it is shown, as well as the network, city, station call letters, and channel number, in addition to stating what you consider objectionable.

## Evaluating the Script

Finally, after writing your script, check your copy by asking yourself these questions.

1. Do I begin in an attention-getting way—to keep listeners from turning off a school program?
2. Overall, what message am I trying to get across to the viewers?
3. Is the program "visual?"
4. What pictures do I need to make the ideas clear?
5. Do my picture statements match the content from audio?
6. Have I selected content that will convey my message?
7. Have I chosen words that will communicate my meaning to the kind of people who will be watching local television at noon on a weekday? Will my vocabulary please or aggravate them?
8. Have I assumed that viewers understand activities and terminology used at my school? If I mention "poli-sci" can I assume they know what I mean?

9. Have I prepared the script to correct form?
10. Have I checked my graphics for four-by-three ratio, legibility, neatness, and professional appearance?
11. Have I provided a cushion?
12. Will this content be in line with your station's prescribed guidelines?
13. Is the program, as it appears in my script, worth spending time to produce and present?
14. If I used school property, school time, and school equipment, is the program content something school officials will be proud to have sponsored?

If it is true that "one picture is worth a thousand words," the television scriptwriter has an obligation to see that the words used add to and emphasize, rather than detract from, the impact of the visual message.

## IT'S A WRAP

Television in the twentieth century is a high-tech enterprise, but each television show or radio program still originates with the ancient art of storytelling. Technology continues to change, but the basics of storytelling remain the same: Create tension and anticipation, develop a sympathetic main character, put your own twist on the classic genres.

Once the story comes together, it's recorded in a script or on storyboards. Media professionals rely on scripts to ensure smooth introductions and conclusions, maintain precise timing, and guide the crew through the production. Many shows, such as newscasts, are completely scripted; others, like talk shows, allow room for some ad-libbing, especially during interviews or demonstrations. The content of scripts should fit with general television guidelines, and writers must obtain permission for any borrowed material, or they risk violating copyright laws.

Detailed planning is one of the keys to success in media. Starting with an excellent story and working from a script helps ensure a polished finished product: A radio or television production that holds the viewer's attention and verbalizes the writer's message.

# 5

# Video Lab

1. **Newsbreak Assignments.** The purpose of this assignment is to give everyone experience in operating the equipment while the director gets experience "calling the shots." It will also allow you to see whether a complete TV script helps the production team. The talent will gain experience "on air" as well. The assignment could be done by each person in class, or you might want to work in teams of two, with the talent and director writing the script together.

a. Write a short newsbreak script similar to the one in Figure 5.5. Choose your stories from the local newspaper. Pick two short stories that will total about one minute in length (thirty seconds each). Write the script word-for-word for this first attempt, showing the director exactly where the talent will be. This allows for precise cues for graphic changes.

b. Pick two stories with pictures (PIX) that can be cut from a newspaper or magazine. The pictures should be large enough so that they can be picked up on camera. Mount them on tagboard. You can place the PIX on separate cameras, or on one camera. If you use one camera, you must allot time to change graphics and have a second camera that goes back to the anchor between stories. Even the opening logo can be on the same camera as the picture for each story.

c. Write a script that will include music and any opening graphic you may wish to show, even perhaps a MS of the studio. Use the sample script in Figure 5.5 as a guide.

d. Write an opening announcement for the booth announcer, as indicated in Figure 5.5.

e. If your studio has facilities for keys, key the name of the anchor sometime during the newscast.

f. Choose opening and closing music for the newsbreak.

g. Write a complete script and create a simple floor plan indicating where the set will be and the anchor's position. Where will the graphics be located? What cameras will pick up the anchor and the graphics? Where will the key originate if your studio does not have a character generator?

h. One person will serve as anchor, and the other will direct the production. If done independently, the writer should serve as talent and give the script to another member of the class who will direct the production.

i. Allow for one rehearsal, then videotape the newsbreak for playback and evaluation later.

j. Evaluate this exercise. Did the production go as smoothly as the script? Why or why not?

2. **Commercial Assignments.** Write a thirty-second TV commercial to sell a product or service. You may use the storyboard technique as shown in Figures 5.6 and 5.7. Remember, TV commercials are different from radio commercials. The straight commercial you hear on the radio would be extremely dull on TV. Viewers expect to see the product and a demonstration of its use. Often more creativity goes into a one-minute commercial than into the program it is sponsoring. The commercial can take many forms:

*Situational or dramatic commercials.* A short drama is presented. This includes writing the dialogue, designing a simple set, choosing a cast, memorizing parts, and producing the one-minute "spot." The product is often the hero of the story—solving family crises, etc.

*Real people commercials.* "Real people" are interviewed to explain the advantages of a product.

*Demonstration commercials.* A sales rep or announcer demonstrates the virtues of a product. This is more like a straight commercial because it visualizes clearly the product's advantages.

To complete this assignment you may work in teams of one or two people.

a. Write a complete TV script for a thirty-second TV commercial.

b. Complete a simple floor plan with set, talent, camera locations, and the necessary graphics.

c. Produce the commercial with the class, and tape the production.

d. If this commercial is a public service announcement or promo for a school func-tion or service, offer it to your local cable company for airing.

3. Take a cutting of four to six minutes from a scene in a play and adapt it for television. You might use the standard video and audio script form. You may refer to published collections of cuttings or teleplays as models. Work in small groups. First write the script using the television format; then design and secure a simple set. Often just simple set furniture will work for this exercise. Find costumes and props, light the set, and produce this play, cutting for television.

4. Children's shows can be fun to write and produce. Take a children's story or folktale and adapt it for television.

5. Some situation comedy series begin "cold." They open with dialogue and an incident, omitting any announcements. Following this "open cold," the credits and announcements are presented and the show proceeds. An "open cold" is a good way to let the audience know what the story will be about. Watch a few situation comedies to see whether they use this kind of opening.

6. Take one of your favorite short stories and adapt it for a television production, using narration with pantomime, a play, a puppet show, or some other format you wish to try.

7. Viewers are always complaining about the number of commercials interrupting movies on network TV. Watch an entire movie (with a stopwatch), keeping track of the total amount of time devoted to commercials.

8. The teleplay format is often used to script a program. Fig 5.14 on page 167 gives guidelines for scripting a teleplay to create a corporate message or television program in such a format. Note that SFX stands for sound effects and MUS stands for music; the voiceover or narration should be written in all upper case.

**FIGURE 5.14**

THE CORPORATE TELEPLAY FORMAT

LOCATION DESCRIPTION
Thoroughly describe the visuals.  Where are you?  What do you see?
Whom do you see? (What do they look like?  What are they wearing?)
What action takes place?  Someone reading this should be able to
clearly picture the scene.

SFX:  Describe sound effects
or background sounds.

MUS:  Describe style and where
it should come UP, UNDER, or OUT.

Dialogue or Narration:
(on camera)

Lip sync dialogue and
narration should be written
in upper and lower case,
single spaced.

Double space between
sentences, and triple
space between thoughts.

VO NARRATION:

SHOULD BE WRITTEN IN

ALL UPPER CASE, DOUBLE

SPACED.

TRIPLE SPACE BETWEEN

SENTENCES, QUADRUPLE

SPACE BETWEEN THOUGHTS.

transition to:
(next scene or shot)

Video column--6 inches (L and R margins, each 1.25")
Dialogue column--2.75 inches (L margin, 2.75"/R margin, 3")
VO narration--2.5 inches (L margin, 4.75"/ R margin, 1.24")

These guidelines for creating a teleplay are provided courtesy of John Holmes, video production instructor at
John Marshall High School, Milwaukee, Wisconsin.

## TAKE TWO

**1**. Why would a television newscast require a complete script for the director and the talent?

**2**. Imagine you are the producer or host of a local talk show. Think of ten questions for the following guests:

    **a**. Mayor or manager of your town or city

    **b**. Your football or basketball coach

    **c**. The program director of the local radio station

    **d**. Principal of your school

    **e**. Student council president

**3**. Why isn't it a good idea for a beginning television performer to memorize his or her speech or use cue cards instead of a script?

**4**. What is the difference between back timing and front timing? Set up an imaginary fifteen-minute newscast, and determine the running time for each story or sequence.

**5**. What is the function of ASCAP and BMI?

**6**. Present an example of a short program where a storyboard script might be more effective than a conventional video/audio script. Prepare a simple storyboard for the program. Use Figures 5.6 and 5.7 as models if you wish.

**7**. Using the teleplay format on page 166, write a script for a short program or message of your choosing.

## ADDITIONAL RESOURCES

Armer, Alan A. *Writing the Screenplay: TV and Film, second edition,* (Belmont, Calif., Wadsworth Publishing, 1993).

Bayer, William. *Breaking Through, Selling Out, Dropping Dead,* (New York, Limelight Editions, 1989).

Berman, Robert A. *Fade In: The Screenwriting Process,* (New York, Wiese Productions, 1989).

Blacker, Irwin R. *The Elements of Screenwriting,* (New York, Macmillan, 1988).

Brande, Dorthea. *Becoming a Writer,* (Los Angeles, Jeremy P. Tarcher, 1981).

Dmytryk, Edward. *On Screen Writing,* (Boston, Focal Press, 1985).

Field, Syd. *Screenplay: The Foundations of Screenwriting,* (New York, Dell Books, 1984).

Goldberg, Lee. *Unsold TV Pilots,* (New York, Citadel Press, 1991).

Idelson, William. *Writing for Dough,* (Los Angeles: Empire Publishing Services, 1990).

Kosberg, Robert. *How to Sell Your Idea in Hollywood,* (New York, Harper Perennial, 1991).

McCarty, Clifford. *Published Screenplays: A Checklist,* (Kent, Ohio, Kent State University Press, Oberlin Printing Co.).

Phillips, William H. *Writing Short Scripts,* (Syracuse, N.Y., Syracuse University Press, 1990).

Polti, George. *The Thirty-Six Dramatic Situations,* (Boston, The Writer, Inc., 1990).

Sautter, Carl. *How to Sell Your Screenplay,* (New York, New Chapter Press, 1992).

Silver, David. *How to Pitch and Sell Your TV Script,* (Cincinnati, Writers Digest Books, 1991).

Smith, David L. *Video Communication,* (Belmont, Calif., Wadsworth Publishing, 1991).

Stempel, Tom. *Framework: A History of Screenwriting,* (New York, Continuum, 1991).

Vogler, Christopher. *The Writer's Journey: Mythic Structure for Storytellers and Screenwriters,* (Studio City, Calif., Michael Wiese Productions, 1994).

# 6

# Producing the Message

Literally, *transmit* means to "send across." In the television studio, the message must be "transmitted," or "sent across," to the camera and microphone with faithful adherence to the intent of the communicator and with consideration for the receiver of the message waiting in front of a television set. Nothing that happens, or fails to happen, in the studio precess must be allowed to distract the viewer from the objective the communicator had in mind.

For instance, if you are transmitting a commercial for a product and your eyes obviously wander to the floor manager's hand signals, the viewer's attention is drawn to your awkward eye movements rather than to the desirable traits of the product you are promoting. Suppose you are presenting an interview with an outstanding science student, and your words are blurred because you do not use the microphone correctly. The people listening to you in front of the television set have to concentrate so intently on hearing the actual words that they cannot focus on the meaning of what you are saying. Suppose your theater group is televising a sorrowful scene. The viewer may respond with hilarity rather than sympathy if the boom mike casts a shadow that makes a telephone pole appear to emerge from the head of one of the tragic characters.

*TV is a collaboration.*

## THE PRODUCTION TEAM

Effectively transmitting the message from the communicator in the studio to the television viewer is a team responsibility. It involves the technicians, who keep the equipment operating efficiently; the di-

169

rector, who orchestrates the human and technical elements into a harmonious whole; the studio crew, who operate the equipment in the studio; the floor manager, who relays the director's instructions to the talent (performers); the talent, or performer, who is transmitting an idea, a musical selection, a dance, or a magic act to a camera and microphone. Any member of this team can create the kind of distraction or interference that prevents the message from getting across to the viewer. All it takes is one person not paying attention to destroy a program.

The talent on a program may never function as floor manager, camera operator, or boom operator. But everyone involved needs to know and understand the full range of job responsibilities in order to assure smooth production.

## FLOOR MANAGERS

The floor manager is the director's representative in the TV studio. Obviously, during a telecast the director cannot give instructions on the PA system because they would be picked up by the microphones. Performers rely on the *floor managers* (sometimes called *floor directors*) for all the cues during the production. Floor managers

**FIGURE 6.1**

Producing a television program is a team effort.

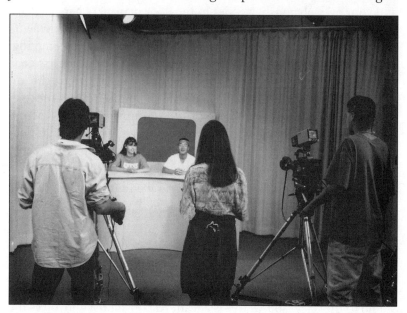

**FIGURE 6.2**

A floor manager relays the director's cues to the talent.

*Many newsroom cameras are now automated and do not need camera operators. Learn many jobs if you wish to be employed in TV.*

cue the talent when they are on the air and remind them how long they have left; floor managers give roll cues for film and tape, and they relay instructions from the director as the show is in progress. They wear a headset that allows them to hear the director's instructions to them and to the camera operators. Floor managers may also give visual cues to stagehands or actually flip graphics for the director.

The floor manager must avoid getting in front of the camera. He or she actually runs the show from the studio because in many stations the control room is not near the studio. Although this is an entry-level position for many TV stations, the role of floor manager is an important one.

## CAMERA OPERATORS

Camera operators are obviously vital members of the studio team. Experienced performers understand the extent to which camera operators can make or break a performance. Some movie actors insist on personally selecting camera operators to shoot their scenes. A camera operator can shoot you at a most uncomplimentary angle, adding pounds to your weight, inches to your nose, and shadows to your eyes.

Camera techniques can help the director establish a viewpoint for the home audience. In *The Selling of the President, 1968*, author Joe McGinniss reported that one of President Nixon's television advisers, William Gavin, recommended that the camera sweep over the audience during a telecast of one of Nixon's speeches. This would show the home viewers what he saw and put them in his position. The camera would make the viewers partners with Nixon, looking through the same eyes.

In many schools and small studios, camera operators may serve on different occasions as directors, audio people, floor managers, or performers when they are not behind their cameras. They may work with a director who gives precise instructions as to their every move, or they may have a director who gives few instructions, depending on them to follow a shot sheet, and frame pictures ready for use. A common arrangement in school studios is to have the operator of a single camera work with the talent and the floor manager during rehearsal, then work on his or her own, with no director, during production. In that way, the camera operator actually functions as his or her own director.

Do not count on a career only as a studio camera operator. Many TV newsrooms are now automated, eliminating the need for camera operators.

### Rehearsal Procedure

If you operate a camera, you will need to check the following procedures:

1. Put on a headset, if there is one, to receive instructions from the control room.

**FIGURE 6.3**
A camera operator listens to instructions from the control room.

2. Uncap the lens, and place the cap where you can find it at the end of the program. Do not carry it home in your pocket by mistake!

3. White-balance your camera so the colors will be true. For most cameras, use a white sheet of paper or tagboard, zoom in so it fills at least 80 percent of the picture area, then push in the white-balance setting for at least five seconds. Other studios may use different means of color setup, depending on their equipment. Check with the director to see how to set color balance in your studio.

4. Determine what f stop you will set the lens aperture to. Most studios use f/5.6 for greatest depth of field. If you want less, open the f stop; if you want more, close the f stop. When you are finished, be sure to close the lens. Many new cameras are automatic.

5. If your camera has a viewfinder, check to see if reflecting lights interfere with the picture. If there is no hood to shade the viewfinder, you can tape on a cardboard reflector.

6. Check cable and AC power lines to be sure that power is coming to the camera and that a picture can be transmitted from the camera.
7. Unlock the panning head, and try panning left and right, and tilting up and down.
8. Truck and dolly across the studio floor to be sure you can move the camera quickly and surely on command.
9. After determining your close-ups, make sure you can zoom without going out of focus during the production.
10. Also check the focus by shooting at a variety of visuals, graphics, and set props.
11. If you are using a shot sheet, check every shot you can frame up in advance to be sure you can give the director and/or talent the picture requested. Your list of shots might look like the one in Figure 6.4.
12. During rehearsals, ask questions whenever you are unsure of what is wanted because you will not be able to talk during the actual production. Even though you have intercom equipment, your voice would be picked up by a studio mike. If the director asks you questions, he or she will be careful to phrase them so you can answer by blowing into the mike, once for *yes* and twice for *no*.

## Production Procedure

During the actual production, your procedure will differ according to the control room facilities and staff available in your setup. Certain procedures, however, are standard in most places.

1. Wait for the tally light on your camera to go out before moving your camera.
2. To keep the picture in focus while your camera is moving, keep one hand on the focus control when you dolly, pan, tilt, or truck.
3. Watch the mike and the camera cables on the studio floor. Do not dolly over them or disconnect them by kicking them out of place. Some camera operators place the cables on their shoulders so the cables will be out of the way as they move the camera.

**FIGURE 6.4**

Shot Sheet: Camera 1
1. Wide shot of classroom
2. Two-shot of teacher and Bill
3. HS shot of Bill
4. CU of key in Bill's hand
5. Two-shot of teacher and Bill
6. HS shot of teacher
7. CU of teacher
8. Wide shot of classroom

4. Look behind you before a fast outward or backward dolly. Knocking over a chair or a set of gongs creates a huge distraction.
5. Be aware (in the periphery of your vision) of any movements that suggest the performer is going to stand, lift a visual, or walk to the side. But concentrate on the viewfinder of your camera, constantly aware that the picture you frame in that viewfinder will be the one that communicates meaning to the viewer.
6. If there are two or more cameras, you are responsible for keeping out of range of these other cameras.
7. If the director permits you to frame shots and select shooting angles, remember that (*a*) pointing the camera upward from a lower angle gives dominance and power to the performer; (*b*) pointing the camera downward on the performer gives him or her the appearance of weakness and inferiority; (*c*) an extreme wide-angle lens can distort close-ups for comic or grotesque effect; and (*d*) an extreme wide-angle lens can give apparent depth to a room, or length to an object angled toward the camera. Notice how the dramatic effect of close-ups is used more often in soap operas than in television newscasts.
8. Any decision you make should fit with the mood and purpose of the show. A tight close-up of a fly on the end of a teacher's twitching nose may be an entertaining reaction shot, but it will be poor television if the aim of the program is to explain how to use the shift key on the typewriter.

**FIGURE 6.5**

A crew checks color balance.

**FIGURE 6.6**

A camera operator checks focus by shooting at a variety of visuals and set props.

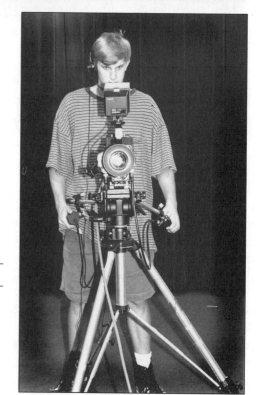

**FIGURE 6.7**
Using the viewfinder, a camera operator checks to see if reflecting lights interfere with the picture.

9. Be sure to check for head room (distance from the top of the talent's head to the top of the screen). Leave a little room to allow for differences between TV sets. When a performer is turned profile, make sure there is "nose room" as well.

## Striking the Set

At the end of the show, close the f stop, replace the cap on the lens, coil the cable, and fasten it neatly. Lock the panning head. Dolly the camera to the side of the studio near a wall. Lock the wheels of the dolly. Assist other members of the student crew in striking or dismantling the set; return all pieces of equipment to their storage location, return all borrowed set props, and see that the studio is in order.

*Audio technicians listen to the subtle effects of tone quality.*

## AUDIO TECHNICIANS

Another crew member of the studio team is the audio technician. Like the camera operator and the floor manager, the technician's duties and responsibilities vary greatly according to the facilities and staff available. In some studios the performers plug in their own mikes and place the lavaliere cord around their necks; in others they do not touch the mikes or any of the audio controls.

In general, audio technicians are responsible for the sound from the mikes and for electronically produced sounds played in the control room or studio. Good audio technicians do more than turn mikes on and off, and volume up and down. They exercise aesthetic judgment, listen to sounds as interpretations of mood, and are sensitive to the subtle effects of tone quality. If you are given the assignment of audio technician, these are some of the duties you will be expected to perform.

1. Check with the director and/or performer to find out what CDs, tapes, carts, and cassettes will be needed. Check cues, mark the script, and mark the CDs and tapes. Check equipment to be sure you know how to operate it at the correct speed, on cue, with all feed lines connected and functioning.
2. Check with the director and/or performer as to what kinds of mikes are needed, where they must be located, and whether they are to be on (live) all the time, or on and off according to cue.
3. Connect mikes and check cables to see that they are out of the way and out of sight if possible.
4. During rehearsals, see that all performers use the mikes properly. Be sure to make this check while they are standing or moving exactly as they will be during production.
5. Write down where each mike is located on the control board. Do not risk turning up two or three pots during the show before the announcer's mike finally comes on.
6. "Get a level" on each performer; that is, determine the volume of his or her voice and the corresponding volume at each mike. Write it down: "Mrs. Mendez, 80–90. Flutist at mike 2, 70–100. John, 75–80." The volume will vary during the performance, but these figures will give you an idea of the range to be expected from each speaker or performer.

**FIGURE 6.8**

An audio technician knows where each mike is located on the control board.

During the performance, "ride gain" (keep a hand on the audio controls and watch the needle that registers the amount of volume being fed through audio lines) throughout the show, ready to anticipate action. It is too late to turn down the volume after a performer shouts into the mike, because the next words may be spoken very softly. It is not necessary to watch every word being spoken. It is all right if the talent goes over 100 percent on the VU meter once in a while, or utters a word softly. Just keep a general check on the volume level.

7. If a lavaliere mike is used, be sure the cord is adjusted to avoid entanglement with beards, long hair, ties, or jewelry.

8. If the boom mike is used, be sure the operator knows when and where he or she can and must move. Check the shadows cast by the boom to be sure they are not visible on walls where camera operators will be framing pictures.

9. After the show, disconnect the mikes and return them to their storage area with cables coiled and fastened. If a portable amplifier has been used, disconnect and store it.

10. Assist other crew members in striking the set and returning the studio to order.

## PRODUCTION ASSISTANTS (PAS)

Production assistants are responsible for the placement and manipulation of graphics and props; they are an important part of the studio team. Production assistants may also help prepare the props and construct suitable stands for displaying visuals.

Their task may be to construct an easel-like stand with an extension at eye level for holding graphics. This "hod," as it is sometimes called, may have the metal spine of a three-ring looseleaf notebook nailed to the top so that graphic cards with three holes punched in the top can be flipped up or down into camera range. The shelf may have ridges or tracks so production assistants can slide graphic cards horizontally into camera range. The music stands used by the orchestra or band work very well as graphic stands. Titles, charts, or any visual will stand up if mounted to cardboard on these stands. You might be able to borrow a stand or two from the band director for production.

A production assistant may be assigned to provide a supply of dry ice to simulate steam, or to number all the graphics on the back in the order of their display on camera. A production assistant will be put in charge of continuity. That is, he or she will make sure that everything on the set remains the same after the camera stops recording until the camera records again. The props and setting must match or the illusion that the scene happened in real time is lost.

A studio prop that production assistants can construct is the strip tease, used for revealing words or numerals one at a time. Words, phrases, or statistics are covered with strips of paper or cardboard, which can be removed one by one to reveal the hidden words or data on cue. Plastic tape on the back of a line graph can be removed an inch at a time, letting the light shine through and giving the effect of a moving graph line.

Many TV studios employ an art director who is in charge of the creative elements of the program. He or she supervises the design and building of scenery and backdrops; makes sure the props needed during the program are obtained; and creates special effects such as rear-screen projections, scenery cut-outs, and light patterns.

## Properties

If you are a production assistant, an interesting challenge to your ingenuity will be the creation of props that look real on camera. For example, you may need to make "synthetic blood," an essential ingredient in so many commercial TV programs nowadays. Catsup can be used for blood on the stage, and in black-and-white films chocolate syrup is satisfactory; but color TV required the development of technicolor and "panchromatic" blood. You can buy a pint of synthetic blood that consist of microscopic red plastic balls suspended in a liquid; it can be thickened or thinned.

## Truth in Advertising

In the television industry, the production assistant's job has been complicated by a regulation intended to protect the consumer from fraudulent claims for products: The FCC (Federal Communications Commission) ruling that only real products can be shown in television commercials. Artificial coloring or synthetic devices cannot be substituted for products on camera. Because the human eye and the camera do not perceive objects and colors the same way, production assistants used to add grenadine to orange juice to keep it from looking like milk, shoe polish to coffee to give it that "rich, full-bodied look," and yellow food coloring to tint spaghetti. The truth-in-advertising regulation requires a commercial television studio to photograph the real item. Fortunately, this does not apply to a school production that remains strictly a closed-circuit operation.

### FIGURE 6.9

A director coordinates the efforts of the whole crew, relying on audio contact for the most part. *Photo courtesy of the Community TV Network, Chicago, Illinois, featuring* the work of *"Hard Cover," a cable program produced and directed by teenagers for teenagers.* ©1992 by Thom Clark, Bryan Clark, all rights reserved.

An ice cream commercial requires gallons of the product, as the melted cream must be replaced after each shot under the hot lights. Filming a 1-minute beer commercial may use up eight cases of beer if egg whites cannot be substituted for the "head," which also melts away under the heat of the lights. So the production assistant must check each item on camera to determine in advance how to make real objects appear real—a most demanding assignment, requiring patience and ingenuity.

## TECHNICAL DIRECTORS AND SWITCHERS

**FIGURE 6.10**

**Sample Floor Plan**

For really effective rehearsals, a floor plan—usually created by the director—is essential. It indicates where each set piece will be, where talent will be located, where cameras will be, where movements will extend, and many more details.

When they are functioning in the studio, the production assistants, audio technician, camera operator, and floor manager are all under the supervision of the director. In many studios, school, cable, and commercial, there is a technical director who operates the switches and buttons in the control room to change from one camera to the other on command from the director: "Take 1. Dissolve to 2. Super 1. Go to black." Passing a command from one person to another can affect the split-second timing needed in cutting from one camera to another, so the director may prefer to be his or her own technical director.

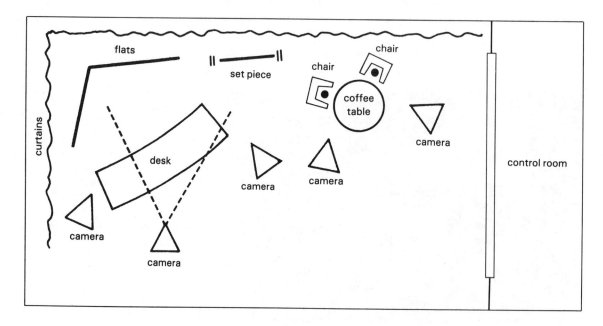

Instead of a technical director, some studios have a switcher who actually pushes the buttons and immediately executes the changes from one camera to another as ordered by the director. Directors often say "*ready* to take one" or "*ready* to dissolve to two" to prepare the switcher for the next move.

## DIRECTORS

In television, the relationships between directors and their teams, and the nature of their responsibilities, differ from those in theater and radio. The stage director of a play has little if any control over the performers once they appear on stage, but may cue lights, sound, and curtain from a position offstage. The radio director, on the other hand, is in constant communication with the cast through hand signals and cues. The TV director has audio contact with the camera operators and the floor manager, who is the director's only contact with the performers.

Television directors, then, have a special communication problem in achieving the effects they wish to create.

*Planning = Power*

### Advance Preparation

Because television directors must achieve a maximum of coordination in a minimum of allotted time, they must prepare carefully in advance. They may call on production assistants for many jobs—timing the script, taking notes at rehearsals, and running errands. Studio time is usually limited and expensive, as is the time of the engineers and technical personnel. Therefore, directors try to make every minute in the studio count. They hold "dry runs"—rehearsals without the cameras turned on. The director makes a floor plan, marking where each set piece will be, where talent will be, where cameras will be, where movements will extend (see Figure 6.10). In short, the director makes all the decisions that simplify and speed up the rehearsal before calling the performers to the studio.

### Picture Sequence

To produce television pictures that will communicate a desired message, you as the director must plan successive camera shots. You must think not only in terms of pictures but the sequence in which the viewer will see those pictures. Suppose the program features a youth symphony orchestra. You will have to instruct camera #2 to frame and focus picture #2 (a close-up of the guest pianist) while camera #1 is taking picture #1 (a wide shot of the entire orchestra). While the viewer is watching picture #2 (the guest pianist) from camera #2, you must instruct camera #1 to frame and focus picture #3 (a shot of the violin section with the first violinist in the foreground). You must think ahead, keeping the viewer's needs in mind and remaining ever aware of the potential and limitations of the cameras you have available. To have the right shots readied and taken at the proper time, you need skill that can be developed only with much practice. To coordinate your work with what everyone else is doing requires visual imagination, efficiency, and advance planning. Even though you have created effective pictures in your mind, the viewer will never see those pictures unless the engineer, the camera operators, and the talent know what you want and are in a position to transmit each picture when you call for it.

**FIGURE 6.11**

A student newscaster is prepared for a close-up anytime.

## Pointers for the Director

Even in simple productions like class exercises, the director can profit by following these suggestions.

1. Rehearse with the performers outside the studio. Correct the way they say and do things before they face the cameras.

2. Work out all the camera positions, angles, and details ahead of time by using a floor plan. Make sure your camera can get all the shots before you walk into the studio. It is expensive to keep a cast and crew waiting as you work out camera positions.

3. Write a shot sheet or cue sheet for each camera operator so he or she will know that the first shot will be a CU of the professor's glasses and the second an HS shot of the professor. Then, if you become too busy or too excited during the show to give each camera operator adequate advance directions, he or she will find them on the shot sheet.

4. Mark difficult-to-remember locations on the studio floor, using chalk or tape. If talent must stand in a certain spot to be properly lighted or to be within mike range, mark that spot on the floor.

5. Rehearse production assistants in the operation of flip cards, pictures on an easel, strip-tease tear-offs, and other properties to be manipulated on cue.

6. Check difficult shots, such as those of a computer keyboard reflected in an overhead mirror. The mirror should be angled and fastened in the best possible position for effective camera work *before* the cast and crew report for rehearsal. Don't keep twelve people waiting while you search for what you need.

7. If you have two copies of a book or picture, one to be held by the talent and the other to be shot close-up in limbo (that is, with no specific background—against a curtain or blank wall), check the distance and size of these shots before the group arrives in the studio. You may want to have one camera operator arrive early to run through these difficult shots.

8. As you plan your shots, remember how small the viewing screen is. Close-ups and medium shots that fill most of the screen will be clearer than a long shot of numerous small objects.

9. Make your instructions to the crew clear, concise, and definite. Use precise languages such as, "Dolly in on the silver cup for a close-up in which we can read the inscription." Then the camera operators know what to do and how they can tell when they have the right shot.

   Make sure you relay all instructions in black-and-white terms, because your camera operators do not have color viewfinders. If you say, "Camera 2, get a close-up of the girl in the green dress," the camera operator will have to look above the camera to find her. Instead, give each girl a number, going left to right. You need only say, "Camera 2, give me a close-up of girl #2."

10. Keep calm. Keep your mind on what you are doing. Losing your temper will only compound any problem.

11. Remember to think ahead. You must always be ready for what's coming next. Think of the next shot or cue and ready the camera operators, audio technician, or switcher.

12. Remember to keep a cover shot that allows you to shoot the entire situation when you are not sure what will happen next. When filming a panel discussion, for example, if you are not sure who is going to talk next, get a shot of the entire group until you know.

13. Concentrate on producing a sound and picture sequence that will communicate the message to the viewer with a single impact and hence without interference.

## VIDEOTAPE OPERATORS

One of the control room jobs is controlling videotape, both for inserting into the program and for videotaping the entire production. In a newscast for your school, it is a good idea to videotape ahead of time sequences around the school. The tape can then be edited and used during the newscast. Later you will learn how to use and edit videotape as well as to shoot remote videotape.

A roll cue counts down the leader from ten to two seconds before the beginning of the tape. Simply cue the tape at the two-second cue. By the time you start the tape, the first word is on the air. The director will usually call for the VTR operator to "roll tape"; then he or she will "take tape," or put it on the air.

The videotape operator is also responsible for taping the entire production on another video recorder. Place a tape (usually a cassette) in the machine and cue it to where the program should start. Make sure both the audio and video signals are reaching the recorder by calling for a check of both systems. The director should tell the VTR to "roll tape" at least ten seconds before the start of the program.

In some cable systems, color bars are inserted for thirty seconds so the operator can adjust the color. Most TV studios have a provision to produce color bars with the cameras. Check with the local cable company on the particulars of the tape configurations. After the program is finished, keep the tape rolling for at least ten seconds. This gives people time to turn off the system or their sets before the tape simply goes off.

## THE TALENT'S RESPONSIBILITIES

No director is skillful enough to communicate a message clearly without the cooperation of the talent. Inexperienced performers may be ill at ease and fail to use the mike properly; they may not cooperate with the studio crew. Directors expect the talent to remain alert and ready for instructions as relayed through the floor manager. If performers miss instructions, forget what message they are sending to the viewer, or fail to understand the demands of the medium, they will cause interference that will distract the viewer, and may in extreme cases obliterate the message from the viewer's consciousness.

As a performer, you have to know how to work with two kinds of production staffs: (1) student groups—most likely to staff your school production center, and (2) a professional studio production staff—with whom you will work if you are invited to appear on a local commercial, cable, or educational station program.

If you are an on-camera performer in a school studio with a classmate as director and an inexperienced camera operator, you will have to think of their problems as well as your own and anticipate what they will do. If you are an on-camera performer in a commercial studio, you will have to follow directions as you receive them and cooperate with the staff in carrying out instructions.

One of the reasons TV performers are so well paid is the impression they give that everything is going well even if it is not. They

*Keep the crew on your side.*

have to be able to take cues while pretending they are not. An inexperienced reporter on cable may nod when a floor manager cues him or her to start; you don't see Dan Rather doing that.

In addition to receiving instructions from the floor manager, most performers in newscasts wear a small headset called an IFB (interrupted feedback) system. This earpiece normally carries the program audio. However, the director can break in and give special instructions. The talent might hear, "Go to Bob Rhodes at City Hall. He's ready for the interview." Or, "We don't have the tape clip ready. Just give the score." Even while the talent is speaking, instructions are sometimes being relayed through this system. Not letting the audience see one's reaction takes a tremendous amount of practice.

As an on-camera performer, you will need to put into practice every principle of effective speaking and communication that you have ever learned. Individuals who express themselves well in their daily jobs sometimes get mike fright and "clam up" on television. Although the following tips were prepared by the Illinois State Medical Society for doctors participating in a televised program, they are equally helpful to students.

1. Do not memorize the script. Conversation should be as flexible and casual as possible. The script is prepared for continuity and cut material, not for specific dialogue.
2. Do not remain too long with any chart or other prop. This is tiring to the viewer. After one or two charts or diagrams have been used for about a minute, walk away, *slowly*, to another part of the set as outlined by the director. Then, when necessary, return to the chart for another brief discussion.
3. Equipment that calls for camera close-ups should be held quietly in the hands and horizontally in front of the body. This is particularly true of shiny objects because of reflection, and of diagrams because of blurred image. Better yet, hold objects and charts on a table so they will not move. When the camera zooms in, the depth of field is so shallow that any movement at all may cause that close-up to go out of focus.
4. A rehearsal without cameras is called a dry run. With cameras, it is called a camera rehearsal. Listen to the instructions given in the studio so that you will know which camera is focused on you without showing the audience that you are receiving signals from the stage director.

5. Do not talk *up* to or *at* a boom mike. This mike is very sensitive. Talk naturally. If you are using a lavaliere mike, don't play with the mike. Any movement will create noise that will be picked up. Don't talk into the lavaliere mike; talk over it as you look into the camera.
6. Do not indulge in long, detailed explanations.... Combine discussion with action.

## Facial Expression: Acting and Reacting

As an on-camera performer, you need to remember that the most frequently used shots of you will probably be head and shoulders. Your facial expression will give the viewer clues as to your sincerity and general attitude. The expression in your eyes is the most revealing way you communicate. When you roll your eyes, you tell the viewer, "I'm only kidding; this really isn't that important." A furtive glance to the side can say, "I'm more worried about that next timing cue than I am about the people starving in Africa." A raised eyebrow can criticize or condemn as caustically as words.

Bowing your head over your notes leaves the camera operator with only the top of your head as a picture communicating your message. Licking your lips or covering part of your face with your hand draws attention to the mannerism and away from the message.

Facial expressions are important to political campaigners trying to persuade their TV audience. The late Hubert Humphrey once said, "The biggest mistake in my political life was not learning how to use television." The National Association of Broadcasters has prepared a booklet to help candidates use this intimate medium more effectively. Among its suggestions are these, which apply to anyone speaking on television:

1. Don't hold the script in front of your face. The audience expects to see *you* on television—not a piece of paper.
2. Add action by moving about—from the desk or table where you are seated to the charts, pictures, or blackboard used to illustrate your message. But don't move about unnecessarily. It will only distract the viewers.
3. Avoid meaningless gestures (such as twisting a pencil, which distracts the viewers) and sweeping gestures, which may be lost to the camera's view.

4. Whether seated or standing, at all times talk directly to the viewer. Keep in mind that the audience is *inside* the camera.
5. Remember that no matter how far from the camera you are, it still is possible to take a close-up of your face. As you have no way of knowing when a close-up is being made, be prepared for one to be taken at all times.

## Body Action

Even though your director may concentrate on head and shoulder shots of you, your gestures and body actions are important. If you are sincerely concerned about what you are saying, your entire body will reflect that tension. So make no attempt to avoid gestures that express what you are feeling. Whether or not they show on camera, they will be evident in the tone of your voice. It is extremely difficult to project an alert, vital tone of voice from a slouchy, overly relaxed body frame. Alway use good posture.

## Restricted Movements

During close-up shots you will need to keep your movements somewhat restricted to avoid going out of the picture frame on the left or on the right. If you extend gestures, the camera will distort and magnify disproportionately those objects close to the lens.

## Memory Aids

The one thing most amateur on-camera performers fear above all is forgetting their lines. Whether the show is ad-lib or scripted, you have a procedure to follow. If your mind "goes blank," you are embarrassed, and the viewer is equally uncomfortable. Even experienced professionals dread "blowing" lines and prepare all kinds of memory aids in advance.

Singers may have the lyrics written on large cue cards held near the camera lens. TelePrompTers mounted on the camera carry the exact words of the script, printed in large letters on a monitor on top of the camera. A series of mirrors and one-way glass puts the script in front of the lens of the camera so the talent can look right into the lens while reading the script. Unless the speaker and the operator of the TelePrompTer rehearse together to establish the most desirable tempo, the speaker may have to speak faster than he or she wishes, or the operator may not be able to pace the roll of script to the speaker's varying tempo.

If you have watched telecasts of the political conventions, you may have glimpsed a one-way vision glass on which words were projected, visible to the speaker but not within range of the camera.

In a commercial, the script to be read may be attached to the back of a box of cereal or dog food as the announcer holds the product at eye level. Books and similar stage props can hide a script on a desk or table.

David Frost, a former talk-show host, did not try to hide the clipboard that held his notes for guest interviews. Talk show hosts such as Arsenio Hall or Joan Rivers may read comments from the back of pictures they are holding up for the camera.

Performers in a dramatic show may look over the shoulders of actors facing them and read their lines or cues on a TelePrompTer or cue card. Run-down lists or key phrases may be written on the studio floor. (Camera operators, beware of shooting low!) Newscasters often use both a script in hand and a teleprompting device. Viewers seem to feel that a report is more authentic if it comes from written copy.

Indeed, there are now so many hidden and visible prompting devices that no on-camera performer need fear going blank. Your only problem is how to read these prompting devices while still appearing to look directly into the camera. With experience, you can learn to look at your notes while the camera focuses on other participants. Just don't give yourself away by glancing at your notes just as the camera returns to you.

## ANNOUNCERS

Announcers may read much of their material off camera in an "announce booth," or they may simply assume a position in which it is natural and acceptable to hold the script in front of them, with no attempt to disguise the fact that they are reading it.

As an announcer, be especially mindful of the way you deliver your material. Your voice should be clear and pleasing, your articulation distinct, and your pronunciation flawless. Columnist Sydney Harris's list of commonly mispronounced words helps you to avoid some of the errors announcers often make.

**FIGURE 6.12**

## A Primer for Announcers

Why don't pronouncing handbooks for radio and television announcers write it large and plain that:

—There is no "heal" in "helicopter," no "pear" in "irreparable," no "eggs" in "excerpts."

—There is no "z" in "absorbs," no "cull" in "culinary," and no "lug" in "luxury."

—There is no "may" in "menu," and no "ay" in "lingerie."

—There is no "peen" in "European," no "pie" in "impious," and no "zidge" in "exigency."

—The word "dour" is of Scottish origin, and rhymes with "moor," not with "our."

—A "glazier" is not an ice-formation, but a man who installs and repairs panes of glass.

—The opposite of "depth" is not "heighth," and the opposite of "weakness" is not "strenth."

—There is no such adjective as "preventative," and no such verb as "commentate"; medicine is "preventive," and commentators "comment."

—There is no "ouch" in "debauch," and no "vay" in "vagary."

—There is no "cue" in "coupon," no "pick" in "despicable," and, above all, no "spit" in "hospitable."

—There is no "dole" in "doldrums," no "he" in "heinous," and no "yum" in "columnist."

—There is no "pea" in "pianist," even when it's a concert pianist; there is no "zoo" in "zoology," and no "bert" in "sherbet."

—The "h" is not sounded in "La Boheme," the "g" is not sounded in "Pagliacci," and "Don Quixote" should not sound like a breakfast cereal.

—A "corespondent" in a divorce case is not pronounced the same as a "correspondent" for a newspaper.

—There are three syllables, not two, in "finally"; three syllables, not four, in "parliament"; and five syllables, not four, in "incidentally."

—There is no "mere" in "premiere," no "mater" in "maitre d'hotel," and no "lounge" in a "chaise longue." There is no "home" in "homicide," no "hew" in "posthumous," and no "hose" in "hosiery."

—The finely expressive word "lambaste" rhymes with "paste" and not with "past."

SYDNEY J. HARRIS

If you are ad-libbing remarks to cover an emergency or adjust to a changing situation, an occasional error in pronunciation might be excused, but it is unthinkable to mispronounce a proper name or a word in a script that you saw in advance of the performance. If you cannot find the name of a composer or the title of a musical selection in your dictionary, ask one of the musicians, preferably the conductor. If you are not sure how to pronounce the names of guests you are interviewing, ask them, even if you have to do it on-camera.

You cannot rely on general rules for the pronunciation of geographic terms. If you mispronounce Des Plaines, Kanawha, Cairo, Terre Haute, Worcester, or Reading, the people who live there will not excuse your ignorance. Try to determine proper pronunciation.

Ask an authority in your school about anglicizing words from other languages. Be consistent in using the native or the Americanized pronunciation of *chic, Goethe, alumnae, Michelangelo, fiance.* Check your dictionary for the correct pronunciation of these everyday words: *penalize, athletics, precedence, address, status, amateur, finance, adult, data.* Errors in pronunciation distract the television viewer's attention away from your message and cast doubt on your authority.

In summary, there are all manner of pitfalls that you, as a television communicator, must avoid as you transmit your message through the camera to people seated in front of their television sets. The more completely you can master production techniques, the more completely you can eliminate interference between yourself and the person receiving your message.

## IT'S A WRAP

Television is truly a team sport. It takes a large production team, working together harmoniously, to create a successful television program. Each member of the team depends on the others, and each production job involves its own special challenges.

Floor managers, also known as floor directors, serve as the link between the director and the talent, relaying instructions from the director and cueing the talent. Camera operators are the viewers' "eyes"; their vital job has been eliminated in some studios by automation. Good audio technicians make sure that each performer is heard clearly, and they make constant, subtle adjustments to the volume, using their aesthetic sense to help set the mood through sound. Production assistants are responsible for placing graphics on the set; they also use their ingenuity to design lifelike props. Technical directors and videotape operators keep the show running from the control room. Performers and announcers use their vocal abilities and acting talent to articulate the message. And directors plan the show and coordinate the efforts of each member of this large team.

No matter which position on the production team you aspire to, it's wise to understand the basics of each job. A comprehensive knowledge of production jobs makes you more employable and makes you a better member of the large interactive group behind any television production.

# Video Lab

1. Imagine you are directing a local program for a cable television public access channel featuring a xylophone player. The host will begin the program by interviewing the guest. After the interview, the guest will walk across the studio to play the xylophone. When the performance is over, the guest will walk back to the chair and resume the interview.

Below is a sample floor plan. Using the elements in Figures 6.13 & 6.14, create a floor plan for the following shots:

a. A two-shot of the interviewer and guest together.
b. A close-up (CU) of each person.
c. A pan shot of the guest walking to the xylophone.
d. A CU of the guest's hands playing the instrument.
e. A pan shot of the guest walking back to the interview area.
f. A two-shot of the interviewer and guest together again.
g. A CU of the interviewer during the wrap-up of the program.

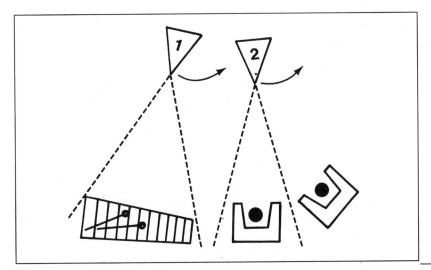

**FIGURE 6.13**

Sample floor plan: Notice that camera one is directed at the xylophone and camera two is focused on an individual.

## FIGURE 6.14

Use these elements for your floor plan.

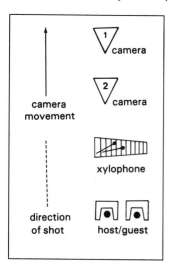

Use dotted lines to indicate camera movements. Use solid lines to indicate the direction of the shots. Vary the width of the angles created by your solid lines to show how much of the scene will be picked up by the camera; for example, a narrow angle indicates a CU of the guest's hands.

2. You are directing an interview show that will use two cameras, two talents, and a coffee table. Using elements in Figure 6.15, make three floor plans. Diagram the location of the props and location of the cameras in each floor plan. Put the types of camera shots (HS = head-and-shoulders shot, LS = long shot, CU = close-up of one person, 2-shot = both persons) you would use for each of the following:

a. The opening shot of the show to establish where the speakers are and the number of speakers.

b. A shot during the guest's description of his or her early career.

c. The shot during the interviewer's closing remarks as he or she thanks the guest for participating in the program.

3. If your TV studio is capable of going remote or you have access to the cable TV company's remote van, plan to televise a school football or basketball game. Or you might televise a less-publicized school sport such as a wrestling meet, girl's basketball game, or gymnastics meet. Prepare a floor plan showing where your cameras will be located. Assign camera operators, play-by-play and color announcers, switcher, audio and videotape technicians, and other necessary personnel. Prepare the broadcast from start to finish, including pregame and postgame coverage. Ask the local cable company to carry the telecast.

4. Assume that a local cable television service has given your school five minutes of a thirty-minute newscast at noon. Write a five-minute script to present on camera. For musical background, you might use a recording of your school song. The station has limited you to three graphics, exclusive of the title cards that it furnishes. You may include a two-minute live interview with a guest from school, either a student or a staff member. Check your script by answering these questions.

a. Which of my news stories will need pictures to make them clear?

b. Have I made a clear distinction between statements of fact and my commentary?

c. Have I cleared the use of pictures with the director?

d. Have I cleared music and music cues?

e. Have I checked statements of fact to verify their accuracy? Is the new Boosters Club president T. *Ellsworth* Brown or T. *Ellison* Brown?

**FIGURE 6.15**

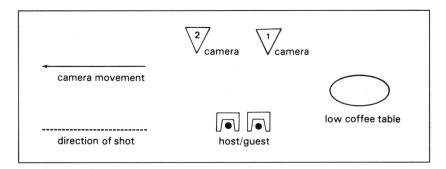

f. Have I timed the script with a stopwatch and recorded the time for the director?

g. If I have included an interview, has that segment been timed—with alternative questions and if-cuts to be used to meet timing cues?

h. Have I cleared all copyrighted material?

i. Have my videotape clips been edited?

Use a videotape recorder to record your newscast and play it back for self-criticism. Be honest as you watch it. Would you turn it off if it were not your own program? What message does it convey about the kind of school you attend, about what is going on there, about your integrity as a reporter, about you as a person?

5. Imagine you are the producer of a local interview program. The program opens with a title card or key title. A host introduces the program and brings out the first guest, who talks for a few minutes with the host and then either demonstrates his or her hobby or performs by singing, dancing, playing an instrument, or reading literature. After the performance, the guest returns and the host asks a few more questions before closing the program with the announcement of future guests. The program closes with music and a closing title or key card. The format is:

a. Opening titles and music

b. Host introduces program and guest

c. Guest demonstrates or performs

d. Host and guest talk

e. Host wraps up

f. Closing titles and music

Write a script that will allow for flexibility and yet will make this work. You will need at least two copies (for the director and the host). Set up a floor plan and produce the program on videotape for analysis.

6. Write a script for a fifteen-minute show for your public access channel. You, as M.C., will interview the coach, co-captains, and head cheerleader on the Wednesday before the basketball game. Check the content of your script with these questions.

a. Have I done my "homework" well by obtaining facts, human-interest items, significant details, and correct statistics on records and events?

b. Do I have a tantalizing introduction that will make viewers want to stay tuned?

c. Do I have well-phrased transitions to lead from the cheerleader to the co-captains and from the co-captains to the assistant coach? Have I prepared substitute statements for "Next we have...."?

d. Do I have questions that will give the coach a chance to say what he or she wants to say, or have I limited the coach with yes and no questions?

e. Have I made it easy for the co-captains to make comments without embarrassment? Have I kidded too much?

f. Are all my questions the same old trite ones, starting with "How did you feel when...?", or do I include some penetrating queries that will elicit fresh viewpoints on this particular sports event?

g. Are all my questions clearly worded so that the interviewee will know what I mean and won't appear stupid as he or she attempts to answer?

h. Do my questions sound as if I have been listening to the previous answers?

i. What comments do I make after an answer? "Oh, I see," may be excused once, but not more than that.

j. Am I trying to get across the same message as the coach and co-captains?

k. Have I thought of my viewers, and tried to ask questions they would like to ask?

Check the form of the script with these questions.

a. Have I used capital letters to distinguish speakers' names, directions, camera shots, music, and sound effects?

b. Have I used arrows and/or underlining to indicate to the technical staff the exact word cue for each action?

c. Is it clear how much time I expect each segment to take?

d. Are the if-cuts clearly marked to indicate passages I may need to omit?

e. Have I included alternative endings, with the exact times indicated, so I can conclude exactly on cue?

f. Have I given credit when using other people's material?

g. Have I cleared the music I wish to use?

## TAKE TWO

**1.** Discuss what general qualities any team should have to function effectively. Consider such elements as cooperation, communication, attitudes, and goals.

**2.** Consider the various duties and responsibilities discussed for each of the positions described. Does any position appeal to you more than another? Why? Why is it important to be aware of all the duties involved?

**3.** If there is another school near you that also has a television studio, ask for permission to visit its con-

trol room during a rehearsal and broadcast. Take your cassette recorder and tape the director's instructions as he or she commands the camera operators, floor manager, and switcher, if one is used. Play the tape back several times to determine how clear the instructions were.

If you have a chance to observe the control room of a commercial station, follow the same procedure. Try to be there during a station break between programs when there are several split-second actions to be timed. Tape the director's pattern for later study if you wish to try your hand at directing.

**4.** Invite a student singer or musicians to perform in your studio. First, listen to the song. Then decide what camera shots should be used. Determine when to cut or dissolve. Videotape the performance and see if your tape enhances the performance of the song. Before taping, watch how performances are directed and shot on network or cable television, such as on MTV.

## ADDITIONAL RESOURCES

Armer, Alan A. *Directing Television and Film, second edition,* (Belmont, Calif., Wadsworth Publishing, 1990).

Broussard, E. Joseph, and Jack F. Holgate. *Writing and Reporting Broadcast News,* (New York, Macmillan, 1982).

Cohler, David. *Broadcast Journalism: A Guide for the Presentation of Radio and Television News,* (Englewood Cliffs, N.J., Prentice-Hall, 1985).

Dmytryk, Edward. *On Screen Directing,* (Boston: Focal Press, 1983).

Hilliard, Robert. *Writing for Television and Radio, fifth edition,* (Belmont, Calif., Wadsworth Publishing, 1991).

Hyde, Stuart. *Television and Radio Announcing, sixth edition,* (Boston, Houghton Mifflin, 1991).

Kirkman, Larry, et al. *TV Acting: A Manual for Camera Performance* (New York, Hastings, 1979).

Mamet, David. *On Directing Film* (New York, Viking Penguin, 1992).

Rabiger, Michael. *Directing: Film Techniques and Aesthetics* (Boston, Focal Press, 1989).

Ravage, John W. *Television: The Director's Viewpoint* (Boulder, Colo., Westview Press, 1981).

White, Ted, and Adrian Meppen. *Broadcast Newswriting, Reporting, and Production,* (New York, Macmillan, 1984).

Willis, Edgar. *Writing Scripts for Television, Radio, and Film* (Ft. Worth, Tex., Harcourt Brace, 1981).

# 7

# Recording the Message

In April 1956, representatives of the National Association of Radio and Television Broadcasters, meeting in Chicago, witnessed the demonstration of a machine that was to have as great an impact on the communications field as the printing press had centuries ago, a machine that could record and store visual images so they could be played back and viewed again.

Prior to this time there were two methods of recording television pictures, both unsatisfactory: the kinescope recording and the disc recording. The kinescope recording was a movie made of the pictures from the television receiver tube, or kinescope. Its quality was unpredictable because it had to go through so many different stages and forms, and it was never very good. The disc recording was unmanageable because of its size. It required a disc forty-two inches in diameter to record less than thirty minutes of sound and picture. After April 1956, however, live television and film moved into second place in favor of this new form of recording—videotape.

> *Videotape has revolutionized television production.*

The videotape recorder looks like a large-size audiotape recorder. The camera and microphone are plugged into the recorder, with its reel of magnetic recording tape. The electronic impulses of television pictures and sound are recorded on this special magnetic videotape. When the tape is played back, the impulses are again converted to picture and sound for viewing on the television screen.

*Camcorders,* with the video recorder built into the camera, allow a freedom enjoyed years ago only by Super 8 film. There are models of camcorders for home use, as well as professional models using VHS, SVHS, HiBand 8 mm video, and digital format tapes.

**FIGURE 7.1**

Camcorders make video
production simple.

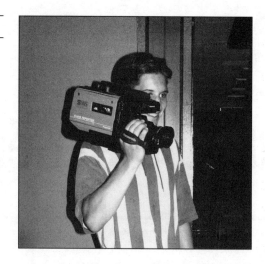

**FIGURE 7.1**

Camcorders make video production simple.

## TYPES OF VIDEOTAPE RECORDERS

Because of their obvious advantages, videotape recorders have become an essential part of a well-equipped television setup. Catalogs
like the *Educational/Instructional Broadcasting Buyers Guide* list
companies manufacturing the various types of videotape recorders.
Magazines such as *Video, Video Systems, Videomaker,* and *Video
Review* often compare the newest videocassette recorders on the
market.

Most of today's recorders for use in schools and industry are
videocassette recorders (VCRs) rather than videotape recorders
(VTRs). Three-quarter inch, one-half inch (VHS and SVHS), and Hi-
Band 8 mm cassettes are being used. Most operate the same as an au-
diocassette recorder: play, record, fast forward, and rewind are the
main functions. However, there are many new features.

### Camcorders

As mentioned earlier, camcorders have the recorder built into the
camera. Consumers have had this feature for several years; JVC's
VHS-C format allows twenty minutes of recording time. Now VHS,
SVHS, and 8mm formats are using standard tapes for up to two
hours recording time. The tape can be played back through the
camera. Formats such as 8mm video allow for special editing features such as "flying erase heads," which provide for glitch-free

stops and starts. Previously this was available only on expensive professional recorders. Professional recorders, such as Sony's Beta Cam and Panasonic's M-II, are portable as well. Many news stations use these recorders to replace the more bulky recorders (and the operator) for news remotes. These use a standard VHS tape but allow for only twenty minutes, as the speed is increased for better quality. SVHS and Hi-8 are found in some broadcast news stations. The difference between consumer grade and industrial grade equipment is decreasing. The professional format of choice is currently Beta Cam SP, increasingly Beta Cam SP Digital.

## Portable VCRs

Portable VCR recording equipment is being made in many formats and sizes, although it is becoming smaller and smaller. For many professional, cable, and industrial uses, the three-quarter inch VCR is still seen but is rapidly giving way to SVHS, HiBand 8, or Beta Cam formats. A three-quarter inch wide videotape allowing for twenty minutes worth of recording time is used, then edited on larger three-quarter inch editing equipment.

With the prohibitive cost of three-quarter inch recorders, many schools now use VHS, SVHS, and Hi-8 recorders. Editors available for VHS, SVHS, and Hi-8 tapes give them professional recording capability.

## Studio VCRs

One-inch VCRs and several digital formats are now all in use in network studios. These are out of the price range of most schools—even colleges—for production classes. Many schools are now getting into video through the use of camcorders, editors, and computers with no plan of ever having a studio.

## OPERATION OF VIDEOCASSETTE RECORDERS

### Suggestions for Recording

Operating a videocassette recorder is similar to recording audiotape. Regardless of the type of recorder you use, the following suggestions will prove helpful supplements to the manual of instructions, which you should always fasten securely to the lid of the recorder.

1. Be sure the recording head is kept free of dust. Minute particles of dust can result in "drop-outs," those imperfections that appear as white flashes on the television screen. Keep the recorder covered while not in use so that dust will not get into it. If you use it often, the recorder's video heads may have to be cleaned. This is not a job for an amateur. Tape head cleaners are available for VCRs. But *do not* do this too often; these cleaners often wear down the recording head. Follow the manufacturer's instructions regarding cleaning.

2. Keep the tape and the recorder in a cool place; videotape, like audiotape, is affected by heat. The videotape consists of a layer of iron oxide dispersion one-sixth the thickness of a human hair, coated on a plastic backing. Heat causes the plastic backing to stretch and distort the dispersion of iron oxide, resulting in imperfections in picture and sound. If you are using a videocassette, it is important not to touch the tape inside.

3. Be sure to have enough tape on hand before the recording begins. The most commonly used lengths of tape are one hour and one-half hour. VCRs have tape that lasts up to six hours of recording time. The best quality on these units is the two-hour speed. Editing system VCRs only operate at the two-hour speed.

4. Identify each tape. Label the tape, the reel, and the box in which you store it. The first shot the camera takes should be a close-up of the identification slate, giving date, time, title, series, director, producer, and technical staff. If the label peels off the reel or the reel gets placed in the wrong box, this "slate" identification on the first few inches of tape will give you accurate information about the show. Do not rely on someone's memory; that person may graduate, take another job, or forget what the tape was.

5. Most videotape recorders have a counter with three or four digits. If the segments are to be taped on one reel, record on the cover box or a separate sheet of paper the location of each segment on the tape. For example:

000–017—Pizza commercial

017–210—*Mary Poppins*

210–271—*The Cat and the Canary*

271–307—Interview with David Letterman

The numbers of these records are not completely accurate and may vary from machine to machine and even within the same machine. Even with that slight variation, it will be much easier to locate a specific athlete between 265 and 275 than to play a dozen snatches here and there. Be sure to set the counter at 000 before recording and again before playback. Professionals often use the SMPTE time code system of marking tapes so that the same frame always comes up with the same number marking it.

6. Catalog the tapes in the same way books are cataloged. Enter the information in two places: on the box containing the tape and on a card in a file box. Record the tape-box information in pencil so it is easy to correct if the tape is erased soon and a new program recorded on it. Because penciled handwriting is easily blurred, many people use type removable labels, which are pasted on the outside of the tape box and can easily be covered by new labels. The card file of information about each tape is easier to go through than shelves of tapes.

   If you have a large supply of tapes, work out some system for numbering them. The library uses the Dewey decimal or Library of Congress system based on the subject area. For instance, in the Dewey decimal system, English literature is 800–899; sports and entertainment, 700–799; science 500–599; and history, 900–999. Some people prefer to catalog the tapes according to the date they were made. Regardless of the method, *be sure to record the number on the card in the file and on the box containing the tape.*

7. Be consistent in your filing method. Most tapes are requested either by subject or by title. Someone will ask for "the tape we did on misuse of drugs" or "that interview we had with Dr. Kwan." You can prepare a cross-reference, with color coding, by pasting various colored dots (available at any stationery store) on the box of tape and on the file card, to indicate director-producer or any other information. In some

schools, the most important information is the name of the teacher giving the lecture. If requests for tapes are usually worded "Dr. Goldberg's lecture," catalog the tape under this name.

8.  In the control-room log, keep a complete record of each recording and playback fed over the air or cable, hour-by-hour through the day and week. This procedure is a legal requirement of a commercial station, a necessity for a public broadcasting station, and a time-saver in a school or college setup. The log should include the names of the producer director, and the control-room staff, such as the engineer and audio technician. A commercial station must include every spot, even a thirty-second commercial, but most schools and closed-circuit facilities find a simplified log adequate.

9.  Note on each tape the length of time it takes, and be sure to *write down the length of time of each recording!* It may not seem important when you are making the tape recording, but months and even years later, it may be necessary to know whether a certain discussion lasted 45:50 or 59:50. Someone will have to spend forty-five or sixty minutes timing the tape—*unless* the time was recorded easily with five strokes of a pen when the tape was completed. Also indicate, if possible, the number of takes in the sequence.

10. Have a schedule, and plan to weed out regularly any tapes that are no longer usable. Evaluate both content and technical quality. If you keep a record of each time a tape is played, either on the tape box or in the control-room log, you will find it easier to judge when it has passed its maximum quality.

    While weeding out the tapes, take a little time for self-criticism. If tape #100 is no better than tape #2, something is wrong. If tapes #60 through #90 follow the same format and pattern, someone is in a rut. If tapes #3 through #76 show that same wilted palm tree and the same brocaded chair, it is time for a change. You do not want a returning alumnus to watch a videotape playback and say, "Yes, that tape was made in our studio. I recognize the smear of paint on the draw curtains."

**FIGURE 7.2**

A closeup of Panasonic's latest SUPERCAM/Camcorder model. *Courtesy of Panasonic Broadcast and Television Systems Company.*

11. If you are using a cassette, index the counter to locate the precise program on the tape, and note the index number for the beginning of the program or sequence wanted.

## Recording Remotes: Electronic Field Production

When videotape is recorded outside the studio, normally only one camera is used and the tape edited to create the illusion that more than one camera was used. Here are some suggestions to make your remote recording more professional and ready for editing. Editing techniques will be discussed in the next section.

1. Plan your remote sequence carefully before you go to the location. If interviewing, think of whom you are going to interview, questions you will ask, and what video you will use to make the sequence as visual as possible. Remember, a "talking head" is *boring*.
2. Make sure you check on all equipment needed before you begin. Wouldn't it be embarrassing to set up the equipment and then discover you forgot a tape? Most studios have a checklist of all items normally needed.

3. Even though most cameras have a mike on top, it is not a good idea to use this mike for anything except "wild audio." Most recorders and cameras also accept a signal from a hand mike. Plan to bring a dynamic mike with a cord of about fifteen feet. This allows you to get away from the camera without sounding as though you are in another county. Take a wind screen in case you are outdoors in a windy location.

4. When interviewing, generally, shoot the interview first. Have the camera set on the person being interviewed; he or she is more important than you are. You might start with a two-shot and then have the camera zoom in on the other person and stay there. After the interview is over, look for video to cover what the subject said; these *inserts* (covered later in editing) can be shown where needed. After the interview, have the camera placed on a close-up of you, which also can be edited into the interview. In TV news this is called a reversal; the camera is reversed and placed on you *after* the interview is over. Shots of a reporter taking notes or nodding are often intercut with the speaker, although many news directors object because they feel nodding indicates approval of what the interviewee is saying.

5. Shoot any cover shots that could be placed into the interview. For example, if you are interviewing the football coach, after the interview shoot players in practice. See if you can pick up any video that relates to what the coach said in the interview.

6. Shoot some other material. The coach alone might be dull, so show the players or anything else at the location that may be of interest. This might give the story a different perspective.

7. Think of a way to show a beginning, middle, and end to the feature. Remember, you do not have to shoot the story in sequence. It can be edited in any order you wish. With a football remote, show practice behind you as you introduce the story.

8. When shooting an event like a fire, generally start with a long shot to identify the location of the situation. With a fire, we usually see an LS of the fire with the trucks, the building, the firefighters, and all the action. The next shot is an MS

with a closer look at the action. Then we go to an interview of a CU of a firefighter. If we started with a close-up, we would lose the identification of where the firefighter is and what is happening. Starting with a close-up, however, may be done to achieve a dramatic effect.

9. Don't forget the principles of good camera work. If outdoors, set for outdoor balance. White-balance the camera. Don't pan too fast or zoom in too much. Bring a tripod; the camera gets very heavy very quickly, and if zoomed in, any little movement looks as if you are shooting in a tornado. In an emergency, the camera operator can be braced against a building or car or anything that might give support. Or tie a piece of string to the handle of the camera, step on the other end, and pull up tightly. This provides some support and makes the camera steadier. These emergency measures do not replace a tripod. A monopod can also work and is easier to carry.

10. Check the lighting. Normally place the sun behind the back of the camera to serve as a key light. If you shoot into the sun, all you will see are silhouettes, and often the light will "flare" into the lens. Large pieces of tinfoil taped to cardboard may help reflect the light and make the shot look better.

11. When you start each sequence or interview, count down on the recorder from ten. When you get to two, count the one and zero to yourself, then start your intro. This allows the editor to pause after you say "two." He or she can simply start the playback, take off the pause on the editing deck, and the sequence will start right on cue.

12. Many of the newer VCRs have a "backspace assemble." This feature allows the recorder to run during an assemble edit so that any glitching will be minimal. This must be compensated for during shooting. After you place the camera on pause, the recorder backs up the tape just a little so that when you hit the start button, the tape will be rolling as you reach the spot where the new recording should begin.

After you finish your last word in shooting any section of tape, count about three seconds before you stop the camera. This allows for backspacing the recorder and for your editing later. Stopping the camera immediately after the last word may "upcut," or cut off, the last words of the tape as you edit. You will be thankful for those three seconds during editing.

## EDITING VIDEOTAPE

A successful television program demands artistic judgment, imaginative directing, and technical skill, but a basic element in its success is the editing of the tape.

In commercial motion pictures, the film editor's talent can make or break the final product, even though it may leave an actor's dreams on the cutting room floor. Videotape cannot be edited like film, by cutting and gluing, because the actual pictures are not visible on the surface of the tape, but it can be edited according to its own properties.

Bob Hope's televised programs of Christmas shows presented to men and women in the armed services all over the world have become classic examples of how hundreds of hours of performances can be condensed into one hour of tape. They emphasize reaction shots of hundreds of service personnel for the benefit of home viewers, including families watching for a five-second close-up of a loved one.

The director of a high school production of *The Mikado* and the videotape editor of a local CBS outlet edited a 3-hour tape of the musical to one hour without distorting the sequence of scenes or the plot.

The tape editor and the engineer in a Denver studio made 375 cuts and splices in eight hours of recorded events of the national Boy Scout Jamboree to produce a sixty-minute telecast. Watch a thirty-second commercial on videotape and count the shots.

The actual process of editing is highly technical and varies according to the type of recorder used. If the director knows that the tape is to be edited, he or she can direct with that fact in mind and provide places where the tape will be easy to cut and splice. For instance, a scene can end with the performers leaving the stage or walking out of the picture frame. The next scene can begin with the performers reentering. The splice can be made at the spot where the stage is empty, with no movement being recorded.

The editor cannot see the images on the surface of the videotape. To determine exactly where to cut, the editor must be guided by the magnetized impulses recorded on the tape.

To understand how editing is done, you must understand how videotape is recorded. Three separate recordings are made simultaneously: audio, video, and a control track. The video portion is recorded in the middle of the tape at a slight slant. Helical scan recorders (all VCRs) are often called "slant tracks" because the picture is recorded in this manner. A series of two (in most VCRs) video heads are located in a bar or drum that spins rapidly. The videotape is wrapped around this drum, and the two heads pass over the tape, giving the tape-to-head speech necessary for placing the video information on the tape. After the tape passes over the video heads, it passes a stationary head, with the audio information recorded at the top and the control track information at the bottom of the tape (see Figure 7.3).

The control track allows videotapes recorded on another machine to be played back on your machine. The control track is similar to the sprocket holes in a film; it makes sure the tape is going across the recording and playback heads at an exact speed and location. The tracking pulses are not seen in the program but are necessary for proper playback. Most video recorders have a tracking control that can be moved to ensure the best picture during playback.

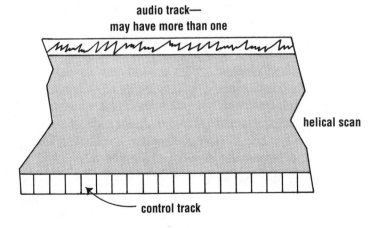

audio track—
may have more than one

helical scan

control track

**FIGURE 7.3**

The videotape editor must be guided by the magnetized impulses recorded on the tape. Three signals are recorded: the picture, the sound, and the field pulses consisting of quarter-inch spaced blips.

Unlike audiotape, videotape editing is not done by physically cutting the tape. In earlier days, the videotape editor did cut the tape, editing it like film. Today, editing is an electronic process whereby the tape is *dubbed* onto a second tape by the use of an electronic editor. At least two machines are needed to edit a tape.

Most consumer VCRs are not really meant to edit videotapes, but you can accomplish some simple "crash" edits. Do not expect glitch-free or roll-free edits with these because they do not have the flying erase heads that allow for clean, professional edits.

To edit on a nonediting recorder, do the following:

1. You will need two video recorders; one will playback the raw or unedited tape, and the other will record the final tape in the order of final playback.
2. You will need a set of dubbing cables for the best recording. Inexpensive audio cables with "RCA"-type audio plugs will do.
3. Connect the cables from the audio and video "out" of the playback recorder to the video and audio "in" of the machine you will record into.
4. Place a new tape in the deck you are recording into. Place the recorded tape into the playback deck and cue to the first segment. It will be much easier if you have logged the start of each sequence by noting the number on the meter. Be sure to reset the numbers to 000 before you start.
5. Listen for the countdown on the tape. When the reporter reaches two, push the pause button.
6. Start the recording deck and play for a few seconds to build up speed, then let up on the pause button on the playback deck.
7. Play past the end cue of the first sequence, and stop both machines.
8. Cue the exact end on the recording deck and press "pause."
9. Cue the next sequence on the playback deck to two on the countdown.
10. Let up the "pause" on the play deck, and let up on the play deck on the final tape recorder. Keep repeating this until the tape is done. This allows only for assemble-type edits where you must piece the various parts together.

## Industrial and Professional Editing Recorders

Industrial and broadcast grade recorders allow for glitch-free edits. Again, depending on the quality of the machines, some recorders work much better than others. Generally, there are two types of edits: assemble and insert.

### Assemble edit

In an assemble edit, one sequence after another is recorded or assembled. You start outside the gym with a stand-up introduction. You then go into the gym and voiceover basketball practice. Next you interview the coach. Interviews with the team members follow, and you conclude again outside the gym. These need not be recorded in sequence, but this becomes the final order of the tape through an assemble edit. Editing consoles range from very inexpensive editors to computer-controlled systems costing thousands of dollars. Even though the quality of the edit varies, the type remains the same.

### FIGURE 7.4

The JVC Edit-Desk is a state-of-the-art videotape editing system. *Photo courtesy of JVC Professional Products.*

An assemble edit simply allows you to go from the end of existing tape to another sequence with as little interruption as possible.

### Insert edit

Insert edits allow the editor to go from a piece of recorded tape to a new videotape and then back to the original tape with no interruption in the original tape. Perhaps you are interviewing the football coach before a big game. As he speaks, you would like to show the players in practice. You took footage of practice after the interview, so cue it up in the playback deck and insert just the video into the recording, keeping the original audio track. Go back to the coach's interview when needed. You could also insert a close-up of you taking notes. You can see the possibilities of insert editing.

Again, if you take a cable access course, most cable companies will show you how to edit with their professional recorders. Videotape editing is really an art form that, with practice, allows for some very creative videotapes. You do not need expensive materials to practice editing techniques. There are special editing VHS, SVHS, and HiBand 8 decks that will give professional edits. TV stations use three-quarter-inch, one-inch, SVHS, HiBand 8, Betacam, MII, or digital recorders for editing.

**FIGURE 7.5**

Students edit a videotape program.

## USES OF VIDEOTAPE

As you improve your taping skills, your uses for videotape will increase in number and variety. They are as numerous as the kinds of machines available and as varied as the creativity of the directors and the technical skill of the operators. For example, because the playback of a videotape enables both the performers and the production staff to see themselves as others see them, an important use of videotaping is constructive self-criticism. In the minds of performers are visions of what they want to convey to their audience, visions sometimes so vivid and clear that they think they have transmitted them to the cameras. Only when they actually see what comes across can they determine whether or not they communicated effectively (at least as far as the camera is concerned).

## Tape Library

Videotapes provide a valuable record of events. Recordings of performances and significant moments in personal or professional life, not to mention recordings of historical events, can be saved for future viewing and reviewing. On a practical note, for commercial and school television stations, videotapes can be stored, under proper conditions, and become a reference library. Such a library can also save the day in an emergency. If the lights burn out in the studio, if the camera blows up, if the talent breaks a leg, a tape can be hauled out of the library, and the show will go on!

In addition to networks and broadcasting stations, various organizations have videotape libraries. The Public Broadcasting Service maintains a library of videotapes that circulate among the educational television stations or are fed to them. There are television libraries, like the Great Plains National Instructional Television Library at Lincoln, Nebraska, which rent and sell videotaped series and programs to educational stations, universities, and schools. The Public Television Library sells schools videotapes of the television programs seen on the Public Broadcasting Service.

**FIGURE 7.6**

Recordings of movies in laser disc format do not deteriorate with age as recordings on videotape do. *Photo courtesy of Panasonic Broadcast & Television Systems Company.*

At the local level, universities and a few public schools maintain libraries of videotaped lesson and reference materials, programs, and supplementary materials. These are placed in a dial-access information-retrieval system. When someone dials the number of a taped lesson or program, the system feeds it into the television receiver in a library carrel.

## NEW TECHNOLOGY: THE DIGITAL REVOLUTION

We have entered the Information Age—where anything and everything is recorded on the microchip. The technology of media is advancing and expanding every day, in ways we can't even imagine. Our world—not just telecommunications and media, but our whole way of life— is being overwhelmed by the Digital Revolution.

With the advent of digital technology, methods of recording have changed radically. Compact discs are the most popular example; they are as popular as tapes and have made records obsolete. There are many other examples. Digital technology basically works like this: When you record something on tape, it gets worn as it ages, and the quality decreases. If you've ever listened to an old tape that you haven't heard for years, you've probably noticed it doesn't sound as good as it once did. Also, the tape becomes brittle with age and can snap and break. Every time you listen to a tape, or watch a video, you wear away part of the magnetic strip that contains the information. When a CD is made, the information (music) is converted into numbers. Incoming information is sampled at 44,100 times a second and compressed into digital "numbers" of sixteen bits each (on standard equipment). This prevents any deterioration with repeated use. The CD is simply reread by a laser, but never touched physically. Tape heads and record needles eventually damage tapes and records. The laser is nothing but light, so it can't do any damage.

Compact discs are not the only digital format. Laser discs have movies recorded on them and have been around as long as videotapes. Videotapes became more popular simply because you can record over them. However, you can now record on some CD and laser disc players, although these models are still fairly expensive. DATs (digital audiotapes) are competing with compact discs, though they will have no real advantage when recordable compact discs enter a reasonable price range.

## Advantages of Digital Technology

What are the advantages of laser and compact discs? For one thing, they don't deteriorate with age. You could still be listening to the compact discs that you own now when you're a lot older. But there are other advantages as well. Random access allows you to skip to any part of the disc. You can skip to your favorite songs on a compact disc, and program them in any order you choose. This becomes invaluable in editing. Also, the picture quality is much stronger with digital equipment. Movie buffs own laser disc players because they can see beautiful, epic films like *2001* and *Apocalypse Now* with the best possible picture.

Digital technology has completely changed the field of television and film. Some video editing systems are completely digital, with everything stored on computer. This is called nonlinear editing. The greatest advantage of this system has to do with rerecording. When you copy a signal on video, by copying something from one videotape to another, you lose part of the picture quality. Each copy is called a "generation." Most videos have only four or five "generations" before the picture is unwatchable. With digital equipment, you can rerecord something as many times as you want without losing any picture quality. This is possible because the video is recorded as numbers, being reread each time. There are other advantages to digital editing as well, though. The time saved in nonlinear editing is mind-boggling: Think how much faster you could edit if you could see any shot instantly with the push of a button. Also, with nonlinear editing systems you can insert a shot without re-editing the rest of the video. This is because it is stored like a computer program rather than recorded on an analog tape. Top-grade studios record everything on computer without ever using videotape. These are called, not surprisingly, *tapeless studios.*

Digital equipment provides a better quality picture and faster production time. Many TV studios are going all-digital as a result. The time-base corrector (TBC) was one of the first advances in digital video processing. It has been around for about twenty years. It can scan a videotape image and improve its quality, taking out any "glitches" by converting the image to digital.

> *Digital technology has made the "tapeless" television studio possible.*

## HDTV, Computers, and Moviemaking

One of the biggest and most important digital advances is HDTV—high definition television. It marks the biggest advance in television since color came along in the 1960s. HDTV provides wide-screen TV images nearly as clear and bright as 35mm film, and crisp digital sound. It will take a different type of television set to receive HDTV broadcasts. Basically, the electron gun inside an HDTV set scans in a different manner. Both sets have a TV screen containing tiny pixels that are illuminated when the gun scans across them in rows. In regular television sets, the gun skips every other row and then goes back across. With HDTV, the gun scans every row in sequence, providing a clarity impossible with ordinary sets. Networks will broadcast on both regular television and HDTV. HDTV sets will be very expensive at first. However, the Federal Communications Commission (FCC) has set a date for some time after the year 2000 when normal television signals will no longer be broadcast, and you will only be able to watch HDTV.

With digital television, the differences between computers and television, as well as film, will be blurred. Already the gaps have closed immensely in the past thirty years. Special effects for films such as *Jurassic Park* and *Terminator 2* are generated entirely by computers, providing more realistic effects than were possible just a few years earlier. Picture quality on television will be strong enough to have implications in factory automation, medical imaging, even national security. And some time in the future, virtual reality and computer-generated actors will become a reality.

Video is rapidly matching the quality and clarity of picture and sound found in film. This will save millions for moviemakers, whose biggest expense can be film and processing. The independent film market will explode. Already we are seeing the "camcorder generation" of filmmakers begin to enter Hollywood. Robert Rodrigues, a filmmaker in his twenties whose first film, *El Mariachi*, was a smash hit at film festivals in 1992, began by making videos on his camcorder and editing them with two home VCRs. Innumerable avenues are opening for creative young people interested in video and film. This is the best time in history to be interested in media as a career.

## IT'S A WRAP

Videotape and digital technology have revolutionized the way television programs and movies are recorded, improving the picture and speeding up production in the process. With digital technology, we can look forward to the clarity of high definition television and the limitless possibilities of virtual reality. As the quality of video improves, young and/or independent producers can realize their moviemaking dreams without needing the backing of huge Hollywood studios. State-of-the-art computers used to generate special effects are creating television and movie magic.

Technology has not eliminated the need for talented directors who know what to shoot, who understand the proper sequence and the best angles, who spot that unexpected detail that delights the viewer. Camcorders and portable videocassette recorders provide such professionals with high-quality editing features at a reasonable cost; they make the technically difficult but essential job of editing a little easier.

For you, the technical progress in the field means access to affordable, quality equipment while you're still a student, and greater media career opportunities once you graduate. Now is an excellent time to enter the dynamic world of television and video production.

# 7

# Video Lab

1. Produce a music video using a single camera shoot and videotape. If you cannot locate a group or singer, have a performer or "talent" lip sync to a popular recording. A suggestion for this program: Record the presentation from start to finish on one tape, and use another for inserts using the original audio. It is hard to match lip syncs from tape to tape. What inserts would you include in the production?

2. Produce a short sequence on one aspect of your school and offer it to your local cable company. Perhaps you could film a magazine-format program about your school to be shown on cable. Some schools produce a weekly newscast for in-school showing. Each week several stories are edited and used in the newscast. Many schools now produce a series of features on their school and use this as a video yearbook.

3. Prepare a local documentary on a subject of interest to your school or area. You might cover the Fourth of July celebration, a winning team's season, or a special event within your school.

4. Videotape and edit a school athletic program for your community. Perhaps you can feature a volleyball or wrestling tournament to generate public interest. Show some matches and interviews with athletes and coaches. Plan to produce the program either for your school or for the public access channel of your local cable company.

## TAKE TWO

1. Instant replays have improved television sports viewing. Debate whether referees on the field or court should have access to immediate playback.

2. What is the basic difference between an assemble edit and an insert edit of videotape?

3. What three recordings are made on videotape simultaneously?

4. Imagine you are producing a segment of a local cable company's magazine program. You are assigned to cover the opening of the local swimming pool for the season. Explain how you would cover this story using a camcorder. What shots would you use? Whom would you interview? How would you introduce and close the story? Plan the development of this segment from start to finish.

5. Videotape is being used today to record weddings and graduations. Imagine that you have been hired to videotape such a ceremony. Plan the shooting from start to finish. Think of the visual element; what would you want to *show* during this program?

## ADDITIONAL RESOURCES

Anderson, Gary H. *Video Editing and Post-Production: A Professional Guide, second edition*, (White Plains, N.Y., Knowledge Industry Publications, Inc., 1988).

Caruso, James R., and Mavis E. Arthur. *A Beginning Guide to Producing TV*, (Englewood Cliffs, N.J., Prentice-Hall, 1982).

Millerson, Gerald. *Video Production Handbook*, (Boston, Focal Press, 1992).

White, Gordon. *Video Techniques*, (Boston, Focal Press, 1982).

Yoakam, Richard, and Charles Cremer. *ENG: Television News and the New Technology*, (New York, Random House, 1985).

# Considering Careers in Media

After you graduate from high school, there are a variety of ways to pursue a career in media. Although there are a growing number of opportunities, careers in media can often be hard work and pay very little. If you pursue a job in broadcasting, the film industry, or the television/video production field, it should be because you enjoy the work. Success in this field depends on determination. This is not a field to enter for high earnings or security. However, it is a very interesting and challenging field, and some people have become very successful at it. We will outline the basic jobs that are available, but first here are some things you should be considering:

## PREPARATION

### College

It is difficult to excel in any field today without a college education. If you plan to go to college and are interested in majoring in film, broadcasting, or communication, you will have, in essence, two separate hurdles to jump. The first is the university itself; you must pass the basic university requirements before even being considered for a certain major. Then you must get into the department or arts school at that university. Universities base their requirements on grades and aptitude tests. Some are stricter than others, so you should be working to keep your grade point average as high as possible. Arts schools and communications departments usually ask for a portfolio or writing sample. You should look for a school with a strong department in the field that interests you. If you're interested in TV or radio, apply to a college that has a working radio or TV production facility so that you can gain experience.

## Portfolio

You should be making a video portfolio of the television programs and videos you work on. This will be useful in a number of ways. When you apply for college, if you major in the media arts, the college may ask to see a video of the work you've done. This can help you get into the school you choose, and it may also give you faster access to higher level courses or internships. A portfolio can also help you to apply for jobs and for grants. Grants or funding to produce your project may help a great deal if you try to work independently in the film world.

If your programs have been viewed or used by any groups, you should document that usage for inclusion in your portfolio. Even an award for a local video competition will show that you are serious about your work.

**FIGURE 8.1**

Student broadcasters at a college radio station gain experience as part of their education. *Photo courtesy of WONC, North Central College, Naperville, Illinois.*

## Internships

The experience you can gain as an intern is also invaluable. If you are unable to get in the school you want, it may be worth taking internships while studying at another college. This experience can help you get into a more selective school, and it will improve your chances of getting a job. Even if all you're doing is filing videotapes, you're meeting people. These people may help you get jobs that may not be advertised. This is a business that relies heavily on "networking" and making connections; knowing someone at a TV station or production company can help a great deal in getting you your first job. Every internship is an opportunity to check out potential fields of study and employment. Even discovering that you dislike an area is beneficial because that helps you narrow your focus. You should also be willing to work without salary, as a lot of good internships provide no pay. Many people have succeeded by doing all the work they could as an intern, and getting noticed. Now, here's a list of possible career choices in media.

## BROADCAST, NONBROADCAST, AND CABLE TV

This is probably the biggest area of growth in media. With cable, hundreds and hundreds of channels are being created with a need for product. And with HDTV, the quality of television becomes much closer to film. Small, local stations are now being nationally broadcast because of cable TV. The basic jobs in a television station are management, programming, and engineering.

## Management

People with management training and skills oversee every aspect of studio production. This includes station management, guest relations, studio scheduling and operation, budgeting, clerical staff, and relations with the networks or cable affiliates. These people are not involved with actual television production. They deal with outside relations and make decisions involving programming, cost, sales, and supervision. They must respond to the needs of the community they are broadcasting to or the corporation they are serving, in order to keep profits from dropping. Television is a business like any other, and it must meet the needs of its audience.

> *At small TV stations, the programming and production departments are one in the same.*

## Programming

Programming is where all of the creative, "idea" work is done, as well as the production of the shows. Programming includes sports, news, special events, political broadcasts, religious broadcasts, films, training, education, commercial, promotional, and corporate image creation. In larger stations, the production staff and the programming staff are separate. The programming staff decides on the content of the shows, arranging time slots, sorting through audition tapes and TV pilots, and overseeing production. If a station focuses on educational broadcasts, they decide what is "educational." If a show is running low in the ratings, they decide whether to change its time slot or drop the show. They also often come up with the concepts for shows that will later be produced. The head writer for a TV show is part of the programming staff. In film, the director has the most power on the set. In television, the head-writer of the show has that honor. The director of a show changes from week to week, but it is the writing staff that remains constant and decides what happens on the program.

## Production Staff

The production staff involves everyone who directly helps with making the program. This includes directors, camera operators, audio technicians, control-room technicians, graphic artists, floor managers, and lighting technicians. Some people in production may never enter the set of the show. These include graphic artists who sit at a computer during the show's production, or a remote crew sent out on location to record a local event. The atmosphere in a TV studio during production is inevitably chaotic to the distant observer, and sometimes chaotic even to those who are running the show. If you are interested in a job in production, you will most likely start with an internship working as a gopher for the technical staff. This way you can observe how the studio works and get basic training. It is those who are most persistent, and offer a lot of assistance for little or no pay, who eventually get promoted.

## Engineering

Engineering includes all of the technical personnel in a station. This is an essential department; no television station can broadcast if it is not broadcast quality. The technical personnel are responsible for the design, operation, installation, and maintenance of the studio's equipment. Often engineers will be involved with the production, handling certain equipment and lights. They could also be working in the quiet seclusion of the transmitting station or off in a repair shop. Learning the skill of maintaining and repairing equipment can make you extremely valuable to a station. Often a school or station will have one person on hand whom they rely on for all of their repairs. You can earn good money and have a relatively secure career, providing you keep up with the changing technology.

## News

You may be interested specifically in broadcast journalism. Some colleges have special programs that combine journalism and a broadcast TV/radio background. Again, you should find a school with a small TV or radio station, one that broadcasts a weekly or daily news program. Also, you can work as an intern in a local newsroom. Often the anchors also write or cover one of the big segments on the show. Other times they simply read the news that a staff of writers has put together earlier. The pressure to create a new show every day makes broadcast news a very frantic and stressful field to enter, but it is also very exciting.

## ADVERTISING AND PUBLIC RELATIONS

## Public Relations

This is an enormous field. Nearly all companies and stations employ people for public relations. Public relations firms are often hired to help the executives of a company learn how to project a certain public image. These firms teach executives how to behave in stressful interview situations. Even politicians hire public relations people to carefully construct the proper image; since the advent of television, elections have basically been won or lost based on image. Also, stations have a public relations department to publicize them. Notice the ads in local newspapers and on TV for a certain news program, and you will realize the importance of public relations.

*Many television production careers exist in the advertising field.*

## Advertising

Advertising is a huge industry. There are probably more television producers and directors working for advertising agencies than for actual television stations. They form the creative production branch of the industry, the "idea people." The other, larger part is made up of management. The two key types of managers are account executives and brand managers. The "idea people" are assigned products by account executives, and they compete for the chance to produce a commercial for the product. The brand manager represents the company that makes the product. This is a high pressure industry, but it offers an opening into the film/TV business for a lot of directors, writers, producers, and actors. Actors often rely on commercial work to pay their salary, as these are the only acting jobs that pay a lot for a small amount of work (unless you're famous, of course). Actors can work for months in a small theater production, living off the residuals of a commercial job.

## FILM PRODUCTION

There are differences and similarities between the film and TV industries. It is difficult to say which is harder to get into. To a certain degree it depends on your approach. Like any business, Hollywood relies a lot on connections, and a lot of people have succeeded because they "knew somebody." If you're most interested in the production end, the conventional approach is to start working as a P.A.—production assistant, or a gopher—and work your way up. This can take a long time and depends on your eagerness, charisma, and luck. "Craft people"—including gaffers, technicians, grips, art directors, set designers, assistant directors, camera operators, cinematographers, and sometimes directors—enter the business this way. Film is a collaborative medium, and on a good film a number of people deserve credit for the outcome. This varies from film to film. Martin Scorsese's films owe a great debt to the cinematographer; whereas in Bernardo Bertolucci's film *The Conformist*, the real star is the art direction. Increasingly, successful directors are film school graduates. Craft people or technicians must gain entry into highly selective guilds and unions.

## Writing

If you're a writer, getting into Hollywood is a whole different ball game. You must go through the fabled and debilitating process of "pitching" your script to producers. Unlike in television or theater, the writer is on the bottom rung of the power ladder in film. Every production company has a staff of writers on call to take over a script once it's bought. Generally a writer has very little control over what happens to a script once it's bought by a producer. This process of hiring people to do rewrites is intended to improve the script, or give it more mainstream appeal. However, because Hollywood writers get credit in a film according to how many scenes they create—not how many lines they change—the script sometimes becomes a muddled and incoherent mess as writers compete for billing. After selling a few scripts or "spec scripts"—sample scripts written for existing shows or original movie scripts—and having them produced, a writer may gain more creative control.

Most writers who get any respect in Hollywood, however, have come from a literary or theatrical background and have already made a name for themselves. Successful producers in Hollywood usually come from the offices of Hollywood corporations. They have worked their way up the traditional corporate ladder; many have MBAs and law degrees. They can come from other places as well; many successful writers, directors, and actors—such as Spike Lee, Robert Redford, Goldie Hawn, and Sally Field—turn to producing to increase creative control over a film. Popular actors produce films they want to star in, in order to push the film successfully through the Hollywood mill. In this way, many great films with limited commercial appeal have been made.

*In most cases, a writer loses control over a script once a producer buys it.*

Except for the production company that funds the film, the producer has the most control over a film's outcome. He or she decides who will direct and star in a film, how the money will be spent, and whether the film is progressing according to plan. After the producer, the director has the most control. The director is considered to have complete creative control over a film, although sometimes the producer makes creative decisions as well. This is why many writers try to direct or produce as well, to control what happens to their script.

**FIGURE 8.2**

Computer-generated video graphics play an integral part in television, film, and video production today. *Photo courtesy of Corplex Systems Group, Lincolnwood, Illinois.*

## COMPUTERS

This field is by far the fastest growing in the media industry. Non-linear editing, HDTV, digital recording, and computer animation are overtaking media and taking on new horizons. Computers are making the impossible possible. The state-of-the-art special effects in *Jurassic Park* are just the beginning: The future will bring computer-generated actors and virtual reality films. Computers are blurring the lines between video, film, and television.

To enter the field of computers in media, you should major in a computer science program in college, or study computer graphics at an art school. You could focus on special effects for film, or study to be an HDTV technician.

These are the basic jobs available in the media industry.. Most people who get jobs in the industry have a college education, and most have some sort of portfolio to show off their work. You must be ready to compete with these people for a career. The media field is a vast industry that caters to a variety of interests. You may be business-minded and interested in becoming a producer or a station manager;

perhaps you are more "creative," and want to be a movie director or writer. Whatever your area of interest, work constantly to improve your skill. If you want to be a writer, you should work on writing every day. If you want to be a station manager, you should look into internships and apprenticeships at local studios. Always keep your mind on your goals because it takes a lot of hard work to have a successful career in media. That's why it's not a good career to enter for money. It must be a labor of love, or you won't be determined enough to succeed and endure the difficult aspects of the media industry.

Consider your future and career options as you read the following speech delivered by Brianne Murphy, currently Director of Photography for the television series "Love and War" and the first woman to become a member of the American Society of Cinematographers. Ms. Murphy addressed this speech to student filmmakers at the 1990 National Student Media Festival in Anaheim, California.

> *Most media jobs require a college education.*

## CREATIVELY BEING THERE

*Brianne Murphy, A.S.C.*

I once thought that speech wasn't very important...that I wouldn't have to think much about saying things with words. I would express myself using a camera and balancing and managing light to say what I felt. If I'd had a movie camera when I was a kid, I probably wouldn't have bothered learning how to talk.

It's just as well that I did...it helps a lot when I find myself looking at all your faces wondering what I'm going to say.

I'm going to talk about "Creatively Being There." That's an expression I heard recently from Price Hicks [Director of Education, Programs, and Services of the Academy of Television Arts and Sciences]. It took me by surprise, and I thought about it. It means a lot. It's a good idea. Latch onto it for yourselves.

I've looked at the tapes of this year's winners and have seen some extraordinary work. Are the winners here? Would you please stand so that those of us who are already in the industry will recognize you when we see you again? Congratulations. Are any of the losers here? Please stand. You deserve to be congratulated for enduring rejection. You are learning one of our industry's prime lessons: Be rejected, *but keep coming back.* This is only the beginning. Congratulations to all of you and to your long-suffering teachers.

I wish I had had a movie camera when I was a little girl because I figured out that at some mysterious time grownups *suddenly completely forgot* what it felt like to be a child. They forgot and could never again remember. So I knew that this would happen to me too. (I'd write down my feelings on paper to help me to remember...when that horrible thing of forgetting happened to me. Of course I lost the paper.) If any of you believe that this is true, you can now tell us with your cameras what *you* feel and have it preserved for yourselves when it comes time for you to understand kids and *you* have forgotten...imagine...forgotten what it feels like to be a kid! Well, you know what you're feeling *now*, and you can tell us with your cameras...so do it before you forget.

I went to college planning to become a teacher and a journalist...It's a wonderful thing to teach. But then I discovered the art of making movies and for a while I thought I was a moviemaker instead...you know, you can't be a moviemaker without being a teacher and a journalist.

I understand that you come from schools all over the United States and from other countries as well. I personally went to twenty-three schools all over the place. You know where I learned the most?...at the *movies*! Oh, I learned to read, write, and count in the classroom. I learned a bunch in the classroom.

So why do I say I learned from the movies? Look at what my generation and some of yours have gotten from the movies. We learned that beautiful women smoked and blew smoke out their noses in candlelit cafes. Many of those beauties are dead...died of cancer.

We learned that macho men, daring, handsome, patriotic heroes, kind doctors under stress, *sports legends*, all smoked cigarettes.

God...what horrible lessons the moviemakers were putting before us!

We were taught that a cocktail or two or three was a gracious habit...that a good swift shot of whiskey was what you deserved if you just saved the whole frontier or needed a bullet removed.

We watched our teen idols drinking and driving fast cars and killing themselves.

No, nobody was telling us that we were being turned on to alcoholism and drug abuse, but that's exactly what was happening.

Next the moviemakers suggested that drugs were funny or glamorous and "mind expanding." They suggested that free love and infidelity were O.K. Pretty soon many people who loved the movies were confused, addicted, paranoid, terminally ill, suicidal, and fed up.

I'm sure no one deliberately set out to corrupt moviegoers....There was no way to know what a powerful force the movies were going to be.

We learn a lot of good things from the movies and from TV. We've seen some of the world's finest books on film: *Mutiny on the Bounty*, *Wuthering Heights*,...,*A Tale of Two Cities*, *Batman*.

We've traveled the world, *Out of Africa*, to India with *Ghandi*, and everywhere with Encyclopaedia Brittanica and National Geographic and with independent travelogue makers.

We've gotten to know a lot about exotic animals and the importance of their care and preservation through Jacques Cousteau, *Gorillas in the Mist*, and hundreds of animal kingdom pictures.

Another fascinating form of filmmaking is the documentary and news genre. I shot news and documentaries, and I've got to tell you... *that's exciting*. Every day is different, and you're right in the middle of what's going on. What you shoot really makes a difference.

We have marched with Martin Luther King and listened to his speech at the Washington Monument. We have seen what war looks like in Central America, what student rebellions look like in China; we've watched spaceships take off and land; we've seen presidents inaugurated, a president assassinated, hostages taken, planes crash, a little girl rescued from a cold dark hole, civil wars, and civil rights clashes....We've seen oil spills that threaten the wildlife, ecology, community. We've seen toxic waste and Chernobyl; we've been made aware of all sorts of dangers.

Daily we learn through the horrible news stories about death, hate, destruction and disaster...and that drugs are all around us. Only the well aware and strong and the people committed to living wholesome, worthwhile lives are going to escape its clutches...all this because people like us, like you and I, have chosen to make the art of telling and teaching, the art of moviemaking our profession and, therefore, our *responsibility*.

You see,...we're all teachers. What are we going to teach? Every time you pick up a camera, you're making a suggestion...an impression. It's up to *you* just *what* you teach. You can build a person by giving hope, giving the facts, the impression that will make him do or feel or act a certain way, or...you can turn your talent into a destructive, negative force. The choice is yours.

I came here to congratulate you and hopefully inspire you to do great things with this wonderful head start and opportunity you have through your talent and good work, your excellent schools, and your dedicated teachers.

I don't mean to sound like another "Just say no" commercial; it's only that I'm so overwhelmed by the enormity of your responsibility that I had to share these thoughts with you.

You probably want to know what life as a Hollywood cinematographer is all about.

Is it glamorous?

Sure it is if you love hard work, long hours, constant creativity, travel, dust, dirt, soundstages, movie stars, bit players, extras, actors, explosive egos, a good scene well played, a masterful director, an inspired cinematographer, color, lights, makeup, costumes, hard work, long hours, dust, dirt...sure, it's the most glamorous thing in the world.

On a Hollywood set the director of photography or cinematographer is in charge of the photography and therefore in charge of the entire technical crew, since everyone's efforts are concentrated in the same direction; putting the image on the screen.

I work most closely with the director. She or he will tell me the look and the feeling she'd like from the movie. We discuss mood, feelings, what's important. Once I'm sure that what I'm about to create with light, shadow, movement, and texture is in sync with the director's vision, then I go to work with all the other members of the crew so that each of us may contribute our best.

Every picture starts with a new script. Here it is that the whole process starts...with the written word...and our ideas of communicating with pictures alone is a fallacy. The director and I had to exchange ideas with words, and I have to tell my crew what's going on...with words. In a nutshell, if you're going to be a filmmaker, be sure that you're literate. It's all part of a big picture called "*Communication.*"

Study literature, art, geography, history, music, people...not just in school but wherever you can...it's all part of the moviemaking process.

Then you've got to learn the tools of your trade, the cameras, the lights, and how to **make** them work for you. Watch the pros, see their work, learn all the tricks of the crafts. There are more than two creative positions on the set. Investigate them all; you might be surprised.

I've shot many pictures. I don't know if you've seen any, but now that you know me I hope you'll start reading the credits. When you do start reading credits, you're in for a happy surprise when you realize all the great jobs there are.

…Currently you might catch *Sidewalk Motel*, which tells us a disturbing amount about the homeless people…*In the Best Interest of the Child* is a Movie of The Week…about the child abuse problem that must be uncovered and dealt with. Afterschool Specials are particularly powerful in putting before us problems such as *Sixteen and Getting Straight*, about young people who were addicted to drugs and their attempts to get straight; *Student Affairs*, about sexually transmitted diseases; or *Five Finger Discount*, about kleptomania.

There used to be an expression about movies: "If you want to send a message go to Western Union." Wrong. *Entertainment* is a far more powerful communicator.

Each episode of *Little House On The Prairie*, *Father Murphy*, and *Highway to Heaven* had something to say. We all have something to say…the object is to say it responsibly.

The question I think I'm asked most often is, "How do you get started in the world of filmmaking?"

When I started in the business there were no film schools, and the art of moviemaking was a carefully guarded secret handed from father to son. What to do? *Creatively be there.*

I… started by running away with the circus. That's a story in itself, and I'm not suggesting that any of you do that. Today there are hundreds of safe, sane, intelligent, and lucky ways

to get in the business if that's what you want.

My first opportunity to operate a motion picture camera came when I was working as a script supervisor/makeup person on a picture called *Man Beast The Abominable Snowman*. We were 6000 feet up in snow covered mountains when they discovered that the yeti suit was too small for the actor, but a perfect fit for the camera operator…they put the camera operator in the monster suit and let me operate the camera!…So don't let anyone tell you that "being there" isn't important.

Another way—

See if there is anyone in your community who is going to make a video or film production.

How can you get in touch with this person?

What you want to do is get a job on that production doing *anything* they'll let you do…no, they're not going to ask you to direct or to be the cinematographer.…They might need someone to run errands, to make phone calls, to sweep the floor, to help with the makeup, hair, or wardrobe.

They might just tell you they don't need you at all…they have everyone they need…and they probably do…there's a line for every job in your hometown as well as here in Hollywood.

So they don't want you. Maybe they made a mistake, and they really do but don't know it. See if there is something they need that you can help them to get. Maybe if you are there every day, observing, taking notes, watching what people do, you can learn aspects of filmmaking you never dreamed of—just stay out of the way and avoid eviction.

OK, say they never did hire you on that one…they even chased you away. See if there is a church, or hospital, a senior citizens group, or a day care center that needs a little film or tape made for them for raising funds, or influencing the citizens, or something like that. Go to the organization and offer your services and talents, and those of your willing friends—for free....

Convince them that you can deliver. Present them with a reasonable budget to cover your costs so your folks don't end up paying...and soon you'll be making pictures. Build yourselves good reputations. Do what you say you're going to do.

Be early, work late, show enthusiasm!

You're entering what I consider to be the most exciting and rewarding profession there is.

*Reprinted by permission of the author.*

It's going to be difficult because the competition is overwhelming, the rejection is recurring, and the sense of humor you'll need is going to be your life jacket as well as your flak jacket.

Learn to be a good Assistant Something...manage to work with a good teacher and role model...a good master will give you your deserved break, and then you can set your own style. Don't try to start at the top...the fall is too fast if you haven't climbed the stairs.

You've already taken the first steps...never be afraid...Start doing it, and the power to do it will come to you. Spread your wings...soar above your inhibitions. Innovate...experiment...initiate...create...You have no limits except those of your imaginations.

## IT'S A WRAP

Perhaps you daydream of becoming the anchor on the local news, a successful television actor, or a famous Hollywood producer. What can you do now to work toward those goals? Education and planning are the key. Keep your grades up so that you can enter the college or drama school of your choice. Develop a portfolio of your best work. Investigate internships and less-than-glamorous entry-level jobs.

Keep an open mind as you consider career options, and remember the vast scope of the field. Your options are many: management, programming, production, writing, engineering, public relations, advertising. Investigate them all; you never know where you ultimately will find your niche.

You face a future filled with long hours, hard work, and stiff competition, but you also are entering an industry that offers tremendous creative rewards. Whatever your final job title, you will be part of a unique process that provides information and entertainment for millions.

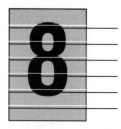

**8**

# Video Lab

1. As a class project, invite professionals in local media to visit your class. Be sure to indicate what areas of their careers you would like them to address. They can inform you on ways to pursue a career in their field.

2. As a group project, arrange a visit to a media production facility, such as a local cable TV station.

## TAKE TWO

**1.** Watch the credits at the end of a TV show or movie, then pick a job and research what that position covers and how one can enter that profession.

**2.** Obtain catalogs from several universities that offer media studies programs; compare the requirements and classes offered.

**3.** As a class project, call or write a television or radio facility and ask what internship opportunities are available and what qualifications are required to obtain them.

**4.** Research and compile a list of career fields, other than the television and movie industry, in which TV and video production skills would be necessary or desirable.

## ADDITIONAL RESOURCES

American Film Institute Staff. *Getting Started in Film,* (Englewood Cliffs, N.J., Prentice-Hall, 1992).

American Film Institute Staff. *The AFI Guide to College Courses in Film and Television, Eighth Edition,* (Englewood Cliffs, N.J., Prentice-Hall, 1992).

Cann, John. *The Stunt Guide* (Action P.A.C. Int., 28293 Bochdale Avenue, Canyon Country, Calif. 91351, 1991).

Noronha, Shonan F.R. *Opportunities in Television and Video Careers,* (Lincolnwood, Ill., VGM Career Horizons, 1993).

Stempel, Tom. *Storytellers to the Nation: A History of American Television Writing,* (New York, N.Y., The Continuum Publishing Company, 1992).

# Glossary

**access channel.** Channel used on a cable TV system whereby citizens may produce TV programs to be shown to the community (different from local origination).

**ad lib.** Speech or action that has not been written or rehearsed.

**AFTRA.** American Federation of Television and Radio Artists; talent union.

**analog.** A signal that varies smoothly between certain ranges.

**analog sound recording.** Audio recording system in which the electrical sound signal fluctuates exactly like the original sound stimulus over its entire range.

**aperture.** Diaphragm opening of a lens; usually measured in *f*-stops.

**arc.** To move the camera in a slightly curved dolly or truck.

**ASCAP.** American Society of Composers, Authors, and Publishers; collects royalties for performance of copyrighted material.

**aspect ratio.** The proportionate size of the television screen, three units high and four units wide, with the long side horizontal.

**assemble edit.** An edit on videotape where portions of a TV program are pieced together and the end of one sequence edited to the beginning of another.

**audio.** The sound portion of television and its production. Technically, the electronic reproduction of audible sound.

**backlight.** Spotlight from behind the performer, lighting the hair and shoulders and separating the performer from scenery behind.

**barn doors.** Metal covers hinged to the front of a spotlight to regulate the spread of the light beam.

**blooper.** A mistake, usually a slip of the tongue, such as "Open tape, roll talent, cue mike," or the famous one, "I present the President of the United States, Hoobert Heever."

**BMI (Broadcast Music Incorporated).** Collects royalties on copyrighted music performed on radio and television.

**boom.** Microphone suspended on end of a movable metal arm attached to a floor stand.

**busy.** Background so elaborate or detailed

that it distracts; design so intricate that it produces a flicker or jiggling effect on the television screen.

**cable television.** (1) Distribution system for broadcast signals via coaxial or fiber-optic cable. (2) Production facility for programs distributed via cable.

**camcorder.** A portable TV camera with a built-in videorecorder.

**cart.** Video or audio tape cartridge cued instantly for commercial messages or music.

**CATV (community antenna television).** TV distributed to receivers via cable from a master antenna.

**CCD (Charge-Coupled Device).** Also called *chip*. A small, solid-state imaging device, used in cameras instead of a camera pickup tube. Within the device, image sensing elements translate the optical image into a video signal.

**CCTV (closed-circuit television).** TV distributed to specific television receivers but not broadcast to the general public.

**CCU (camera control unit).** Remote equipment used in a television room to operate the television camera.

**character generator.** An electronic processor like a keyboard that inserts lettering into the TV picture.

**chroma key.** A special effect; certain colors (usually blue or green) are keyed so that a performer can be inserted in front of computer graphics or film.

**clear.** To obtain permission to use copyrighted material.

**close-up.** Photographing objects or people at close range. Listed as "CU" on a script or storyboard; variations include the ECU (Extreme Close-up) and MCU (Medium Close-up).

**coaxial cable.** Shielded cable through which television pictures and sound are transmitted.

**CD (compact disc).** A small, shiny disc that contains information (usually sound signals) in digital form. A CD player reads the encoded digital data via laser beam.

**continuity.** (1) Script; (2) content of show; (3) logically related sequence of events.

**control room.** Area where director, switcher, technical director, and audio technician work during the program.

**copy.** Any portion of the program that is written word-for-word.

**cover shot.** Picture that shows entire set or entire group of performers.

**crawl.** Graphics or credit copy rotated upward in front of the video image.

**credits.** List of people who participated in the production and performance of a television program.

**cue.** (1) Signal for various production activities. (2) To select a certain spot in the videotape or film.

**cue card.** A large, hand-lettered card that contains copy, usually held next to the camera lens by floor personnel.

**cushion.** Words or music that can be included or omitted as needed to meet time requirements.

**cut.** An instant switch from one picture to another without fading.

**definition.** The degree or amount of detail clearly visible in a television picture.

**DEG (digital effects generator).** A computer-controlled special effects generator that provides many special video effects.

**depth of field.** The area in which all objects, located at different distances from camera, appear in focus.

**depth of focus.** The distance between the TV lens and the subject on camera.

**digital recording.** Recordings that convert sound or visual information into a numbered code for perfect re-recording without any deterioration through use. DAT is digital audio tape.

**dolly.** (1) Tripod or pedestal that supports the camera and enables it to be moved in all directions; (2) to move the camera toward or away from an object.

**dry run.** A rehearsal without cameras.

**dub.** The duplication of an electronic recording. Dubs can be made from tape to tape, or from record or disc to tape and vice versa.

**EFP (electronic field production).** *See* ENG.

**ENG (electronic news gathering).** Name often given to the portable TV equipment for gathering remote newscasts.

**ESS (electronic still store).** A process whereby a single image or graphic can be stored on a video disc for newscasts.

**establishing shot.** A long shot or wide shot to orient viewer to the setting or situation.

**FCC (Federal Communications Commission).** One of the U.S. government's administrative agencies, charged with regulating interstate and foreign communication (broadcasting) in or from the United States.

**feed.** To transmit or send the television signal from one source to another.

**fill light.** A light originating from the opposite side of the key light; it removes some of the shadows produced by the key light.

**film clip.** A section clipped from a motion picture to be shown independently of the rest of the reel.

**flat.** A piece of standing scenery made of a wooden frame covered with muslin or canvas.

**flip cards.** Graphics on cards of the same size that can be changed by flipping one after the other on or off the easel or *hod*.

**floor plan.** A plan of the studio floor and set showing the walls, the main doors and the location of the control room.

**FM (frequency modulation).** Static-free broadcasting characterized by more faithful reproduction of sound.

**focal length.** Distance from center of lens to surface of camera tube (short lenses have a wide angle of view; long lenses have a narrow angle of view).

**footcandle.** A unit of illumination, the amount of light produced by one candle one foot away from a portion of an object.

***f*-stop.** The calibration on the lens, indicating the aperture, or diaphragm opening (and therefore the amount of light transmitted through the lens). The larger the *f*-stop number, the smaller the aperture; the smaller the *f*-stop number, the larger the aperture.

**genre.** A distinctive group or type of story, movie, or television program that follows a recognizable pattern and can be categorized by style and purpose. Examples include the horror film, the police drama, and the television comedy.

**graphics.** Two-dimensional visuals; cards, flat pictures, printed or lettered signs.

**hod.** An easel for holding graphics or flip cards.

**IFB (interrupted feedback system).** A small earpiece worn by talent through which the director gives special instructions during a telecast.

**infomercial.** A contraction of "information" and "commercial." An infomercial is usually 30 minutes in length and thinly hides its commercial message in a program format.

**in media res.** A method of storytelling in which the story begins in the middle of the action; then there are "flashbacks" and "flashforwards."

**insert edit.** An edit on videotape whereby the editor goes from an existing sequence to a new one and back to the old sequence (differs from an assemble edit).

**intercom.** Intercommunication system among studio and control room personnel; headset with or without microphone.

**key light.** Principal source of illumination; sometimes called *modeling light.*

**kill.** To cut out or remove.

**level.** Audio volume; "get a level" means to check the volume.

**limbo.** Any area of the set having no scenic background; used for displays, easels, etc.

**lip sync.** Synchronization of sound and lip movement; spoken lines recorded

simultaneously with filming of the action. Usually, the script will make this reference (OC for on camera) at the the beginning of the scene.

**live.** (1) Direct transmission of a studio program at the time it is originated or performed; (2) turned on, such as a *live* mike.

**LO (local origination) programs.** Programs produced by a local cable company to be telecast over its system.

**loop.** A large circle of film or tape used in dubbing sessions. If you want to re-voice an actor's reading, you "loop it." The actor stands in a recording studio watching the projected film loop on the screen, which keeps repeating until the actor has matched his or her voice to the movement of the lips on the screen.

**minicam** (also *microcam.*) Lightweight, often self-contained, portable video camera for ENG taping.

**monitor.** A television set used in the studio for checking what is being picked up by a camera or what is being broadcast.

**NAB (National Association of Broadcasters).** An organization of commercial broadcasters.

**NAEB (National Association of Educational Broadcasters).** An organization of noncommercial or public broadcasters.

**omnidirectional.** A type of pickup pattern in which the microphone can pick up sounds equally well from all directions.

**P.A.** Production assistant.

**PBS.** (Public Broadcasting Service). A system of public TV stations that broadcast noncommercial and educational programs.

**pan.** To move the camera horizontally while pedestal remains stationary.

**pix.** An abbreviation for pictures.

**PL.** The phone line or intercommunications system among control-room staff and studio personnel.

**pole cats.** Extension poles between studio floor and ceiling, used to support scenery and graphics.

**portfolio.** A folder or videotape of samples of your work, showing your strengths and experience.

**pots.** Short for *potentiometers;* volume control dials on an audio board or console.

**pre-empt.** To acquire television time for high-priority programs by excluding regularly scheduled programs.

**props.** Properties; objects used to decorate the set or used by performers.

**PSA.** Public service announcement, a noncommercial message broadcast by a television station.

**quality.** A dimension of light related to its hardness or softness.

**rating.** Percentage of television households with their sets tuned to a specific station in relation to the total number of television households.

**ride gain.** To manually keep the audio or video levels within acceptable limits.

**roll.** (1) Graphics (usually credit copy) that move slowly up the screen, often called *crawl.* (2) Command to roll tape or film.

**scrim.** A gauzelike addition to the lights that illuminate the set. A scrim (also *silk*) is a thin piece of translucent cloth used to diffuse and soften the light.

**SESAC (The Society of European Stage Authors and Composers).** Collects royalties on materials it has copyrighted.

**shot.** The picture taken by the television camera.

**shot sheet.** A list, in order, of the shots a camera is to take

**slow motion.** A scene in which the objects appear to be moving more slowly than normal. In film, slow motion is achieved through high-speed photography and normal playback. In television, slow motion is achieved by slowing down the playback speed of the tape which results in a multiple scanning of each television frame.

**soft news.** Television news features such reports on other programs on the network, health and nutrition specials, or film reviews; added to the regular daily news to make the news program more entertaining.

**stand-by.** (1) A warning cue for any kind of action in television production. (2) A button on a videotape recorder that activates the rotation of the video heads or head drum independently of the actual tape motion. In the stand-by position, the video heads can come up to speed before the videotape is started.

**stock footage.** Previously shot scenes of all kinds, found in stock footage libraries. The initial charge is for making an examination print or tape of the footage requested, plus a per-foot charge for the footage that is actually used in a commercial. Stock footage includes historic newsreel footage, scenic locations in all types of weather, as well as every imaginable type of sports or stunts.

**storyboard.** A series of either art frames or photos which depict the planned-for video and audio (the storyline) of a commercial or PSA.

**strike.** (1) To remove objects no longer needed in the show; (2) to take down scenery.

**studio camera.** Heavy, high-quality camera and zoom lens that cannot be maneuvered properly without the aid of a pedestal or some other type of camera mount.

**super.** The simultaneous showing of two or more full pictures on the same screen; often letters or numbers over a picture.

**switcher.** The engineer or production team member who does the video switching (usually the technical director); also, a panel with rows of buttons that allows the selection and assembly of various video sources through a variety of transition devices, and the creation of electronic special effects.

**switching.** A change from one video source to another during a program or program segment with the aid of a switcher.

**take.** (1) Signal for a cut from one video source to another. (2) Any one of similar repeated shots take during videotaping and filming. Sometimes *take* is used synonymously with *shot*.

**talent.** A collective or individual name for television announcers, performers and actors.

**tally light.** The small red light on a camera indicating when that camera is on the air; also called *cue light*.

**TD.** The technical director or switcher, who operates switching controls changing from one camera to another by cutting, dissolving, fading.

**TelePrompTer.** The brand name for a mechanical prompting device that projects moving (usually computer-generated) copy over the lens so that the talent can read it without losing eye contact with the viewer.

**test pattern.** The line picture used by technicians to align the picture properly.

**title.** Studio title card or slide or an electronically generated title.

**truck.** To move the camera and dolly laterally, left and right.

**unidirectional.** A type of pickup pattern in which the microphone picks up sound from only one direction.

**video.** The picture portion of a telecast or production activities that are not broadcast.

**video cassette.** A plastic container that holds a videotape; the tape moves from supply to takeup reel, recording and playing back program segments through a videotape recorder. All VTRs except the 1" VTR use cassettes.

**video disc.** A recordlike disc that can store digital video (picture) information. Needs a special playback device.

**videotape.** A plastic, iron-oxide coated tape of various widths (from 8 mm to 1 inch) for video technical code and audio recording.

**virtual reality.** A complex graphics and optics system, in which someone can "walk through" a three-dimensional computer generated (graphics) environment. All the "virtually real" factors exist only in the computer and are "experienced" only by wearing headgear linked to the computer system.

**visuals.** Articles, pictures, or other properties seen on television. When a distinction is made between two- and three-dimensional visuals, the two-dimensional visuals are called *graphics.*

**voiceover.** An announcer's or actor's voice heard on the audio track without that person being seen on film. On a script or storyboard such voices are listed as "VO."

**zoom.** To change focal length of lens in and out, near and far; gives the effect of dollying without moving the camera.

# Index

Fade, 54
Faders, 95
Fairness Doctrine, 7
Federal Communications Commission
    (FCC), 6–7, 181
    Fairness Doctrine by, 7
    truth in advertising ruling by, 181–82
    and use of HDTV, 218
Field, Sally, 229
Fill light, 82, **89**
Film, 33–34
    control over, 229
    disadvantages of, 33
    special effects with, 84
Film production, careers in, 228–29
Flats
    back view of, 75
    construction of, 73–74
    vise grips for, 75
Floodlights, 81
Floor managers, duties and responsibilities
    of, 170
Floor plan
    for rehearsals, 182, **195–96**
    for three camera production, 74, 76
Floor stand microphone, 92–93
Fluid head, 51
Focal length of camera lenses, 44–46
Foster, Jodie, 137
Four-by-three aspect ratio, 65, 84
Frequency modulation (FM) radio, 32,
    100
Frequency range of microphones, 99–100
Fresnel spotlight, 80, 81
Friction head, 51
Front, 82
Front timing, 155–56, **166**
Frost, David, 191
*f* stop, 460

**G**

Gain control, 95
Game shows, scripting for, 147
"Gangbusters," 10
Gangster film, 138
Gavin, William, 172
"General Hospital," 10
Generating element, 100
Generation, 217
Genre, 137–38, 138
    biographical film, 140
    comedy, 139
    gangster film, 138
    horror film, 139–40
    police drama, 138
    sci-fi-film, 140
*Ghost Train,* 29
Go-ahead signal, 11
Government regulation, of radio and televi-
    sion, **21**
Graphics
    aspect ratio, 65
    rule of six for, 65–66
    techniques for preparing, 66–70
Gray scale, 82
Great Plains National Instructional Televi-
    sion Library, 215

**H**

Hall, Arsenio, 191
Hand microphone, 95
"Hard Cover," 181
Hawn, Goldie, 229
Hayes, Helen, 110
HBO, 7

# W

# X

# Z

# NTC COMMUNICATION BOOKS

**Speech Communication**
ACTIVITIES FOR EFFECTIVE COMMUNICATION, LiSacchi
THE BASICS OF SPEECH, Galvin, Cooper, & Gordon
CONTEMPORARY SPEECH, HopKins & Whitaker
CREATIVE SPEAKING, Frank
DYNAMICS OF SPEECH, Myers & Herndon
GETTING STARTED IN ORAL INTERPRETATION, Naegelin & Krikac
GETTING STARTED IN PUBLIC SPEAKING, Carlin & Payne
LISTENING BY DOING, Galvin
LITERATURE ALIVE, Gamble & Gamble
PERSON TO PERSON, Galvin & Book
PUBLIC SPEAKING TODAY, Carlin & Payne
SELF-AWARENESS, Ratliffe & Herman
SPEAKING BY DOING, Buys, Sills, & Beck

**Media Communication**
GETTING STARTED IN MASS MEDIA, Beckert
PHOTOGRAPHY IN FOCUS, Jacobs & Kokrda
TELEVISION PRODUCTION TODAY, Bielak
UNDERSTANDING THE FILM, Bone & Johnson
UNDERSTANDING MASS MEDIA, Schrank

**Business Communication**
EFFECTIVE GROUP COMMUNICATION, Ratliffe & Stech
HANDBOOK FOR BUSINESS WRITING, Baugh, Fryar, & Thomas
HOW TO BE A RAPID READER, Redway
MEETINGS: RULES & PROCEDURES, Pohl
SUCCESSFUL BUSINESS SERIES
WORKING IN GROUPS, Ratliffe & Stech

For a current catalog and information about our complete line
of language arts books, write:
National Textbook Company
a division of NTC Publishing Group
4255 West Touhy Avenue
Lincolnwood (Chicago), Illinois 60646-1975 U.S.A.